Give the Holy Spirit a Chance

Garrie F. Williams

REVIEW AND HERALD® PUBLISHING ASSOCIATION
HAGERSTOWN, MD 21740

Copyright © 1993 by
Review and Herald® Publishing Association

The author assumes full responsibility for the accuracy of all facts and quotations as cited in this book.

This book was
Edited by James Cavil
Designed by Bill Kirstein
Type set: 11/12 Garamond Book

Unless otherwise noted, Bible texts in this book are from The New King James Version. Copyright © 1979, 1980, 1982, Thomas Nelson Inc., Publishers.

Texts credited to NIV are from the *Holy Bible, New International Version.* Copyright © 1973, 1978, 1984, International Bible Society. Used by permission of Zondervan Bible Publishers.

Bible texts credited to NRSV are from the New Revised Standard Version of the Bible, copyright © 1989 by the Division of Christian Education of the National Council of the Churches of Christ in the U.S.A. Used by permission.

Bible texts credited to RSV are from the Revised Standard Version of the Bible, copyright © 1946, 1952, 1971, by the Division of Christian Education of the National Council of the Churches of Christ in the U.S.A. Used by permission.

Texts credited to RV are from the Revised Version, Oxford University Press, 1911.

Bible texts credited to TEV are from the *Good News Bible*—Old Testament: Copyright © American Bible Society 1976; New Testament: Copyright © American Bible Society 1966, 1971, 1976.

Verses marked TLB are taken from *The Living Bible*, copyright © 1971 by Tyndale House Publishers, Wheaton, Ill. Used by permission.

PRINTED IN U.S.A.

98 97 96 95   10 9 8 7 6 5 4 3 2

R & H Cataloging Service
Williams, Garrie F.
    Give the Holy Spirit a chance.

    1. Holy Spirit. 2. Gifts, Spiritual.
I. Title.
        231.3

ISBN 0-8280-0728-4

**To
my oldest daughter and son-in-law
Carolyn and Struan Robertson**

who were used by the
Holy Spirit
to give me edification,
exhortation, and comfort
at a time when they were
needed most.

Acknowledgments

Without the direct help of many people who were instruments of power in the hands of the Holy Spirit, this book would not have been written or published. It is the fruit of countless hours of prayer.

First I thank my wife, Barbara, not only for her support, but also for long hours of typing and reading this manuscript. Her prayers and praise to God never failed. In sickness and in health she had strong faith that this book would be completed in the strength of the Lord.

Penny Estes Wheeler, of the Review and Herald Publishing Association, encouraged me to write a follow-up volume to *How to Be Filled With the Holy Spirit and Know It*. I thank her for her prompting and prayers. The small group that meets weekly in our home prayed as each chapter was completed, and gave words of encouragement. Tom and Carolyn Hamilton prayed when the way seemed dark and the task impossible. Janet Lui was led by the Holy Spirit not only into strong intercessory prayer that we could survive the attacks of the enemy, but also to send books and quotations that proved very helpful and timely.

Lay members and pastors across North America and overseas who have read my first book on the Holy Spirit have continued to pray for a follow-up volume to use in their small groups. Their "When will it be ready?" was often an incentive to keep writing.

Thanks to the people who have given permission for their experiences to be used in this book. The stories are all true, although some names have been changed.

Contents

Orientation 9

GIVE THE HOLY SPIRIT A CHANCE

Chapter One: TO SHOW HE IS YOUR FRIEND 11
Study Guide 19

Chapter Two: TO GIVE YOU RESURRECTION LIFE NOW 21
Study Guide 30

Chapter Three: TO SUPPLY YOU WITH ABUNDANT HOPE 33
Study Guide 43

Chapter Four: TO LET YOU HEAR GOD SPEAK 45
Study Guide 55

Chapter Five: TO HELP YOU PRAY IN THE SPIRIT 58
Study Guide 71

Chapter Six: TO GLORIFY GOD'S NAME 73
Study Guide 85

Chapter Seven: TO GIVE YOU VICTORY POWER 87
Study Guide 98

Chapter Eight: TO SHATTER SELF-CONTROL 100
Study Guide 111

Chapter Nine: TO GIVE YOU A HOUSEHOLD OF FAITH 114
Study Guide 128

Chapter Ten: TO GIFT YOU FOR HEALING MINISTRY 131
Study Guide 144

Chapter Eleven: TO MAKE WORSHIP MEANINGFUL 147
Study Guide 159

Chapter Twelve: TO GIVE YOU VISIONS AND DREAMS 161
Study Guide 173

Chapter Thirteen: TO BRING THE GREAT RENEWAL 175
Study Guide 188

References 190

Orientation

This book builds on the foundation of my first book on the Holy Spirit, *How to Be Filled With the Holy Spirit and Know It*, which has not only been widely read but also used in study groups in a number of countries. In many places people have said, "We have studied your first book on the Holy Spirit and know that we have been filled with the Spirit, but we want to understand more about how we can keep strong in our new experience and have a part in the final great revival." This new book will not deal with basic questions such as how to be filled with the Holy Spirit, what are the signs of that filling, and many other details covered in my first volume on this topic. It will assume that readers will already have that basic knowledge and experience.

Wherever I go, people have very similar questions about the Holy Spirit: "What is the difference between Pentecostal, charismatic, and evangelical Christianity?" "How can I keep renewed in the Holy Spirit by prayer and Bible study?" "Are there revelations from the Holy Spirit today that supersede the Bible?" "Why does the Holy Spirit use small groups as the basic units for Christianity?" "How are the healing gifts of the Holy Spirit revealed most powerfully in small groups?" "Why are spiritual gifts so effective in team ministry?" "What is the connection between the Holy Spirit and true worship?" "How can I know whether or not a dream or vision is from the Holy Spirit?" "What is the secret of Holy Spirit power for victory over sin?" "What relationship is there between the Holy Spirit in me and my salvation by Jesus Christ?" "How will I be able to recognize a true revival?" "What basic steps can I take to help the last great revival take place?"

I have tried to answer these questions and more about the Holy Spirit in a practical rather than a deeply theological way. I want the answers to be understood in the neighborhoods in which you and I live, not just in church seminaries or sanctuaries. If my answers are theories you discuss and forget, I will have failed, but if they result in new ministries, changed lives, and great revivals, I will not cease to praise the Lord.

Let me repeat some information from *How to Be Filled With the Holy Spirit and Know It* concerning the small group study guides in this book.

I have written with neighborhood study groups, households of faith, foremost in mind, while at the same time realizing that many of these groups may actually meet in churches, on college and academy campuses, and at various retreat and seminar situations.

The study guides use relational and inductive questions that are not primarily for teaching but rather for discussion and interaction. Relational questions help us understand God, ourselves, other people, and the world around us. These questions do not major in presenting intellectual facts, but rather lead into an understanding of what is involved in strong and positive relationships in these four critical areas.

Inductive Bible study has been called discovery Bible study. This type of study has been used with small groups for hundreds of years. Basically, in inductive Bible study there are three questions asked of each part of Scripture: "What does the text say?" "What does the text mean?" and "How can I apply this text and live according to Scripture today?"

If you are studying these guides in a small group, it is important that the group leader understand a few basic principles of facilitating a group. The leader does not have to be concerned about being a teacher and knowing answers to complex theological questions. Rather, the group leader guides the group in discovery, discussion, prayer, and sharing with one another, as well as encouraging group members in outreach and growth of the group. It is good if each group can have a leader, an assistant leader, and a host or hostess. In this way the group will function successfully and, as it grows, may even want to divide into two or more smaller groups. It is best if the group does not reach beyond 12 or 14 members, as this will limit the opportunity for discussion and interaction.

Small group leaders will find great encouragement if they can meet with other leaders on a regular basis. In this regular meeting they can receive, especially from their pastor, encouragement, help, and inspiration that they, in turn, can share with their own small group in the weekly Bible study.

There is much evidence that the enemy of souls did not want this book written. His attack was many times direct and severe, yet the Holy Spirit always triumphed with the mighty power by which He makes us super-conquerors. I pray that you also will know the great strength of the Holy Spirit and will be able to be victorious in your life and ministry. The Holy Spirit is your special friend. Give Him the chance every day to reintroduce you to your loving Father in heaven and your wonderful Saviour, Jesus. I pray that you will know today the eternal resurrection life that the Holy Spirit gives you.

CHAPTER ONE
▼

Give the Holy Spirit a Chance
To Show He Is Your Friend

"Is the Holy Spirit your friend?" Some Christians are surprised by this question because they have thought of Jesus as a sympathizer, the Father as a problem to be appeased, and the Holy Spirit as a rather unpredictable emotional force.

Let me tell you what I have discovered, along with millions of other Christians around the world. The Holy Spirit is an amazing and delightful friend. He reveals not only the full beauty of Jesus, but also the love of the Father, which He pours abundantly into the hearts of all who are open to Him (Romans 5:5). He is the Spirit of truth. Give Him a chance today, and He will show you what a great friend He is.

If you are puzzled about the reason for suspicion about the Holy Spirit, a little history may help clarify the situation. A few facts from the past can turn on lights that enable us to see and walk in the safe path of truth.

A Friend of New Testament Christians

Before His death and after His resurrection, Jesus promised the Holy Spirit to the disciples (John 14:25; Luke 24:49; Acts 1:8). They obviously could see that this was a gift to be excited about, because they prayed, praised, and ministered with great joy while they waited the coming of the Comforter (Luke 24:49-53; Acts 1:14).

After the disciples received the great outpouring of the Holy Spirit in Jerusalem on the feast day of Pentecost, they made their listeners fully aware that the gift of the Holy Spirit was also for them (Acts 2:38, 39). The Holy Spirit was a friend to be shared, not a danger to be feared. Numerous references to the Holy Spirit in the book of Acts indicate the intimacy of the early Christians with the Holy Spirit. In fact, they worked so closely that they could say, "It seemed good to the Holy Spirit and to us" (Acts 15:28).

Paul speaks of the love of the Spirit (Romans 15:30). Twice he says we have fellowship with the Spirit (2 Corinthians 13:14; Philippians 2:1, 2). Often joy and the Holy Spirit are linked together. This is hardly the way one would relate to an enemy. You can trust the Holy Spirit; there is no doubt about it. He will lead you into truth and fill your heart with joy and peace (Romans 15:13). When you begin to accept the Holy Spirit in this way, you are in step with the New Testament Christians. In fact, as Paul told young Timothy, the Holy Spirit enables you to keep your grip on all the good things that God has given you (2 Timothy 1:14).

The New Testament Christians believed that in the swirling whirlwind of crisis the Holy Spirit provides a storm shelter of assurance and joy (1 Thessalonians 1:5, 6). Now, that's the sort of friend to have. No wonder New Testament Christians were so powerful. They had authority! They could say to trouble, "You may batter us and bruise us, but we cannot be defeated. We have a Friend who is so strong that He can encapsulate us in Jesus' love every moment. Because of Him we can rejoice even if we have to suffer for Jesus, because He guarantees that our mortality is swallowed up by eternal life." Now, you will not read those exact words in the New Testament, but look at what it has to say about the New Testament Christians' Friend in such places as 1 Peter 1:2-14 and 2 Corinthians 5:4, 5.

Following a seminar I was teaching in Wales a lady indicated that she appreciated the material presented but then stated, "I differ from you on one part. I do not believe the Holy Spirit is a person. To me, the Holy Spirit is the life force of God."

"So you consider the Holy Spirit to be an 'it,' " I replied. We laughed for a few moments about the implications of being an "it." I think even neutered animals would be indignant about such a designation. We then reviewed the fact that the New Testament Christians considered the Holy Spirit to be a personal friend, even though some impersonal metaphors such as wind and water are used to describe Him, and the word for "Spirit" in the New Testament is in the neuter gender.

I like the explanation of this given by Dr. John Rea, professor emeritus of Old Testament at Regent University and an editor of the *Wycliffe Bible Encyclopedia*. He says, "It is true that the Greek expression *to pneuma* for 'the Spirit' is neuter in gender and grammatically requires a neuter pronoun. Nevertheless, the masculine demonstrative pronoun *ekeinos* ("that one" or "he") is used repeatedly in Jesus' statements as recorded by the apostle John to refer to the Comforter, the Holy Spirit, the Spirit of truth (John 14:26; 15:26; 16:8, 13, 14). Meanwhile, the New Testament makes a distinction between divine power and the Holy Spirit as a person: 'God anointed Him [Jesus] with the Holy Spirit and with power' (Acts 10:38, NASB); and 'our gospel did not come to you in word only, but also in power and in the Holy Spirit and with full conviction' (1 Thessalonians 1:5, NASB)." [1]

When the New Testament Christians spoke about their friend the Holy Spirit, they obviously recognized Him as a person. In fact, they mention a lot of the Holy Spirit's activities in a way that showed they knew Him as someone as real as themselves or their beloved Jesus. The Spirit searches (1 Corinthians 2:10), knows (verse 11), teaches (verse 13), gives gifts as He wills (1 Corinthians 12:7-12). He loves (Romans 15:30), He can speak (Acts 8:29), He can be lied to (Acts 5:3, 4). The Holy Spirit can be grieved (Ephesians 4:30) and even insulted (Matthew 12:31).[2]

Yes, as the New Testament Christians would no doubt say to you, please give the Holy Spirit a chance to be your friend today.

The Twentieth-Century Transition

"We are very worried about our young people," a church leader said recently. "Some of them believe that the Holy Spirit is giving them dreams and visions." While the possibility of such direct communication with God today is rather frightening to many people and should be carefully tested by Scripture, the Bible states clearly that the Holy Spirit will give dreams and visions of significance to both men and women, young and old. There is a lot of evidence that the Spirit will be particularly active in this way just before the second coming of Jesus (Joel 2:28, 29; see chapter twelve). In view of this, it is interesting to notice how the twentieth century has seen the Holy Spirit come into focus in a very dramatic way. Tragically, though, the Holy Spirit has been perceived by a large part of Christianity as an enemy rather than as a friend. Powerless Christianity has masqueraded as pious and pure while some Christian excesses have professed to represent the exuberance of Holy Spirit exultation.

Mark and Sonya wanted to be part of a Spirit-filled fellowship but were puzzled about the variety of attitudes to the Holy Spirit they encountered in different denominations. "Can you explain the difference between Pentecostal, charismatic, and evangelical churches?" they asked me, hoping to find an easy answer that would clear the way for friendship with the Holy Spirit. My reply generalized the situation a little, but I offered them this explanation: "Mark and Sonya, Pentecostalism is a movement of independent congregations and some rapidly growing denominations that usually state that the paramount evidence of the baptism of the Holy Spirit is the gift of tongues. They also highlight other miraculous gifts and speak a lot about spiritual warfare and holiness.

"Charismatic renewal is a movement within many mainline Protestant and Catholic churches. It emphasizes the availability of all of the gifts of the Holy Spirit but does not generally dogmatize that any one gift is the sign of

Spirit baptism, although there is an acceptance of tongues, healing, and other miracles.

"Fundamental evangelicalism, on the other hand, stresses that truth—biblical truth—is the sign of the Holy Spirit's ministry and that most of the gifts of the Spirit were primarily for New Testament times and concluded when those New Testament revelations were completed."

After my explanation the young couple naturally wanted to know how all this got started, so I shared with them a little of the history I had learned in my own quest for an understanding of the ministry of the Holy Spirit in the twentieth century.

Pentecostalism is usually considered as beginning in 1906, when William J. Seymour, a Black holiness preacher, received what was believed to be the true gift of tongues and miracles at revival meetings on Azusa Street in Los Angeles. Although Pentecostalism came under continuing attack from other Christian and secular groups, it expanded quickly and continues to be the most rapidly growing Christian movement in the twentieth century.

Pentecostals have largely overcome derogatory titles such as "Holy Rollers," which came from the extreme forms of worship that were demonstrated by some early enthusiasts and radical groups throughout this century. A large part of Pentecostalism is much concerned about holiness and victorious Christian living.

The "second wave," as Peter Wagner calls it,[3] of the Holy Spirit's work in this century came in the 1960s, when mainline denominations found large numbers of their members becoming open to the gifts of the Holy Spirit. Catholics and Protestants began to practice healing, the casting out of evil spirits, and speaking in tongues, along with all the other spiritual gifts. In Catholicism this movement is often spoken of as beginning at the University of Notre Dame in the early part of 1967, although in 1966 the *National Catholic Reporter* told of Pentecostal experiences among Roman Catholics at Duquesne University in Pittsburgh. There a group of people, realizing their own deep spiritual needs, had come to God and had prayed earnestly together for the presence of Jesus to fill their lives.[4] The Catholic and Protestant charismatics did not call people into new independent congregations or churches, but rather became subgroups in their own denominations.

The fundamentalist, evangelical, gospel-centered denominations growing out of the sixteenth- and seventeenth-century European Reformation movements see the Scriptures as the greatest work of the Holy Spirit (2 Timothy 3:16; 2 Peter 1:20, 21). Along with this is Jesus' promise that the Holy Spirit will lead people into all truth and glorify Jesus (John 16:13, 14). Evangelicals fear that the subjective experience of gifts such as prophecy, tongues, and interpretations, as well as discernment and a word of knowledge, will undermine the authority of the Bible as the supreme manifestation of God's will and work for humanity. They explain that the evidence of the Holy Spirit in a person's life is that one will understand conversion, will exalt Jesus and witness about Him, and accept and obey the great truths of God's Word.

Mark and Sonya's next question was understandable. It is one I have asked, and I would not be surprised if you haven't been thinking about it also. "Are these positions irreconcilable? Does there have to be an unbridgeable canyon between the gifts of the Spirit and the Spirit of truth? Will there be a "third wave" of the Holy Spirit when the Spirit and truth come together?"

We should look at this carefully, or we may make the mistake of the disciples who wanted Jesus to stop those who were working miracles in His name but were not part of the disciples' team (Mark 9:38-40).

Sometime ago I was surprised to discover in a secondhand bookstore a paperback published by the evangelical printer Zondervan entitled *Let's Quit Fighting About the Holy Spirit*. The author, Peter E. Gillquist, begins by looking at the problem we have just discussed: "Oftentimes entire fellowships of believers split over disagreements on the gifts of the Spirit. Or two people who have been close in the bonds of Christ for years no longer share Him with intimacy and oneness because one of them receives a manifestation of the Spirit with which the other disagrees. It's tragic how Satan has used to *divide* us the very means God gave to unite us. The Holy Spirit was given to the body of Christ to make us one." [5]

Riding the Wave With a Friend

Although I don't profess to be a skilled surfboard rider, I have always found body surfing to be an exhilarating experience. The warm water and powerful surf of the Australian east coast beaches always drew my family to vacation at the seaside even when we lived in a seaside suburb of Sydney. There is nothing like "catching a wave" and riding it to the shore with what seems a high wall of water pushing you at tremendous speed.

Occasionally I would catch the wave the wrong way, and my children would laugh when they saw my feet appearing in the air as I went through the "washing machine" turbulence in front of the breaker. To miss a wave often meant floating like a jellyfish in the lifelessness that followed, hoping that another good wave would soon appear.

An emphasis on Spirit without truth has left some people, even Christian movements, in a "washing machine" of turbulence and unrestricted emotionalism, while truth without Spirit has left other Christian groups floundering in a sea of lifelessness and even in anger and persecution of those who do not agree with their perceptions of right and wrong. G. B. Thompson quotes a French writer who says, "The Spirit and the Word, the Word and the Spirit, are two things indissolubly united by God. A theology which separates them is not worthy of the name. 'The Spirit without the Word' is, with some, personal inspiration with all its illusions, or mysticism in its bad sense, if not fanaticism with all its errors. On the other hand, 'the Word without Spirit' is, for some, orthodox intellectualism with its desolating dryness, or, what is still worse, rationalism and its errors; for others it is a prolongation of their childish comprehension of the Word, the want of peace and confidence in the promise of God, of assurance and rejoicing over our reconciliation with Him through faith in Jesus Christ, and it also is a delay in sanctification. Let us avoid these two extremes with equal care; while we hold the Book, let us lift our hearts to Him who makes us able to read it with profit; in the union of the Word and the Spirit, and there alone, is there entire safety for our souls." [6]

I want to ride the wave of Spirit and truth, moving ahead powerfully toward the delightful "shore" of Jesus' second coming. It is certain that your friend and mine, the Holy Spirit, wants you to give Him a chance today to confirm His gift and ministry in your life. Let me tell you now how I explained this to Mark and Sonya. You may have other insights that you can add as you prayerfully listen to what God has to say.

Because the Holy Spirit is our friend, He is concerned that we are not deceived, so naturally He will be constantly revealing truth to us. That's what is nice about true friends—you can always trust them. Jesus linked the Spirit and truth together a number of times. He said we must worship in Spirit and in truth (John 4:24). In fact, in a later chapter we will notice how the union of Spirit and truth energizes and revitalizes worship. It is in His final discussion with His disciples before Calvary, however, that Jesus gives His clearest picture of the importance of uniting Spirit and truth. Let me interject a word of concern here. When we talk about truth, it is not just an intellectual understanding of various doctrines of the Bible. It is definitely much more personal than that. Jack Hayford, pastor of the Church on the Way, in Van Nuys, California, a charismatic pastor and author of the beautiful song "Majesty," which is sung by most Christian denominations today, voiced this concern in this way: "The essential point to understand is that we are not dealing with a generalized or academic approach to the Bible. Hearing and studying the Word of God are both very desirable practices and are both taught in the Scriptures. But hearing without doing and studying without applying are dangerous to even the most sincere among us (see

James 1:22). What keeps the Word of God at hand—ready for confrontation with flesh or devil—is allowing the Holy Spirit to infuse it into your spiritual system. Spirit-filled living calls for hearing, studying, doing, and applying the Word, for then all become joyfully dynamic with the Holy Spirit's aid." [7]

The Holy Spirit is the Spirit of truth (John 14:17). In His teaching ministry the Holy Spirit, because He is your friend, will reveal the truth regarding sin, righteousness, and judgment (John 16:8). The second time Jesus calls the Holy Spirit the Spirit of truth He says that the Spirit will guide people into all truth (verse 13). But please remember that this revelation of truth will be progressive, because even Jesus Himself did not overwhelm people with information that was beyond their limits of coping. "I still have many things to say to you," Jesus said, "but you cannot bear them now" (verse 12). That is what a friend is like.

Sometimes Christians want to judge the type of Spirit others have by the amount of truth they appear to be believing or practicing. "Why don't they believe this doctrine or that? If they were really filled with the Holy Spirit, they would be doing what I think is right." But the Holy Spirit knows the right time and place for all knowledge of truth. He does not overwhelm. Of course, the greatest truth the Holy Spirit reveals is concerning Jesus (John 15:26; 16:14). Jesus is the Truth.

Now, does all this emphasis on truth eliminate spiritual gifts as part of the joy our friend the Holy Spirit shares with God's people? Obviously not, because spiritual gifts remain as part of "the truth" until the very end of time. The gospel commission spreads the good news of salvation to all the world in every age. "He who believes and is baptized will be saved" (Mark 16:16), Jesus proclaimed, then emphasized that miraculous signs will follow those who believe (verses 17, 18). There is no indication that signs and wonders are any more restricted to the Apostolic Age than is "believe and be baptized." In fact, Paul states that those who await the return of Jesus will come behind in no gift (1 Corinthians 1:7, 8). And he clearly outlines what those gifts are (1 Corinthians 12). Joel's prophecy concerning prophecy and visions resulting from the outpouring of the Holy Spirit certainly applies to the time near to the Second Coming. The Holy Spirit actually uses these gifts to bring people to the knowledge of truth (Ephesians 4:11-15).

Attorney Tom Hamilton and his wife, Carolyn, were excited when they told me of an interesting study they had typed out from the introduction to a book that was written more than 100 years ago. The introduction author, James White, addressed the subject of the denial of spiritual gifts, which was taking place in many churches in the middle of the past century. As these denominations struggled to find a balance between Spirit and truth, he says,

"The gifts have been superseded in the popular churches by human creeds. The object of the gifts, as stated by Paul, was 'for the perfecting of the saints, for the work of the ministry, for the edifying of the body of Christ, till we all come in the unity of the faith.' These were Heaven's appointed means to secure the unity of the church. . . . The gifts were given to secure the state of unity. But the popular churches have introduced another means of preserving unity, namely, human creeds. These creeds secure a sort of unity to each denomination; but they have all proved inefficient, as appears from the 'new schools' and 'reformed' of almost every creed-bound denomination under heaven. . . . And the smaller sects who reject human creeds, professing to take the Bible as their rule of faith and practice, yet reject the gifts, are not a whit better off. In these perilous times they shake to fragments, yet crying, the Bible, the Bible! We, too, would exalt the Bible, and would say to those who would represent us as taking the gifts instead of the Bible, that we are not satisfied with a part of the Sacred Volume, but claim as ours the Bible, and the whole Bible, gifts and all." [8]

When the great message of the three angels of Revelation 14 circles the world in the last days, Spirit and truth link together, as Jesus said in John 4, to enable God's people to truly worship the Creator-God (Revelation 14:6, 7). So the Spirit and bride (the church) will link together to say to all people, "Come and drink of the Water of Life" (see Revelation 22:17).

Mark and Sonya opened their lives fully to Jesus and knew the beautiful experience of being filled with the Holy Spirit. Sometimes, even in the middle of trouble, they would feel like shouting hallelujah and jumping for joy. One day they came to me with some exciting news. "Look what the Holy Spirit has revealed to us as we have been praying in the Bible. We've found out something very interesting about the Ten Commandments."

They went on to give me a detailed explanation of this wonderful new truth they had discovered, and then concluded by saying with real determination, "We have asked the Lord to help us change our lifestyle so we can live and worship according to His Word."

I want to be riding the last great "wave" of the Holy Spirit and truth, don't you? It is exciting to have a friend like the Holy Spirit. He has a lot of beautiful surprises in store for us as He links Spirit and truth. Give the Holy Spirit a chance today. Give Him a chance to show you He is your friend.

SMALL GROUP STUDY
Chapter One

Cohesive Contrasts

Small groups bring together people of many different personalities and cultures. Bonding can happen very quickly when people are willing to talk about themselves in a way that enables others to get to know them and relate to them. Here is a question that will help group members learn about each other in this first meeting together.

Who was your best friend, outside your immediate family, when you were 12 or 13, and what influence did this person have on your life?

Concentrating on the Word
Study Text: John 14:12-21

The Holy Spirit brings Jesus into our lives. What are some of the ways Jesus may choose to reveal Himself to us (verse 21)?

Through the Word _____ Through other Christians _____
Through prayer _____ Through a vision or dream _____
Through miracles _____ Other _____

What are some ways "commandments" (verses 15, 21) and truth (verse 17) can safeguard a Christian from deceptions?

_____
_____

In verses 12-21 Jesus indicates several times the miraculous use of spiritual gifts and the way these will be united with a right relationship to truth. List and compare these two facets of the Spirit's ministry.

Gifts	Truth
_____	_____
_____	_____
_____	_____
_____	_____

Which of the following would be involved in doing the work of Jesus?

Teaching _____ Healing _____ Preaching _____
Miracles _____ Others _____

What qualities of friendship does Jesus imphasize when He introduces the Holy Spirit to His followers?
_____
_____

If you could choose a new friend today—a friend for life—what qualities would be most important to you? Why?
_____
_____

Why could it be that the Holy Spirit does not reveal all truth to all people at the same time?
_____
_____

What lessons do you think Christian denominations can learn from Jesus' linking of Spirit and truth? In what ways do you see this as having special signifiance as the time of Jesus' return comes very near?
_____
_____

Conversation With the Lord

Conclude your small group meeting with a time of conversational prayer, centering on praise, needs within the group, and intercession for others outside the group. Finish your prayer time with the Lord's Prayer and also pray for the "empty chair," asking the Lord to lead each group member to someone who can be invited to join the group next week.

Committing the Word to Memory

This week, write out a verse from John 14:12-21 and share it with someone as soon as possible.
_____
_____

CHAPTER TWO
▼

Give the Holy Spirit a Chance
To Give You Resurrection Life Now

Have you ever felt dead? I mean lifeless. Perhaps it happened in the morning when it was time to get up. Maybe you felt dead in the middle of the day or in the middle of church worship or after a few years of school or marriage. "I have no energy, no sparkle; I don't have any interest in life." Most people have said something like that at some time. Perhaps the lifelessness has been caused by a physical ailment, overwork, shock, chemical dependency, sudden memories of childhood abuse, failure, or deliberate sin.

Whatever the cause, two things are certain. First, the dead need resurrection, not criticism or artificial inspiration. Second, there is One who can raise the dead. Every person has the potential to walk in abundant resurrection life. Are you really alive today? It can surely be the case. Give the Holy Spirit a chance. The dead can be raised.

Look at Jesus

Demonstrations are usually very interesting. A new plane demonstrates its maneuverability at an air show; a cook demonstrates how to make an appetizing entrée. Large groups of people demonstrate their solidarity behind a particular ideology or principle. History's greatest demonstration came when God the Father revealed the Holy Spirit's resurrection power when He raised Jesus from the dead. Look at Paul's explanation of this: "And what is the exceeding greatness of His power toward us who believe, according to the working of His mighty power which He worked in Christ when He raised Him from the dead and seated Him at His right hand in heavenly places" (Ephesians 1:19, 20). No wonder Paul uses superlatives. This resurrection power is certainly exceedingly great power. Paul emphasizes this power a number of times in Ephesians (e.g., 3:7, 20; 4:10). Peter agrees that it was the power of the Holy Spirit that God used to raise Jesus from death (1 Peter 3:18).

Have you ever noticed how the New Testament Christians centered their preaching and teaching on the resurrection of Jesus? They were totally convinced that it actually happened. Peter and John were willing to go to prison for this teaching (Acts 4:2). Resurrection witnessing jumped onto center stage when the Holy Spirit was poured out with great power on Peter and John's prayer team. "And when they had prayed, the place where they were assembled together was shaken; and they were all filled with the Holy Spirit, and they spoke the word of God with boldness. . . . And with great power the apostles gave witness to the resurrection of the Lord Jesus. And great grace was upon them all" (verses 31-33).

Yes, the Holy Spirit empowered a mighty resurrection witness. Paul proclaimed the resurrection to the Sadducees, who didn't believe in resurrection at all, and to the Greek philosophers, who thought it was a joke (Acts 17:31, 32; 23:6-8).

During a seminar I was teaching at a university a few years ago a number of students posed a question about Jesus. "What evidence is there that He rose from the dead? Surely this is just an early Christian myth."

As these students pressed me for an answer, I thought of a lot of good books that have been written on the evidences for the Resurrection. These include *Who Moved the Stone?* by lawyer Frank Morrison.[1] But first I began to pray that the Holy Spirit would give me the wisdom and boldness of the early Christians. "Think about this," I suggested. "A group of frightened disciples were radically changed into men who were willing to die for their faith. That change certainly didn't happen on the basis of a stolen body. The Pharisees were most upset that the disciples were boldly proclaiming the resurrection of Jesus. All those Pharisees had to do to shut the disciples up was to produce the body." I imagined the ancient Jewish equivalent of the CIA or KGB scouring Palestine for the body, without success. Jesus was alive.

"Here is another point to consider," I told the students as we became more absorbed in the topic. "The first letter to the Corinthians is considered an authentic document, and it is here that Paul claims to know of more than 500 people who saw the resurrected Jesus. Paul implies that people could still talk to most of these witnesses. All of them would give the same testimony—Jesus is alive!" (1 Corinthians 15:5-7).

Recently I saw a notice on a power pole at a street corner. It read: "Anyone witnessing an accident on this corner last Friday please phone. . . ." Even one witness would be helpful; two would be much better. But if you have 500 witnesses, you are safe in court; you've got an airtight case. J. B. Phillips, whose paraphrased Bible has been very popular, once stated that C. S. Lewis, a great Christian writer, twice appeared to him after Lewis had died. Phillips could have been dreaming, but 500 people don't all have the same dream at the same time. The 500 Paul referred to actually saw the real Jesus. The devil thought he had conquered at Calvary, but on the Resurrection morning he realized his defeat. Jesus is alive.

One Easter weekend in Portland, Oregon, I spoke to a large congregation in a church that had been beautifully prepared for a Resurrection celebration. As I rolled away the styrofoam stone from the front of the tomb all the congregation stood and we sang with great enthusiasm that Christ is indeed alive. It was a very moving moment for each one of us.

Yes, we serve a living Saviour. Jesus is alive. Give the Holy Spirit a chance to help you fully understand this today.

Resurrection Now

"Pastor, I just don't know what to do about my son. He has turned his back on his family and God, and is ruining his life with drugs, satanism, and evil living." The father, Joe Tully, was distraught. Tears rolled down his face. "Please pray for my son. There is nothing else we can do." We did pray many times and asked the Holy Spirit to surround this young man with Jesus' love and to bind up Satan and his evil forces.

One day many months later Mr. Tully rushed into my office. "I can't believe it!" he shouted. "Mike has come home and he's a Christian. I just can't believe it; it's just as if he has risen from the dead." Mike's experience was like that of the prodigal son, who "was dead and is alive again" (Luke 15:24).

Notice how Paul explains the life-giving power of the Holy Spirit: "But if the Spirit of Him who raised Jesus from the dead dwells in you, He who raised Christ from the dead will also give life to your mortal bodies through His Spirit who dwells in you" (Romans 8:11). I like that verse. It is powerful. We don't have to wait for the second coming of Jesus to receive resurrection power; we can have it now. We can be alive now. We can come out of the tomb of defeat, despair, and spiritual death.

Give the Holy Spirit a chance today. It is often said that there are many different lifestyles, but that is not true. Genuine Christianity is the only lifestyle; without Jesus, all else is a death style.

Let's take a few minutes to review the steps that lead to resurrection life. Before conversion the Holy Spirit is with people, leading them to the Scriptures, where they can discover the principles of the gospel. At conversion a person becomes the dwelling place of the Holy Spirit, who comes into the life, seals the new Christian with God's family name, and guarantees the eternal inheritance (Ephesians 1:13, 14).

Until a person becomes a dwelling place of the Holy Spirit, he or she belongs not actually to Jesus, but to the world.[2] "But you are not in the flesh but in the Spirit, if indeed the Spirit of God dwells in you. Now if anyone does not have the Spirit of Christ, he is not His" (Romans 8:9).

Separated from God, even the healthiest sinner is in a state of spiritual death. If that seems a bit hard to believe, just think about Paul's very definite statement to Timothy: "She who lives in pleasure is dead while she lives" (1 Timothy 5:6). This is the resurrection that God seeks to give. He wants to raise people out of spiritual death. The problem is that the "dead know nothing" (this is rather a homiletic use of Ecclesiastes 9:5). In fact, the spiritually dead usually think themselves to be quite all right. So the Holy Spirit works through born-again Christians and the Word of God to stimulate a desire for life in the spiritually dead.

When a person chooses to allow that resurrection to take place, the transformation is remarkable. "He who is trying to reach heaven by his own works in keeping the law is attempting an impossibility. There is no safety for one who has merely a legal religion, a form of godliness. The Christian's life is not a modification or improvement of the old, but a transformation of nature. There is a death to self and sin, and a new life altogether. This change can be brought about only by the effectual working of the Holy Spirit."[3]

I want to ask you a personal question. Are you conscious that you are spiritually alive today? If not, give the Holy Spirit a chance now to give you life. Just bow your head in prayer and say, "Dear Father God, I recognize my great need of You. I come to You confessing my sins and opening my heart for You to come into my life. I accept Jesus as my personal Saviour and thank You that right at this moment I believe I have life as a child of Yours through the resurrection power of the Holy Spirit. Praise the name of Jesus. Amen." If you have prayed that prayer, I say "Amen" for you. You are alive! Hallelujah!

Often those who are cultural Christians do not realize their need of Holy Spirit resurrection life. I became a Christian as a teenager and was truly born again as I accepted Jesus as my Saviour. I preached the everlasting gospel for 10 years as a layman, but after 20 years of professional ministry Christianity became a lifestyle, a culture, rather than a vital connection to God. I could explain the Bible to others but was blinded to my own desperate need. My egotism and self-satisfaction could be shattered only by a new, personal understanding of the cross of Calvary. My experience with Jesus had become ritualistic, superficial, cultural, and professional.

Perhaps you have had the same experience. I once saw the remains of a Greek tanker wrecked on the California coast, and it reminded me that the Lord allows us to be "broken on the Rock." A situation arises that reveals our deep need, and suddenly we become aware that all the good intentions in the world will not be enough to raise us from spiritual death. Only Jesus can do that, through His Holy Spirit.

That sort of experience came to me. Suddenly the facade was shattered; I tried to run from reality and act holy, but I was only deceiving myself. The Holy Spirit convinced me of sin, and the wages of sin is death. But praise God, the Holy Spirit also leads to the cross. I had helped many others throughout my life, but who would help me to the cross in this time of desperate need? Thank God that He was able to use three friends, Christian attorney Dr. Tom Hamilton and his wife, Carolyn, who are the founders of Living Tree Prayer Ministries, and Janet Lui, who is chairperson of the Mega Los Angeles Intercessory Prayer Taskforce. Their belief in prayer and the resurrection power of God was not theoretical but alive and personal. They were friends who saw me through God's eyes and did not crush and destroy, but were used by the Holy Spirit to lead me to Jesus, the Rock of Ages. There I could not only understand my brokenness but also experience healing and resurrection power.

After eight hours of continuous prayer and fellowship in the Word with full repentance and surrender, I experienced a consciousness of new resurrection life. Anointing took place, and we celebrated the Communion with joy together. The Holy Spirit was given a chance, and He raised the dead. If you are in the midst of brokenness today, pray the sinner's prayer and give the Holy Spirit a chance to raise you up. You can be sure He will do it now. I know; He has done it for me.

It is exciting to meet someone who is alive in Jesus through the power of the Holy Spirit. Paul knew some people like that in Ephesus. Listen to what he says, and notice that he can give a testimony of his own journey from death to life. "And you He made alive, who were dead in trespasses and sins, in which you once walked according to the course of this world, according to the prince of the power of the air, the spirit who now works in the sons of disobedience, among whom also we all once conducted ourselves in the lusts of our flesh, fulfilling the desires of the flesh and of the mind, and were by nature children of wrath, just as the others. But God, who is rich in mercy, because of His great love with which He loved us, even when we were dead in trespasses, made us alive together with Christ (by grace you have been saved), and raised us up together, and made us sit together in the heavenly places in Christ Jesus, that in the ages to come He might show the exceeding riches of His grace in His kindness toward us in Christ Jesus" (Ephesians 2:1-7).

When we belong to Jesus, we are counted as being raised from the dead with Him. He didn't wait until we were good enough. He did it while we were dead in sin (verse 5). Just as Jesus died for us while we were sinners (Romans 5:8), so He was willing to raise us up on the basis of His love and grace and our willingness to accept His gift of everlasting life.

Please don't consider yourself a Christian while you are still living in the grave. Just as the Holy Spirit says to the church at Sardis, some people seem to have a name that lives (Christian), but they are spiritually dead (Revelation 3:1). I have been in that position myself a few times, even as a pastor. It is possible to have the name of some denomination whose founders were alive in Jesus and who understood the beautiful union of Spirit and truth, yet be spiritually dead. If you have accepted Jesus as your Saviour, begin to live the resurrection life of victory and joy today.

On the Throne With Jesus

As we give the Holy Spirit a chance, He will reveal to us that God considers us not only alive with Jesus but also as sitting in heavenly places on the throne with Him. Now, that's almost too good to believe. "Even when we were dead in trespasses, [God] made us alive together with Christ (by grace you have been saved), and raised us up together, and made us sit together in the heavenly places in Christ Jesus" (Ephesians 2:5, 6).

When my wife and I visited Westminster Abbey recently we saw the throne on which the monarchs of England have been crowned for many centuries. Visually it is not a very impressive throne, but its history is incredible.

Perhaps the most ornate throne I have seen was the Peacock Throne of the shah of Iran, in Teheran. It is breathtaking. It originated with the Mogul Empire in India and was taken to the successor of ancient Persia by Nadir Shah in 1739. But God's throne, where Jesus is seated, obviously knows no comparison in size or grandeur to any earthly king's seat.

I was enjoying the hospitality of Dr. Jim and Kim Cady in Palos Verdes Estates, in California. Kim, using her new Kereoke voice system, sang for me a number of beautiful songs. One of these was based on Psalm 45:6, 7: "Your throne, O God, is forever and ever." Many of the homes and gardens in this part of Los Angeles are magnificent, but they obviously pale into insignificance when compared with God's eternal throne.

Don't trade anything in this world for your place on the throne of heaven with Jesus. Only God's children can be seated there. That's why the Holy Spirit witnesses to those He has raised that they belong to the royal family of God. "The Spirit Himself bears witness with our spirit that we are children of God" (Romans 8:16).

To Give You Resurrection Life Now

Some modern British history can help us understand how Christians with resurrection life are counted as being on the throne with Jesus. When King Edward VIII of Great Britain abdicated in 1936 to marry Mrs. Wallis Simpson, his brother George came to the throne. In George, who become known as George VI, was George VII, Elizabeth II, Charles, and his son William. If George VI had not come to the throne, all these other people would be virtually unknown—including Diana, the popular princess of Wales. The new royal Windsor line was represented in George VI.

You were represented at the resurrection by Jesus. You are reckoned by God as being on the throne with Him. Don't give that up for anything. Give the Holy Spirit a chance today to confirm you in certainty of resurrection life.

My maternal grandfather lived until he was 100 years old. As far as I know, he was an atheist all his life. He did not die in fear of death, but tenaciously clung to his belief that death is the end—an eternal nothingness. But through faith in Jesus we believe that death is not the end. The Holy Spirit has given us ample evidence of that by raising Jesus from the dead.

There is even more telling evidence the Holy Spirit gives us. That is the evidence of lives changed by the Holy Spirit's resurrection power. When the prophet Ezekiel saw the strange vision of the dry bones that became beautiful but lifeless bodies, he was privileged to give to the people a great message of hope. "I will put My Spirit in you, and you shall live," the Lord said (Ezekiel 37:14). As the New Testament teaches, it is at conversion that the Holy Spirit comes to dwell in a person's life. Then we see the greatest evidence of the Holy Spirit's resurrection power—a life transformed from death to life. Look at the way the Lord had previously explained this to Ezekiel: "I will give you a new heart and put a new spirit within you; I will take the heart of stone out of your flesh and give you a heart of flesh. I will put My Spirit within you and cause you to walk in My statutes, and you will keep My judgments and do them" (Ezekiel 36:26, 27). You can see how, once again, as we studied in chapter one, the resurrection life of the Holy Spirit blends Spirit and truth together in a very beautiful and wonderful way.

In a meeting with pastors I listened to a young man tell of his experience with the resurrection power of the Holy Spirit. I asked his permission to share with you a little of his story. It confirms again, 20 centuries after Jesus rose from the dead, that the Holy Spirit still has this incredible power.

In 1986, after three years of marriage, Michael Harris and his beautiful Fijian wife, Amber, were making the long, tedious drive from Ventura, California, to Las Vegas, Nevada. At 2:00 a.m., with the cruise control set on 70 miles per hour, Michael fell asleep at the wheel. The car hit the guardrail and flipped over four times, throwing Amber through the windshield. Michael was unhurt, but he soon discovered that Amber was paralyzed from the chest down.

"No car would stop to help us. It was about 7:30 a.m. when we finally got Amber to the hospital," Michael told me as he relived again the terrible anguish of that accident. Michael and Amber were not Christians, although Amber had been brought up in a Christian family.

In a recent telephone conversation Amber revealed something to me that confirmed the Holy Spirit's ability to use even the vaguest memory of spiritual things a person may have. "While I was lying there injured in the desert, and later for months in the hospital, the Holy Spirit brought scriptures to my mind, plus the words and music of old hymns. It was as though I was in school with the Holy Spirit."

What happened in that terrible accident was eclipsed only by the tragedy of Michael turning to cocaine, marijuana, and alcohol as he tried to bury his mental and emotional pain. "Here's some drugs," his friends said to him. "They will help you get over the things that have happened to you so you can enjoy life again."

It soon became obvious that Michael was in no state to care for his paraplegic wife, so when Amber left the hospital six months later, she returned to her family in Fiji. "When I went to Fiji, a lot of things happened," Amber said. "I was crying for Michael, and God showed me to 'seek first' His glorious kingdom." Amber learned to believe in prayer.

Amber's mother and sisters tried to convince her that witchcraft could help her walk. "I had to choose between my mother and God," said Amber. "I told her, 'I don't want to walk if it's through witchcraft.'" So Amber moved in with an aunt who lived nearby.

For eight months Amber and her loved ones prayed for Michael. "Even 3-year-olds were praying for me," said Michael as he told me the story. "Amber had now given her life fully to the Lord. When I called and wanted her to come back to me in the States, she said that she could not do it unless we joined a church."

One morning as Michael got out of bed and looked in the bathroom mirror he saw a young man whose life was being completely ruined by drug addiction. He looked at the drug tracks in the veins in his arms, and he knew that only the Man with scars in His hands could save his life. There in the bathroom that morning he cried out to God: "Lord, I know You exist; I submit to You. Please give me the victory over these bad habits that are ruining my life."

The cure came instantly. "It happened right there on the spot," said

Michael. "I had no more urges for marijuana, cocaine, or alcohol."

That very day Amber arrived from Fiji. Now they are both baptized and Spirit-filled. Michael quit his government job to devote himself "entirely to ministry work," which concentrates on helping in drug recovery homes, rescue missions, prisons, and convalescent homes in southern California. Amber has begun a special wheelchair ministry in Los Angeles. "There are so many people out there to reach; I'm glad I don't have to walk to do that," Amber explained. This confirmed the fact that I had discovered Amber to be a woman of great faith, experiencing with her husband the resurrection power of the Holy Spirit.

There is no doubt that Jesus is alive, and His people are alive with Him. I listened to the beautiful bass voice of Michael Harris singing "Touch by Me, Holy Spirit, Touch by Me," and I knew that God would continue to raise the dead as Spirit-filled Christians like Michael and Amber bring the healing touch of Jesus to all who are dead in trespasses and sins.

Give the Holy Spirit a chance. If you are alive in Jesus today, let the Holy Spirit work His resurrection ministry through you.

SMALL GROUP STUDY
Chapter Two

Cohesive Contrasts

The Holy Spirit will quickly bring your group into what the New Testament calls *koinonia*, which means communication and partnership. This word is often translated in the New Testament as "fellowship." Always be sensitive to new members joining the group as a result of the "empty chair" principle. Today continue to get to know each other by sharing answers to the following question:

When you were quite young, who impressed you most as being a person of life and energy?

Concentrating on the Word
Study Text: Ephesians 2:1-10

What is the most convincing evidence for you that Jesus is actually alive?

_____
_____
_____

List some of the comparisons Paul makes in Ephesians 2:1-10 between spiritual life and spiritual death.

_____   _____
_____   _____
_____   _____

Can you think of other instances in the Bible when the Holy Spirit played an important part in a resurrection or new creation? Write down these references and compare them with the findings of other group members.

_____
_____

How do you feel about God's categorization of unconverted people as "dead"?

Shocked _____ Puzzled _____ In agreement _____

Skeptical _____ Other _____
Why? _____

List some similarities and differences between spiritual and physical death.

Similarities	Differences
_____	_____
_____	_____
_____	_____

If you feel comfortable doing so, share with the group an experience of going from the dry bones experience (as Ezekiel calls it) to that of life through the power of the Holy Spirit.
_____
_____

In what ways are Spirit and truth linked together in both Ezekiel 36:26, 27 and Ephesians 2:1-10?
_____
_____

What do you consider to be the most important differences between the "death styles" of the world and the "lifestyles" of Jesus?
_____
_____

If you could purchase for yourself the most comfortable and beautiful chair, what would it be like?
_____
_____

How does it make you feel knowing that God considers you as sitting on the throne with Jesus?

Proud _____	Mystified _____
Gratified _____	Humble _____
Excited _____	Powerful _____
Royal _____	Other _____

As you consider your resurrection life, do you agree with Paul in his use of such superlatives as "exceeding greatness," "mighty power," "great love," "exceeding riches"? Why?

_____

_____

Conversation With the Lord

Include some worship time in your small group fellowship. Perhaps you would like to sing together or read a psalm together before you pray. Now spend some time in conversational prayer. Once again, center on praise, needs within the group, and intercession for others outside the group. Finish your prayer time with the Lord's Prayer together, and also pray for the "empty chair," asking the Lord to lead each group member to someone who can be invited to join the group next week.

Committing the Word to Memory

This week, write out a verse from Ephesians 2:1-10 and share it with someone as soon as possible.

_____

_____

Chapter Three

Give the Holy Spirit a Chance
To Supply You With Abundant Hope

The French emperor Napoleon once said, "Leaders are dealers in hope." Every now and then you meet a hope dealer. Hope dealers inspire you. They give you courage. They change your life. Hope dealers help you feel that you can carry on.

You may be rather surprised about this, but one of the first things the Holy Spirit will do after He has raised you from the dead is to fill you with such incredible hope that you will be able to start a dealership right where you live.

Listen to this: "Now may the God of hope fill you with all joy and peace in believing, that you may abound in hope by the power of the Holy Spirit" (Romans 15:13). Not only is our God the great God of hope, but the Holy Spirit actually causes people to "overflow" with hope. When something overflows, it just pours onto everything around it. David said, "You anoint my head with oil; my cup runs over" (Psalm 23:5).

Sometimes you meet people overflowing with hope. This is actually an evidence of the Holy Spirit filling their life. A favorite book of mine on the life of Jesus says, "In describing to His disciples the office work of the Holy Spirit, Jesus sought to inspire them with the joy and hope that inspired His own heart."[1] Yes, Jesus was a hope dealer, and so were His disciples after they were filled with the Holy Spirit on the day of Pentecost.

The same author talks about the hope dealership of the disciples. "The glad tidings of a risen Saviour were carried to the utmost bounds of the known world.... Under their labors there were added to the church chosen men, who, receiving the Word of life, consecrated their lives to the work of giving to others the hope that had filled their hearts with peace and joy."[2] Give the Holy Spirit a chance to fill you with hope today.

Hope in the Bible is not a feeling, but a person—the God of hope represented in His people by the indwelling presence of the Holy Spirit. That's why the psalmist said, "You are my hope, O Lord God" (Psalm 71:5). Jeremiah confirms the personality of hope when he says, "Blessed is the man who trusts in the Lord, and whose hope is the Lord" (Jeremiah 17:7). The hope that is generated in Christians by the Holy Spirit is not wishful thinking about the future but absolute certainty in Jesus.

A prisoner soon to be released from an Oregon penitentiary told a Christian visitor, "When I get out of here, it will be almost impossible for me to get a job, a good job, but I have been offered a job as a cook. Not a cook in McDonald's, nor in the kitchen of the Sheraton, but a cook in a crack house. In just a few weeks I can earn $30,000 supplying crack to dope dealers." I had the opportunity myself, years ago, to be a dope dealer. Once in Baghdad and once in Bangkok I had the chance to buy for a few hundred dollars enough drugs to sell on the streets back home for hundreds of thousands. With a supply like that I could have been a dealer, a dealer in dope. But when as a teenager I gave my life to Jesus and was filled with the Holy Spirit, I made a life commitment to be a hope dealer for the Lord Jesus Christ.

Paul emphasizes that hope overflows in the human heart through the power of the Holy Spirit (Romans 15:13). This means that the Spirit-filled Christian has a supply of Holy Spirit hope to share with others. No matter what you deal in, you have to have a supply. If you are going to deal in farm machinery, you need a supply of equipment. If you are going to deal in flowers, you need a supply of flowers. If you are going to deal in fish or fancy work, you need a supply. To be a hope dealer, you must have a supply of hope. Let me tell you how you can have enough hope to supply all who are in desperate need.

The Basis of Hope

In Romans 5:1, 2 Paul establishes the basic principle for hope dealership. "Therefore, having been justified by faith, we have peace with God through our Lord Jesus Christ, through whom also we have access by faith into this grace in which we stand, and rejoice in hope of the glory of God." Notice Paul concludes these verses by saying, "Rejoice in the hope of the glory of God." This hope is worth having. When you possess the hope that Jesus Christ offers through the Holy Spirit, you can rejoice and be glad, you can sing, you can praise the Lord.

In Old Testament times much of the hope of God's people was centered in the Messianic expectation. They were looking forward to the coming of Jesus. In the Old Testament, it seems, there was no neutral ground of future expectations, only fear or hope. But in the New Testament the Holy Spirit reveals that hope is realized in Jesus Christ. In Jesus we can rejoice, because He has made possible an inexhaustible supply of hope. Notice what Paul says

Jesus has done to make the supply of hope accessible: "Therefore, having been justified by faith, we have peace with God through our Lord Jesus Christ" (verse 1). Jesus died not only for the sins of Christians but also for the sins of the whole world. Jesus provided justification for the whole human family. He made it possible for every person to be counted just as if he or she had never sinned.

To make the supply of hope abundant in the Christian's life, the Holy Spirit works to create an absolute assurance of salvation through the blood of Jesus. Through the Holy Spirit there is clarity in the mind of the Christian that he or she is accounted righteous by God because of faith in Jesus. So the Holy Spirit convicts not only of sin and judgment but also of righteousness (John 16:8). In fact, Paul states that the kingdom of God is righteousness, joy, and peace in the Holy Spirit (Romans 14:17).

Just before the 1988 elections the Libertine Party leader, who was running for president of the United States, indicated that one of his prominent platforms was to legalize drugs. With drugs legalized, there would be an unlimited supply. What a tragedy that would be. But Jesus came and legalized justification. He made possible an unlimited supply of justification. As the old hymn says: "My hope is built on nothing less than Jesus' blood and righteousness." He supplied sufficient righteousness for all people. Every person who accepts Jesus' offer of justification can have access to the peace that Jesus makes possible, and therefore can have an abundant supply of hope.

Look again at verse 2 in Romans 5. Paul uses the word "access": "Through whom also we have access by faith into this grace." Martin Luther, commenting on these verses, stated that Paul makes clear the fact that we are not just saved through Jesus or through faith, as if one supersedes the other. Luther says in his commentary on Romans, "Both must be together that we may have access into this grace in which we stand." Dope addicts struggle to find access to a supply. Dope houses on the streets of Portland have escalated the crime in this city until it has been reported in *U.S. News & World Report* that Portland, Oregon, in 1990 had the highest crime rate per ratio of population of any city in the United States.

Look at what the Holy Spirit has done. He provides a supply for hope dealers today. He has made access to that supply possible through faith. "For through Him we both have access by one Spirit to the Father" (Ephesians 2:18). Once the Holy Spirit has convinced you of the righteousness you are accounted as having through Jesus' work of justification, you will not approach God's throne with timidity or fear, because the Spirit will continually assure you of your complete acceptance by God. As Paul said: "In whom we have boldness and access with confidence through faith in Him" (Ephesians 3:12). The supply of hope is not obtained by some Christian form of crime or works; it is a gift of grace. It doesn't have to be stolen; it is freely available. Give the Holy Spirit a chance to give you a super supply of hope today.

Sometime ago my wife and I bought a house. Because we were a little concerned about other people having keys to the house we decided to change the locks, and with the new locks came three keys. We moved into the house on Friday, and the next night our 17-year-old daughter, Sharon, went out to a school social function. She took her key with her so she could get into the house when she came home late in the evening. In fact, I said like a good father, "Please be home by midnight," and then added, "Make sure you let yourself in, because I am not feeling well." When she arrived home just before midnight, instead of opening the door with her key she rang the doorbell. I had to get up out of bed and go down to the door. The first thing I said, of course, was "Where is your key? Why didn't you use it?" She replied, "I lost it." Perhaps you know what it's like to feel you have lost your key of faith. You feel that you cannot open the door and find access to the hope that Jesus has provided for you. But I want to tell you today that the Holy Spirit continues to offer you the key of new faith. Our daughter found her key the next day and we were glad about that, but how much more rejoicing there is when spiritually we reach out and accept the offer of grace that God has provided for us.

When the disciples were filled with the Holy Spirit, "great grace was upon them all" (Acts 4:33). That grace gives us a sufficient supply of hope to enable us to be dealers in that which is worth more than any thrill the world can offer. Like the New Testament Christians we can "rejoice in the hope of the glory of God."

Years ago in New Zealand and Australia teenage girls would often receive a wooden chest called a glory box. Into that glory box they would put all sorts of treasures that they were preparing for the day when they might get married and have a home and family of their own. When I came to the United States I found that the term *glory box* was not used, so I was surprised recently to see, in a magazine, pictures and diagrams of *hope chests*. I read in the article a little of the history of how hope chests originated in Europe in the fifteenth century. They reached the peak of popularity at the time of the Renaissance and eventually made their way to the U.S.A. Very often they were made with cedar. Into these hope chests young ladies placed linen and other wonderful things that were being prepared in the hope that a marriage would eventually take place. But the joy of hope in Jesus Christ is more substantial than a cedar box. The inexhaustible supply of hope in the Lord Jesus Christ provided through the Holy Spirit is more wonderful than a glory box or hope chest can ever be. "Now may the God of hope fill you with all joy and peace in believing, that you may abound in hope by the power of the Holy Spirit."

The Building of Hope

I have never met anyone who was excited about being in trouble, have you? However, many people have testified of good that came out of bad situations. "And not only that, but we also glory in tribulations, knowing that tribulation produces perseverance; and perseverance, character; and character, hope" (Romans 5:3, 4). It seems that the Holy Spirit grows true hope out of experiences of fearing, doubting, and despairing. There is a cross at the heart of the Christian faith. There is the valley of the shadow of death. But in the midst of it all the Holy Spirit reveals that through Jesus Christ there is the sense of possibility—the hope and joy of resurrection.

Just as the born-again Christian has resurrection life now spiritually through the exceptional power of the Holy Spirit, so also the Holy Spirit points forward to the day when physical death will be destroyed and God's children will be glorified totally with their Lord. Out of the suffering of humans who are persecuted or harassed for their belief in justification and righteousness through Jesus, the ultimate hope of resurrection joy shines like a flashlight on a moonless night in the mountains. "For we through the Spirit eagerly await for the hope of righteousness by faith" (Galatians 5:5).

Now, the hope of righteousness by faith is not righteousness by faith. Spirit-filled Christians already are counted righteous in Jesus. The blazing hope righteousness by faith brings is the redemption of the body (Romans 8:23), which for those who have the firstfruits of the Spirit growing and flowing in them is as certain as the spiritual resurrection the Holy Spirit has made possible at conversion. Look at the remarkably concise way Paul links together regeneration and justification with hope and eternal life as he talks to Titus about the Holy Spirit. "Not by works of righteousness which we have done, but according to His mercy He saved us, through the washing of regeneration and renewing of the Holy Spirit, whom He poured out on us abundantly through Jesus Christ our Savior, that having been justified by His grace we should become heirs according to the hope of eternal life" (Titus 3:5-7). Pray about the key points in those verses and notice again the regeneration or resurrection life spiritually that the Christian has now. Observe that through Jesus the Holy Spirit is poured out abundantly so that

He overflows and as a result there is an awareness of justification by God's grace, and hope flourishes in the life.

If you give the Holy Spirit a chance, He will build true hope in you as He guides you through the most difficult experiences of life. As the German theologian Jurgen Moltmann said in his *Theology of Hope*: "In the power of the Spirit who raised Christ from the dead, they (His followers) can obediently take upon them the sufferings of discipleship and in these very sufferings await the future glory."[3]

When we moved into our new house, my wife and I, because of our love for walking, looked around the area for somewhere close by where we could enjoy some good exercise. Within a block of our home we found a place with beautiful green grass and lovely trees, paved walking trails and a view of Mount Hood, Mount St. Helens, Mount Adams, and Mount Rainier in the distance. What a place to walk, but there was only one problem with this beautiful walking location. It's a cemetery! It's a little sad to look at the gravestones as we walk by and think of all the lives and tragedies that they represent. One area that we walk through caused my wife to shed a few tears initially because it is where many little babies are buried. But I have noticed on some of the graves, words of hope and encouragement, words of confidence and certainty. That is what hope is really like.

True hope grows out of tribulation and conflict, as Paul explains in Romans 5:3, 4. Just before one Halloween while walking through the cemetery I noticed on one grave a pumpkin painted with a funny face. I said to my wife, "That must be a little child buried there and the parents have come and placed this funny face on the grave in memory of this little life." I was quite surprised when I walked over and looked at the gravestone closely and discovered it was that of an 82-year-old lady. A sense of humor even in a cemetery! The Holy Spirit enables hope dealers to minister in the darkest hours of tribulation and trouble.

Roy Fairchild in his *Guide to Counseling the Depressed* has stated that a common characteristic of depression is the loss of hope. A founder of Gestalt therapy states that many depressed people have "catastrophic expectations," while another psychologist has stated that depressed people believe in the "never syndrome." "Things will never get right, things will never get better, it will never work out well, I will never pass the examination, I will never get a job, I will never have enough money to do this or that, my family situation will never be better." Never, never, never.[4]

In ancient times Christians faced tremendous pressures and persecution. As Paul says in the third verse of Romans 5, Christians can "glory in tribulations, knowing that tribulation produces perseverance; and perseverance, character; and character, hope." Out of the conflict of a situation that could degenerate into a catastrophic tragedy the Holy Spirit develops character by the realization that all the hope plus joy and peace that God offers is available now. As Fairchild states, true hope, biblical hope, is not a utopian fantasy of the future; it is a reality now.

Hope dealers are not just painting of a glorious tomorrow, but are showing how we can experience through the Holy Spirit what God has for us today. God does not offer just sweet peace in heaven above; He offers us life, joy, and forgiveness now.

Recently in London I turned off Fleet Street and walked up Fetter Lane, where for more than 200 years stood a little Moravian chapel. This Moravian chapel was the place where John and Charles Wesley and George Whitfield, together with 60 Moravians and four other Anglican clergy, received a great infilling of the Holy Spirit on January 1, 1739. As I looked for the chapel I discovered that it had been destroyed by the bombing raids that had swept over London in the early part of World War II. Only a plaque stands now in memory of this famous spot. The effect of Wesley's conversion and filling of the Holy Spirit was absolutely amazing. He became a horseback hope dealer, traveling more than 4,500 miles annually. Wesley's hope dealership was so effective that within his lifetime more than 130,000 people rallied around him as charter members of Methodism. By the middle of the next century there were more than 12 million followers of Wesley, each one still inspired by their hope dealer founder.

In his journal on Monday, September 3, 1739, John Wesley wrote of the beautiful experience he had sharing with his mother concerning the great confidence and assurance a newborn Christian has in the Lord Jesus Christ. "I talked largely with my mother, who told me that, till a short time since, she had scarce heard such a thing mentioned as the having forgiveness of sins now, or God's Spirit bearing witness with our spirit: much less did she imagine that this was the common privilege of all true believers." This remarkable Christian woman went on to give her words of assurance, saying that "I knew God for Christ's sake had forgiven me all my sins."[5] Suzanna Wesley was not only the mother of 19 children, but also, because of a hope and joy in Jesus, became known as the mother of Methodism. The blessed hope of Jesus' second coming, the new creation to which Christians can look forward, eternal bliss that God has offered His people—all of these can have present reality in our lives today through the Holy Spirit.

With the wonderful assurance of salvation there is a supply of hope that the Holy Spirit makes readily available. That's why I am asking you to give the Holy Spirit a chance to help you be a hope dealer today. Remember, we do not merit hope or earn it by enduring tribulation. But it is in tribulation that the character of the true hope dealer is revealed. The person who knows the intensity of pain and suffering, sin and tragedy can through Holy Spirit witnessing power share with others the hope that is possible in Jesus Christ.

The Blossoming of Hope

"It's raining, it's pouring, the old man is snoring . . ." I seem to remember that song from my year or two in a New Zealand kindergarten. "Pouring" conjures up a vision of abundance, generosity. God says, "I will . . . pour out . . . such a blessing that there will not be room enough to receive it" (Malachi 3:10). He will pour out His Spirit (Joel 2:28). He will pour water on the thirsty (Isaiah 44:3). Paul sounds excited as he tells how hope will ultimately blossom in the life of a hope dealer. "Now hope does not disappoint because the love of God has been poured out in our hearts by the Holy Spirit who was given to us" (Romans 5:5). Through the power of the Holy Spirit the amazing love of God floods into our hearts. Love is the fruit of the Spirit and supersedes all spiritual gifts. Love is the character of God and is greater than faith and hope, because love is their basis (1 Corinthians 13). With love comes a hope that never disappoints, a hope that is not like the cheap and transitory emotions that Hollywood offers.

A young man committed suicide recently because, as he said in a note he left behind, "my girlfriend just doesn't love me anymore." God's love never disappoints, never changes; that is why the hope dealer's supply of positive power is never in question, never in doubt. Dope dealers concentrate all their life and energy on getting people hooked on misery, driving them into a living hell, but hope dealers, filled with the Holy Spirit, concentrate on revealing to others a joy and peace that is contagious. Through the Holy Spirit they communicate the love that has been poured into their hearts. They give the people courage to move ahead, to carry on, to really reach their true potential. As Napoleon said: "Leaders are dealers in hope."

Philip was a young man who had attended a Christian school but somehow slipped away from the Lord and found his life moving in a negative direction mainly because of his constant habit of drinking alcohol. It seemed that Philip had many hurdles to overcome. Both his parents were alcoholics. They had struggled to do their best for him, but he rapidly followed the same path that his parents had taken. Philip moved to the big city and one night after some rather heavy drinking he went out with a friend to find a dope dealer. That night, back in their room, Philip and his friend injected the heroin they had bought. It killed them both instantly.

To Supply You With Abundant Hope

Many young people from the inner city streets gathered for the funeral. I had expected a few Christian relatives and no more, so I was surprised to see the chapel crowded with young people from all walks of life listening intently, many of them thirsty for hope. I laid aside my prepared funeral notes and began to talk to them about the conflict between good and evil, right and wrong, hope and fear. I prayed silently, "Lord, help me today to be a hope dealer. Lord, pour into the hearts of these people, by the power of the Holy Spirit, Your love, Your peace, and Your joy." Immediately I noticed the power of Jesus beginning to work. As I preached and as I spoke to many of these inner city young people afterward, I knew that they had become conscious of a different power that day—the power of a hope dealer. In a society and a culture rapidly being destroyed by drugs, some of these young people had seen the light of Jesus. I was able, as Peter said, to give a reason for the hope that was within me, "with meekness and fear" (1 Peter 3:15).

The world needs hope dealers today. It needs young people and older people who will accept the joy of Jesus for themselves and then, through the power of the Holy Spirit, share their hope to others who are in desperate need.

At the end of the eighties I spoke about hope dealers to more than 1,000 students on a college campus. Afterward many students came to me and expressed the conviction that the Lord had brought to them during that meeting. "We want to become hope dealers on this campus and in this community," many of them said. Soon the Holy Spirit enabled hundreds of students to become involved in small groups where the love of Jesus became the foundation of nurture and outreach ministry. Not only many students but Christians of all ages around the world are participating in Homes of Hope, a small group movement concentrating on fellowship, outreach, Bible study, and prayer.

Inner city police struggle with the tragedy of a crack house manufacturing dope on almost every city block. Soon the devil will have to face the reality of a Home of Hope, or whatever these small groups may be called, dealing love from every neighborhood and community. From dormitory rooms, apartments, flats, houses, and even mansions, hope dealers share their supply. The lonely, discouraged, defeated, sick, the spiritually needy in every strata of society, find a hope that will never disappoint.

I was in New Zealand for a series of revival meetings when I spoke to a young man who had attended high school there with my oldest daughter, Carolyn. He asked me what she was doing now, and I told him that she had graduated from college and was teaching high school in Sydney, Australia. Then I asked him what he had done with his life since leaving high school.

He replied, "My family broke up, and I went into alcohol and drugs. It seemed that my life was going rapidly downhill. But I praise God that He led me to meet a man who brought to me a knowledge of Jesus. Through His wonderful help I was able to turn my life around and now am doing all I can to share the love of Jesus." He told me about the small group Bible study that he was leading each week and about some of the non-Christians who came to the Home of Hope and were helped there. One young man who had attended the group told him, "I feel so close to God in this group. It is changing my life." Today that young man is also a hope dealer.

This is my invitation to you today. Give the Holy Spirit a chance to give you a hope dealership now. The supply is plentiful and available. "Now may the God of hope fill you with all joy and peace in believing, that you may abound in hope by the power of the Holy Spirit" (Romans 15:13). If you have been justified by faith you have peace with God through our Lord Jesus Christ, and you can rejoice in the hope of the glory of God. Even in the middle of big trouble, through perseverance and the strength of Jesus you can develop a character that will be a revelation of hope, and that hope will not disappoint, because the love of God will be poured into your heart by the Holy Spirit, who is given to you.

SMALL GROUP STUDY
Chapter Three

Cohesive Contrasts

Small groups have been called Homes of Hope because it is here that nurture and encouragement can flourish. Here is a sharing question that will help the group understand each other even a little more than has happened in the past two weeks.

Apart from a religious leader, what person during your lifetime inspired you with the most hope? What happened? Did the hope prove dependable or did it eventually disappoint?

Concentrating on the Word
Study Text: Romans 5:1-5

In today's study text what balance do you see between words of fact (e.g., "justified") and words of feeling (e.g., "rejoice")?

_____
_____

List some of the ways you see hope as a fact and hope as a feeling. What difference does it make?

_____
_____

Until you studied this chapter, what was your concept of hope?
Vague _____ Unlikely dream _____
Remote possibility _____ Frustration _____
Disappointment _____ Positive assurance _____
Other _____

What is your understanding of hope now?
_____

Look at Romans 15:13 and discuss some of the connections you see between the power of the Holy Spirit and true hope. What indications have you seen in your own life of the necessity of supernatural power to produce hope?

_____
_____

In verses 3 and 4 Paul takes three steps from tribulation to hope. Do you agree with his evaluation of tribution as something Christians can glory in? Why?

_____
_____

Apart from the gospel, what one thing do you believe can bring lasting hope to humanity? In what way do you see it as being far inferior to what Jesus has to offer? Is there any way your suggestion is better than the gospel?

_____
_____

If you were asked to give a talk on the danger of drugs to a group of junior high school students, what would you list as the most decisive reasons for total abstinence? How would you contrast these reasons with true hope?

_____
_____

Paul connects love and hope together; in fact, the love of God, he says, is the real reason God's hope will never disappoint. Humanly speaking, in what ways do you see true love as the basis of unfailing hope?

_____
_____

Conversation With the Lord

Concentrate prayer on praising God for specific hopes. Then pray for all the necessary qualifications for hope dealership. In your conversational prayer time, sing together songs of hope. Pray for others within the group and outside the group who need hope in specific situations. Conclude by praying for the "empty chair" and sharing the Lord's Prayer together.

Committing the Word to Memory

This week, write out a verse from Romans 5:1-5 and share it with someone as soon as possible.

_____
_____

Chapter Four

Give the Holy Spirit a Chance
To Let You Hear God Speak

I once worked with a Christian lady who had a strong faith in God, especially in His willingness to hear even the most timid, simple prayer of one of His children. No matter how crushed, hurt, or guilty a person felt she believed that God will always hear and answer with forgiveness, courage, and hope. I agreed with my secretary every time she told me of the remarkable ways she had seen proof of God's unfailing love. But coupled with this belief she had a practice that I was a little skeptical about. "I pray and then open my Bible, and God has a message from that page that just jumps straight out at me," she explained. Then she added, "It is always just what I need for that day or situation." I joked about this method at times, telling her of the man who closed his eyes, opened his Bible, and put his finger on a verse that said, "Judas went and hung himself." Being uncomfortable with that verse, he turned to another, only to find that he was pointing to one that said, "Go thou and do likewise."

This skepticism of mine did not seem to discourage my secretary's faith in God's ability to speak to her through His Word, and I am glad of that now, because a number of times I was stunned by direct, positive, and absolutely pertinent messages from the Lord that she shared with me in that way. In fact, one of them I still have marked clearly in every Bible that I use. I was facing a very discouraging time and was wondering how I was going to adjust to some negative circumstances that had arisen when at a very critical moment my friend spoke very clearly to me. "I have been praying about your situation, and I asked the Lord to open my Bible to the exact place that will reveal to you His will at this time. Here is what He has given me. Please read it, and never forget what it says."

Slowly I looked at the open Bible, not knowing what to expect, and there were the words that God knew I needed more than anything else that day. Since then I have shared them with pastors in many situations in a number of countries, and the reaction is always the same. "Thank You, Jesus, for the confidence You have brought to me this day." Would you like to know those verses? Well, here they are. God may be speaking to you through them now. "God is not unjust; he will not forget your work and the love you have shown him as you have helped his people and continue to help them. We want each of you to show this same diligence to the very end, in order to make your hope sure" (Hebrews 6:10, 11, NIV).

I will always remember those words of hope that God gave to me from His Word that day. All the overflowing hope given to us by the Holy Spirit (Romans 15:13) actually has its source in the Word of God. "Whatever things were written before were written for our learning, that we through the patience and comfort of the Scriptures might have hope" (verse 4). I still do not make it the practice of following my work associate's particular method of opening the Bible and pointing to a text, but I will never again deny that there are many and varied ways that the Holy Spirit can help us hear God's voice speaking through His Word.

Before we think and pray about some of the lines of communication—power lines—that the Holy Spirit opens between us and the Word, we should consider the very intimate relationship that exists between the Holy Spirit and the Scriptures. I would like to say that the Holy Spirit is the mother of the Scriptures, but perhaps that term is too easily misunderstood in view of all the masculine pronouns Jesus uses regarding the Holy Spirit. Let us just say that the Holy Spirit was responsible for the conception, birth, and postnatal development of the Bible. If you want to understand the Bible and hear God speak through it, then give the Holy Spirit a chance today—He knows all about it.

Birthing the Bible

"Where did the Bible come from? Perhaps it was written by some pious monks in the Middle Ages." Often in secular universities I have been faced with this question. A particularly skeptical speaker may throw in an extra jab, such as "The Bible is full of mistakes and contradictions anyway." Historical and archaeological studies can quickly show that such questions reveal a basic ignorance of a large body of evidence available today. Thousands of New Testament manuscripts dating back to the first century, and Old Testament documents such as the Dead Sea scrolls and other ancient Jewish literature, confirm the fact that the Bible certainly dates from what we call biblical times. On top of this, although we have only well authenticated copies of original biblical writings, the substantial unity of the Scriptures is amazing considering that they were written by approximately 35 to 40 authors over a period of about 1,500 years.

But listen. Let's really pray now that the Holy Spirit will help us understand the way He brought this book into existence and how He can make it explode with new meaning in hearts and minds.

The first step in this whole process is that the Holy Spirit revealed to men and women a message or scenario He wanted them to communicate. It is this step that theologians call "revelation." The Holy Spirit brought God's revelation to Moses, and He also came upon 70 elders who prophesied (Numbers 11:25). Although the first five books of the Bible are considered to be the fruitage of the Holy Spirit's revelation to Moses, we do not have any written record of the prophecies of the 70 elders. The Holy Spirit gives some revelations to people for local ministry only as in the case of Azariah (2 Chronicles 15:1-8).

On the other hand, Paul says the Holy Spirit spoke through Isaiah, and much of his message is universal. Ezekiel was very much aware that the Holy Spirit was giving him visions (e.g., Ezekiel 8:3; 43:5), and in Daniel visions and dreams are mentioned more than 30 times. This type of activity of the Holy Spirit sweeps right through the Bible and finds its climax in Revelation where John was in the Spirit on the Lord's day (1:10). The Spirit took him in visions into the throne room of heaven (4:2). By the Spirit he saw graphic representations of evil (17:3). Finally in the Spirit he saw the New Jerusalem and the ultimate glory of the new creation.

So the Holy Spirit gave all of the information to the people who are recognized as Bible authors. But now millions of people ask, How did these authors get it written down correctly? Let us notice a couple statements that clarify this. "Knowing this first, that no prophecy of Scripture is of any private interpretation, for prophecy never came by the will of man, but holy men of God spoke as they were moved by the Holy Spirit" (2 Peter 1:20, 21).

I like the way evangelical author Dr. John Williams explains this: "Peter's expression, 'moved by the Holy Ghost,' suggests that just as a ship is borne along by the wind in its sails, so were the writers of Scripture 'carried along' by the Spirit of God. Under His sovereign direction they were enabled to pen the infallible Word of God. Peter's careful use of language here recognizes both the divine and human aspects of Scripture. He allows for the conscious involvement of men with all their individuality, he underlines the sovereignty and surveillance of God, which guarantees to us the inerrancy of Scripture." [1] This moving by the Holy Spirit is often called "inspiration," but could be more correctly translated "expiration," because "God breathed out" His Spirit into the Bible writers, enabling them to communicate effectually what they had seen or heard. "All Scripture is given by inspiration of God, and is profitable for doctrine, for reproof, for correction, for instruction in righteousness" (2 Timothy 3:16).

Paul could tell firsthand what it meant to communicate the Word while being truly inspired. "And I, brethren, when I came to you, did not come with excellence of speech or of wisdom declaring to you the testimony of God. . . . And my speech and my preaching were not with persuasive words of human wisdom, but in demonstration of the Spirit and power" (1 Corinthians 2:1-4). God didn't supply a computer software package and then dictate the Bible to His writers word for word; He inspired people and let them write in the style of their own culture and language.

Now, if all this theological discussion seems a bit heavy (or dare I suggest even a bit boring), please do not panic and think that you might not be holy enough to make it through the pearly gates. Just remember this about Revelation and inspiration: God has made certain that there will always be what John Calvin, the French Reformer, called the "self-authenticating nature of Scripture." When you ask the Holy Spirit to lead you through the Bible, you will know for sure that this is God's Word. Just as you are always aware of your affinity with your native land, so when you come to the Word with heart made open by surrender to the Holy Spirit you will be able to say, "I may not understand all or even much about this, but there is something in this Book that affirms within me that this is God's Word." Give the Holy Spirit a chance, and He will give you such a joy in the Word that you will feel like hugging it.

Recently I spoke to church elder Harold Quinn, who told of his experience after returning to his home from an international prayer conference. "We had prayed together a great deal," he said excitedly, "and I believe I was filled with the Holy Spirit. As I drove home, scriptures seemed to be going over and over in my mind; in fact, I began to read the Bible as soon as I could. There was a hunger in my heart for the Bible. I just devoured it. I wanted to be filled with it every day. Sometimes I was even late for work, as I spent so much time each morning just reading and praying in the Bible and capturing for myself so much of its beauty." Not only did this lay leader find himself immersed in the Scriptures, but God soon gave him opportunity to share the Scriptures with someone else. At the time of our last meeting Harold and his wife, Lisa, introduced me to Kelly, whom the Holy Spirit had brought to a knowledge of Jesus through a number of miraculous events. Now Kelly leads a small group and is helping others understand God's Word.

Turning On the Light

I had heard of Presbyterians but never of presbyopia until I discovered that I was having difficulty reading small print. Although at 45-plus I considered myself not much more than a youth, my optometrist informed me that my eye condition was the result of the hardening of the crystalline lens because of advancing age. My new glasses enabled me to read so clearly that I could almost see the fibers in the paper.

In the same way, if you give the Holy Spirit a chance He will enable you not only to see the Word clearly, but to hear God speak through it. First of all, pray for the Holy Spirit to eliminate spiritual presbyopia. Now you will see the deep things of God as He has promised: "But as it is written: 'Eye has not seen, nor ear heard, nor have entered into the heart of man the things which God has prepared for those who love Him.' But God has revealed them to us through His Spirit. For the Spirit searches all things, yes, the deep things of God" (1 Corinthians 2:9, 10). As you pray through Scripture, this will enable the Holy Spirit to draw together truths from each verse and bring them into focus more effectively than the most complex computerized optical system. "Now we have received, not the spirit of the world, but the Spirit who is from God, that we might know the things that have been freely given to us by God. These things we also speak, not in words which man's wisdom teaches but which the Holy Spirit teaches, comparing spiritual things with spiritual" (verses 12, 13).

This is how the Holy Spirit will lead you into all truth. Just today in the library of Multnomah School of the Bible I read through some of the sermons of John Wesley. I like reading Wesley because he was completely filled with the Holy Spirit and knew it following his Fetter Lane experience on January 1, 1739. Wesley was on fire for God and loved the Bible with a deep passion. Listen to what he says in the introduction to his first volume of sermons: "God Himself has condescended to teach the way: For this very end He came from heaven. He hath written it down in a Book. O give me that Book! At any price, give me the Book of God! I have it: Here is knowledge enough for me. . . . I sit down alone: Only God is here. In His presence I open, I read His Book; for this end, to find the way to heaven. Is there a doubt concerning the meaning of what I read? Does anything appear dark or intricate? I lift up my heart to the Father of lights: 'Lord, is it not Thy Word, "If any man lack wisdom, let him ask of God"? Thou "givest liberally and upbraidest not." Thou hast said, "If any be willing to do thy will, he shall know." I am willing to do, let me know, Thy will.' I then search after and consider parallel passages of Scripture, 'comparing spiritual things with spiritual.' I meditate thereon with all the attention and earnestness of which my mind is capable." [2]

Like John Wesley, pray in the Word, verse by verse. Ask the Holy Spirit to show you what He has for you there. You will not be disappointed. My favorite book on the life of Jesus puts it this way: "We should carefully study the Bible, asking God for the aid of the Holy Spirit, that we may understand His Word. We should take one verse, and concentrate the mind on the task of ascertaining the thought which God has put in that verse for us. We should dwell upon the thought until it becomes our own, and we know 'what saith the Lord.' " [3]

George Müller, founder of the great orphanage ministry in Bristol, England, had much the same experience. He explains in his autobiography, "I began therefore to meditate on the New Testament from the beginning, early in the morning. The first thing I did, after having asked in a few words the Lord's blessing upon His precious Word, was to begin to meditate on the Word of God, searching, as it were, into every verse, to get blessing out of it; . . . not for the sake of preaching on what I had meditated upon, but for the sake of obtaining food for my own soul. The result I have found to be almost invariably this, that after a very few minutes my soul has been led to confession, or to thanksgiving, or to intercession, or to supplication; so that, though I did not, as it were, give myself to *prayer*, but to *meditation*, yet it turned almost immediately more or less into prayer." [4]

There is absolutely no doubt that you can hear God speak to you right out of His Word if you pray in the Scriptures this way. I have found seven prayer questions that for me are most helpful. I was explaining these at a camp meeting in Maine recently, and a young pastor, David Holton, tied them to the word "ESCAPES," which made them so much easier to remember. As you pray in the Word, ask these seven questions: 1. "Lord, is there an Example here for me to follow?" 2. "Lord, is there a Sin here I can avoid?" 3. "Father, is there a Command for me to obey?" 4. "What does this passage teach me About You, Jesus?" 5. "Lord, is there a Promise here that I can claim?" 6. "Is there a difficulty that I can Explore at some future time?" 7. "Father, in this passage is there Something I can pray about today?" [5] It is through the Scriptures that "the righteous ESCAPES from trouble" (Proverbs 12:13, RSV). Jesus' way of escape from the temptations of the enemy was "It is written" (Matthew 4:1-11). The Christian ESCAPES spiritual lethargy and comes alive in the Spirit by praying in the Word.

At present I am using a copy of the Gospel of Mark to teach this method of praying in the Scriptures. Using a single book of the Bible can have special benefits. I carry mine with me when I am walking or driving. When the opportunity is right, I can read a few verses and pray about them as I walk or drive on. Although there is not much room in the margins of this Gospel, I encourage people to write in the book their responses to the Holy Spirit's leading as they pray in each part of the Word. In this way the Gospel becomes like a prayer journal. It is most helpful if the response is written in the form of a prayer. I was praying in the Gospel of Mark with a group of pastors in California, and the Lord led us to the story of Jesus calming the storm in chapter 4:35-41. "Lord, please calm the storm in my life," one pastor prayed. Another responded to the Holy Spirit's leading by praying "Jesus, I have felt angry that You seemed asleep when I faced the crisis in my church." I prayed, "Lord, am I willing to take You with me just as You are, or do I want to change You to suit my own comfort level?"

Over the past few years I have been trying to pray through the Bible each year. Sometimes it takes two years. Looking back over the journaled prayer responses in these Bibles is a very interesting experience for me. I use a different version of the Bible each time. Sometimes the formal type, like the King James Version or the *New American Standard Bible*, is a great blessing. Some years I have enjoyed a dynamic version like the New International Version or Today's English Version. Even paraphrases like *The Living Bible* can be extremely rewarding, although doctrinal studies should always be based on a more formal translation.

The Words Bear Fruit

Now, what is going to be the result of praying this way in the Word? What will be the result of giving the Holy Spirit a chance to open your mind to the Word in a new and living way? I can guarantee that a number of things will happen. First of all, you will begin to hear God speak to you right out of His Word.

I am not talking about imagining some secret message, but rather becoming aware of what Scripture is really saying in each situation of life. Some people charged John Wesley that instead of making the Word of God the rule of his actions, he followed only his secret impulses. I like the vividness of his reply in a letter to the bishop of London: "In the whole compass of language there is not a proposition which less belongs to me than this. I have declared again and again that I make the Word of God 'the rule' of all my actions; and that I no more follow any 'secret impulse' than I follow Muhammad or Confucius." [6]

Every Tuesday night we have a small group meeting in our home, and I am always amazed at how the Holy Spirit opens up so many great truths from the Gospel of Mark. Bill and Nancy, Alan and Sonna, Joe and Janinne, Kathy, Denise, Terry, Peggy, and others join Barbara and me to listen to God give words of edification, exhortation, and comfort by the Holy Spirit. Denise found great meaning in her discovery that heaven was torn open at the baptism of Jesus. I have been a minister for 25 years, but I learned more about this in 10 minutes from a young Christian than I had in all my years of study. God spoke by the Holy Spirit right out of His Word about the significance of the violent tearing of heaven at the time of Jesus' baptism and how from this came the gentleness of the dove.

Second, not only will praying in the Word and receiving the illumination of the Holy Spirit lead you into all truth, but it will nurture and sustain you through the pressures and crises of daily life. Even in the most extreme circumstances the scriptures that the Holy Spirit has impressed on your mind as you have prayed through the Bible will not let you down. Billy Graham, writing on the Holy Spirit and the Word, gives a couple illustrations of this: "Many prisoners in the 'Hanoi Hilton' during the Vietnam war were gloriously sustained by the Spirit through the Word of God. These men testified to the strength they received from the Word of God. Howard Rutledge, in his book *In the Presence of Mine Enemies*, tells how the prisoners developed a code system that the enemy was never able to break. By it they communicated with one another, sharing names and serial numbers of every prisoner. They also passed along other messages . . . , including Scripture verses that they knew. Geoffrey Bull, a missionary on the borders of Tibet, said in his book, *When Iron Gates Yield*, that during his three years of imprisonment he was relentlessly brainwashed and would have succumbed if it had not been for the scriptures he had committed to memory. He repeated them over and over to himself when he was in solitary confinement. Through them God strengthened him to face the torture designed to break him down."[7]

Third, praying in the Word and giving the Holy Spirit a chance to let you hear God speak will give you great victory power against the forces of evil within and without. In the Tower of London my wife and I saw many different types of body armor. Although hundreds of years old, they had been carefully made and joined together so that there was no place for enemy weapons to penetrate. Paul lists the most effective armor for Christians in their warfare with satanic forces. But within this impressive detail of defensive materials there is only one offensive weapon: "And take . . . the sword of the Spirit, which is the word of God; praying always with prayer and supplication in the Spirit, being watchful to this end with all perseverance and supplication for all the saints" (Ephesians 6:17, 18).

The sword of the Spirit is the weapon Jesus used when He was tempted. He conquered by saying, "It is written" (Luke 4:1-13). If you have doubts and fears, turn to the Word, pray in the Word until you are strong. Don't give up. Pray in the Word. Give the Holy Spirit a chance to sharpen your sword. Listen to Martin Luther tell of his faith in this weapon. "And though this world, with devils filled, should threaten to undo us, we will not fear, for God hath willed His truth to triumph through us. The prince of darkness grim, we tremble not for him; his rage we can endure, for lo! his doom is sure, one little word shall fell him. That Word above all earthly powers, no thanks to them, abideth; the Spirit and the gifts are ours through Him who with us sideth." [8]

"Why do we have to have all these complicated doctrines?" asked a high school student at a church camp. I explained how, rightly understood, the doctrines of Bible truth you learn as you study and pray in the Word are also a great aid against the enemy. Doctrine is dangerous if it is made a way of salvation. But if it is a wall of protection around a born-again Christian, it will be a great barrier against evil. This is how Paul came into his discussion with Timothy about inspiration. Have a look at this in its context, and the truth will jump right out at you. "But evil men and impostors will grow worse and worse, deceiving and being deceived. But you must continue in the things which you have learned and been assured of, knowing from whom you have learned them, and that from childhood you have known the Holy Scriptures, which are able to make you wise for salvation through faith which is in Christ Jesus. All Scripture is given by inspiration of God, and is profitable for doctrine, for reproof, for correction, for instruction in righteousness, that the man of God may be complete, thoroughly equipped for every good work" (2 Timothy 3:13-17).

Fourth, praying in the Word through the Holy Spirit will provide all the material for witness that a hope dealer needs. It is in this setting of a small group, a Home of Hope, ministering in the neighborhood, that Paul links Scripture and hope together in Romans 15: "Let each of us please his neighbor for his good, leading to edification. . . . For whatever things were written before were written for our learning, that we through the patience and comfort of the Scriptures might have hope" (verses 2-4). This biblical ministry is utilized by the Holy Spirit in a dramatic way. Paul explains how the Holy Spirit uses His Written Word to become the basis of the word that is spoken by believer to believer and by believer to those not part of the Christian family. "Now may the God of hope fill you with all joy and peace in believing, that you may abound in hope by the power of the Holy Spirit. Now I myself am confident concerning you, my brethren, that you also are full of goodness, filled with all knowledge, able also to admonish one another" (verses 13, 14).

In our small group Kathy wondered how she could witness for the Lord. But after she prayed in the Word the Holy Spirit gave her a powerful message for the group: "Lord, I thank You for being such an example of humility," she wrote in her Gospel after praying about Jesus' baptism. Then she shared the message of exhortation God had given her: "If we are willing to follow Jesus' example, He will also give us a ministry, but we must serve in humility and not allow pride to stand in our way." We all affirmed that Kathy could be a preacher with the strong message God had given her. In fact, a few weeks later God gave her the opportunity to witness to a large group. We all prayed for her and were greatly blessed.

After praying in the Gospel of Mark during an early-morning service at a camp meeting in northern New England, men and women came to the microphone and shared what the Holy Spirit had revealed from the Word. The power in their messages was unmistakable. One young man prayed through Mark 4:35-41 in a very moving way. You will understand each part of this prayer if you follow it through Mark's account of the storm on Galilee. "Dear Lord, help us to be prepared to come over onto the other side, to enter into the heavenly Canaan. Help us not to resist You. Help us follow You. Let us accept You even as You are and let You come into our lives. Let us take others with us across. Great storms will arise in our lives in this end-time. . . . Even though the waves beat into the ships, let us not keep You asleep in our lives, but let us awaken You so that You will help us that we will not perish, but will enter into everlasting life with peace and assurance."

A young mother told how God had shown her new principles from these very verses in Mark 4 that would help her in the correct disciplining of her children. Diane prayed, "Thank You, Jesus, for Your promises and care as we witness for You. We know that we can go out in the midst of the storm and can glorify You." These prayers in Mark 4:35-41 reminded me of the Burl Ives song we taught our daughters when they were small: "With Christ in the vessel we can smile at the storm."

Give the Holy Spirit a chance today. He gave revelation and inspiration so the Word could be written. He will give you such illumination today as you pray through verses of Scripture that you will be able to say with confidence, "Listen to what God has spoken to me from His Word. It has blessed me, and I know it will bless you."

SMALL GROUP STUDY

Chapter Four

Cohesive Contrasts

If your group has been meeting for three or four weeks now, you will have come almost to the end of the "honeymoon" stage. People have gotten used to the group and may even feel it is getting into a rut. Two things will help the group in this disillusionment stage. The first is to have variety and spontaneity at each meeting. People will be excited to discover each week that God has new things in store for them. Second, it is time to share some affirmation with each group member.

Begin your group today telling just one way each person in the group has encouraged you. Pray about it. God will give you the right words to speak.

Concentrating on the Word

Study Text: 1 Corinthians 2:1-14

At least seven times in these 14 verses Paul speaks about the Holy Spirit. In what ways do you see the Holy Spirit connected in these verses each time to the communication of God's Word?

_____
_____

How does praying in the Word and learning to hear God's voice in Scripture provide a safeguard against deceptions?

_____
_____

Paul was given the testimony of God (verse 1), which is the Spirit of prophecy (Revelation 19:10). Why would He say that His communication of this was a demonstration of Holy Spirit power (verse 4)?

_____
_____

Look at the whole context of the purpose of Scripture in the light of 2 Timothy 3:14-17. Which of the following statements most clearly defines the main reason God gave all this information that we call the Bible?

1. To give lists of teachings that would be difficult for people to obey. ___

2. To make theology complex enough to keep scholars busy for a lifetime.
_____

3. To glorify Jesus and all the details of salvation and its history. _____
4. To reprimand people so they would feel guilty and bad. _____
5. To set a standard for perfection of life that cannot be reached. _____
6. To protect Christians from error and deception. _____
7. Other _____

What are some things freely given us by God that the Holy Spirit can help us really know (verse 12)?

_____
_____

Tell of some way that comparing spiritual things with spiritual as the Holy Spirit teaches (verse 13) helped you learn a wonderful truth from the Bible.

_____
_____

Paul says spiritual things are spiritually discerned (verse 14). List some ways the Bible seemed different to you before and after your conversion.

_____
_____

Pray now in verses 6-10 and write as a prayer response the things that God says to you from these verses. The whole group may pray silently here for five or ten minutes and then begin to share what each person has written as a response to the leading of the Holy Spirit.

_____
_____

Taking the Sword of the Spirit, which is the Word of God (Ephesians 6:17), list ways in which Bible verses can be used to defeat the enemy.

_____
_____

Conversation With the Lord

Conclude your group meeting with a period of conversational prayer, centering on praise, needs within the group, and intercession for others outside the group. Give the Holy Spirit opportunity to lead you into prayer songs and prayer scriptures that can be shared within this conversational prayer time. Remember to agree with each other in prayer so that no person seems alone in his or her prayer, particularly in bringing the specific supplication to God. Finish your prayer time with the Lord's Prayer, and also pray for the "empty chair," continuing to ask the Lord to lead each group member to someone who can be invited to join the group next week. If the group is growing large because of success with this outreach, pray that the Lord will lead in what way the group can perhaps consider dividing in two.

Committing the Word to Memory

This week, write out a verse from 1 Corinthians 2:1-14 and share it with someone as soon as possible.

_____

_____

Chapter Five

▼

Give the Holy Spirit a Chance
To Help You Pray in the Spirit

Did you know that John the Baptist had a prayer ministry and that Jesus did not teach His disciples to pray until they specifically asked Him for this instruction? Somehow I have always had this reversed, thinking that John the Baptist was only a hyperactivist type of hellfire and brimstone preacher, while Jesus would have moved His disciples immediately into gentle prayer ministries. This illusion was shattered one morning as I prayed in Luke 11. Right in the very first verse I discovered that Jesus' disciples had been apparently standing around watching Him pray when they decided to deal head-on with an issue that had been concerning them. "And it came to pass, as He was praying in a certain place, when He ceased, that one of His disciples said to Him, 'Lord, teach us to pray, as John also taught his disciples'" (Luke 11:1).

Would you like to learn to pray? Then give the Holy Spirit a chance today. He will help you understand not only what it means to pray in the Holy Spirit, as Jude says (verse 20), but also the very close connection there is between the Holy Spirit and prayer. The two are as inseparable as life and air.

"Have you said your prayers?" my mother would ask when I was a child. Many people have learned prayers from parents or church and have fallen into the habit of "saying" them in a rather routine manner. But when the Holy Spirit and prayer are connected so that prayer becomes a power line between a person and God, then the communication is intimate and personal and the effect is remarkable.

Remember the old discussion about which came first, the chicken or the egg? We could find ourselves in a similar contention concerning the Holy Spirit and prayer. Which comes first—prayer that opens a person's life to the Holy Spirit, or the Holy Spirit working in people enabling them to pray? Actually the Holy Spirit Himself will clarify this as we give Him a chance to teach us to pray.

An Invitation for a Friend

In many places around the world I have heard Christians sing a prayer song to the Holy Spirit. Perhaps you have sung it yourself:

"Come, Holy Spirit, I need You,
Come, sweet Spirit, I pray;
Come, in Your strength and Your power,
Come, in Your own gentle way." [1]

An invitation like that is what the Holy Spirit is waiting for. He does not force Himself into any life, but comes with full power when a person is completely open to Him. Here we must remind ourselves of a theological technicality. It is actually at conversion that the Holy Spirit enters a person's life. Study again such passages as Romans 8:9; Ephesians 1:13; 2 Corinthians 1:21, 22; and Ezekiel 36:27 if you are not clear on this point. So when a born-again Christian, who is already the dwelling place of the Holy Spirit (1 Corinthians 6:19, 20; Romans 8:11), again invites the Holy Spirit into his or her life, it is actually a reaffirmation of the conversion experience and a new invitation for the Holy Spirit to have complete residential authority.

This leads us back to our first Bible reference in this chapter—Luke 11. This section of Scripture contains Jesus' most concentrated teaching on prayer. He begins with what has become known as the Lord's Prayer, and then He tells a story about persistence. Finally Jesus brings to a climax His discussion on prayer by saying, "If you then, being evil, know how to give good gifts to your children, how much more will your heavenly Father give the Holy Spirit to those who ask Him!" (Luke 11:13). The original language here indicates that these words could be translated "How much more will your heavenly Father give the Holy Spirit to those who *keep on asking Him*." The word Jesus uses for "keep on asking" is translated as "requesting" or "demanding" in various versions of 1 Corinthians 1:22. Just as Jesus taught His disciples to keep on asking "daily" or "day by day" for bread (Luke 11:3), so they would keep on requesting or even demanding God to give them the gift of the Holy Spirit.

The word "demanding" makes me feel a little nervous, because it does not seem right to think of oneself demanding anything from God. A friend of mine said of his sister's daughter, "She is a very demanding child." Perhaps the little girl suffered from the "I want" or "give me" syndrome. But "ask," as Jesus used it to teach His disciples about praying for the Holy Spirit, can be translated "demand," which means to ask with absolute expectancy. An author who wrote much about the Holy Spirit over a period of 70 years (in fact, in 100,000 manuscript pages, Ellen White mentions the Holy Spirit about 40,000 times) uses "demand" a number of times in connection with the Holy Spirit. "But there is power for us if we will have it. There is grace for us if we will appreciate it. The Holy Spirit is waiting our demand if we will only demand it with that intensity of purpose which is proportionate to the value of the object we seek." [2] "The time of the Holy Spirit's power is the time when in a special sense the heavenly gift is sought and found. . . . The outpouring of the Holy Spirit on the day of Pentecost was the former rain, but the latter rain will be more abundant. The Spirit awaits our demand and reception. Christ is again to be revealed in His fulness by the Holy Spirit's power." [3]

E. M. Bounds was a young lawyer who was a prisoner of war twice during the American Civil War. After his final release Dr. Bounds became a pastor, and it was during his years of ministry that he realized increasingly his dependence on prayer and the Holy Spirit. Each day he arose at 4:00 a.m. and spent at least three hours in prayer, so that talking to God became as much a reality for Edward Bounds as was breathing. Bounds' books on prayer have been Christian classics for almost a century and are still best-sellers today. Listen to what he writes about prayer and the Holy Spirit: "How complex, confusing, and involved is many a human direction about obtaining the gift of the Holy Spirit as the abiding comforter, our sanctifier, and the One who empowers us. How simple and direct is our Lord's direction—ASK! This is plain and direct. Ask with urgency, ask without fainting. Ask, seek, knock, till He comes. Your heavenly Father will surely send Him if you ask for Him. Wait on the Lord for the Holy Spirit. It is the child waiting, asking, urging, and praying, persevering for the Father's greatest gift and for the child's greatest need, the Holy Spirit. . . . In these three words, ask, seek, and knock, given us by Christ, we have the repetition of the advancing steps of insistency and effort. He is laying Himself out in command and promise in the strongest way, showing us that if we lay ourselves out in prayer and will persevere, rising to higher and stronger attitudes and sinking to deeper depths of intensity and effort, the answer must inevitably come." [4] Earlier Bounds said, "The coming of the Holy Spirit is dependent on prayer, for only prayer can compass with its authority and demands the realm where this person of the Godhead has His abode." [5]

If you have a keen sense of humor, you will notice that Jesus told a rather amusing story as He answered the disciples' request to be taught about prayer. This story clarifies what He meant when He said, "Ask, seek, knock." Read this story in Luke 11:5-8. A friend comes to his neighbor's house at midnight seeking bread because a guest has arrived at his own home and custom requires him to give the guest food. He asks his neighbor for three loaves of bread, and although it seems that the neighbor is reluctant to get up and get the bread because the whole family are in bed together, nevertheless eventually he rises up because of his friend's "persistence" and gives him what he asks for. The punch line of the story certainly comes in verse 8, when he says that it was because of his persistence that the friend got all that he wanted. I used to have the idea that persistence meant that we should almost wear God out with our petitions until He says, "All right, give them all they want, or I won't have a moment's peace." Of course that is not the meaning at all. The word Jesus used for persistence (which is translated "importunity" in the King James Version) means "boldly, without shamefacedness." In other words, this is an attitude of absolute expectancy and confidence. The man climbed out of bed in the middle of the night and gave his friend bread because he knew that he could not disappoint one who was totally sure that he would not go away empty-handed. As Pastor Kevin Wilfley says: "I am personally convinced that the three loaves represent the fullness of the Father, Son, and Holy Spirit that is given to us through the ministry of the Holy Spirit as described in John 14. The elements in the bread, water, wheat, and salt are all symbols of the great work of the Holy Spirit."

Now, this may seem strange to you, but it is actually the Holy Spirit who creates in a person's life the deep desire to pray more earnestly for the Spirit Himself. A man told me that he had no desire to marry again after his wife died. But then he fell in love with a delightful Christian lady who lived in a distant city. The love that he had for her prompted him to make long journeys to see her, and expensive phone calls to talk to her regularly. So it is the Holy Spirit in us that motivates us earnestly to seek the Spirit Himself every day. The disciples of Jesus came boldly to the throne of grace as they waited for the outpouring of the Holy Spirit. They were asking, seeking, knocking, and demanding. "These all continued with one accord in prayer and supplication, with the women and Mary the mother of Jesus, and with His brothers" (Acts 1:14). As a result of this praying, the Holy Spirit came with mighty power. At Pentecost they didn't receive just "three loaves"— they got the whole bakery!

Peter and John's prayer team some time after Pentecost again prayed in the Word and came before God with great confidence, resulting in another earth-shattering outpouring of the Holy Spirit (Acts 4:23-33). We will study this small group experience in a later chapter, but notice now as the Holy Spirit is poured out from the throne of grace that "great grace was upon them all" (verse 33). The coming of the Holy Spirit into people's lives is connected to prayer throughout the New Testament. Give the Holy Spirit a chance to create within you the absolute confidence that you can ask for Him again and again and receive more loaves (to use the terminology of

Jesus' story) than you ever believed possible.

Making Prayer Power Possible

Not only can you be filled with the Holy Spirit each day by continuing to ask with the complete confidence that the Holy Spirit creates in you, but you can know that your prayers to the Father in the name of Jesus are actually part of the ministry of the Holy Spirit. Allowing the Holy Spirit to energize and focus a prayer is the basis of what Jude calls "praying in the Holy Spirit" (Jude 20). Look at the way Paul agrees with Jude: "Praying always with all prayer and supplication in the Spirit, being watchful to this end with all perseverance and supplication for all the saints" (Ephesians 6:18).

While it is difficult to make exact distinctions, "supplications in the Spirit" may be defined as direct petitions, urgent requests to God, such as the "asking" and "seeking" we noticed earlier. These supplications are petitions that are of an absolutely critical nature and that are brought to the throne of grace through the Holy Spirit with intensity and urgency. "Prayer," on the other hand, reflects the joy and beauty of worship and adoration, glorifying God and placing within His care all the general concerns that we have for ourselves and others. Paul was very anxious that his friends in Rome include him in this type of prayer, being fully aware that it is the fruitage of the Holy Spirit's love ministry. "Now I beg you, brethren, through the Lord Jesus Christ, and through the love of the Spirit, that you strive together with me in your prayers to God for me" (Romans 15:30).

When my wife and I were newly married we were active members of a church fellowship, and so prayer was a regular part of our daily lives. Our prayers, however, seemed mainly general and rather routine. News of our first baby filled us with excitement, and Barbara bought and made all sorts of pretty things in preparation for the birth. But suddenly our prayers changed to urgent supplications. Barbara was diagnosed as having severe toxemia and was in a very dangerous condition. The Holy Spirit can teach a lot about prayer in a situation like that. A few days before my wife's twentieth birthday little Sheryl was born. She had golden hair and looked pretty and strong. But even a day after the birth Barbara had not yet seen her baby, because of the struggle to recover from the effects of the illness that had almost taken her life. On the evening of the next day after the baby's birth I visited Barbara and stopped by the nursery to admire our beautiful little girl. Reluctantly, after what seemed like only a few minutes with the baby, I drove home, only to find a telephone call awaiting me on my arrival.

"Garrie, this is Doctor Irwin. I am sorry to tell you that your baby has died."

"But that can't be true. I was with her just a few minutes ago," I responded in unbelief.

"After you left, the nurse fed your baby," the doctor explained sympathetically. "Then the nurse left her for a little while, and when she came back she found that the baby had choked and died."

Now my prayers changed again. In fact, there were no words I could speak or even think in prayer at this time. The doctor and our pastor joined me as we tried to break the news to Barbara in the gentlest way possible. The pastor prayed, but I couldn't. My love for God did not change, but it was a long time before I could really pray again. While Barbara was still in the hospital we buried that little white coffin in the grave where my wife's mother had been laid to rest three years before. Over the next few years the Lord gave us three lovely daughters; they sometimes ask about their eldest sister and look forward to meeting her with Jesus on the resurrection day.

I often regret that I did not know the Holy Spirit at the time of that tragedy as I do today. Not only is He the Comforter, but He is the Spirit of grace and supplication (Zechariah 2:10). Even in the most difficult circumstances He will help us pray. Let me share with you some things He has taught me about prayer in the Spirit, because I have seen how helpful others have found these principles when they have learned them in our seminars.

The Spirit's Model Prayer

Coming back once again to Luke 11, we notice in verses 2-4 that Jesus began His instruction on prayer by repeating near Jerusalem, in a more personal form, the prayer He had taught during the Sermon on the Mount in Galilee (Matthew 6). It is the Holy Spirit who makes every part of this prayer possible. Give the Holy Spirit a chance, and He will show you the full meaning of Jesus' prayer today.

"*Father in heaven.*" Because the Holy Spirit is like an obstetrician who leads us through the new birth experience, He also helps us understand our intimate family connection to God. He introduces us to our Father. Because of the Holy Spirit, we can throw our arms around God and say "Abba [Daddy], Father." "And because you are sons, God has sent forth the Spirit of His Son into your hearts, crying out, 'Abba, Father' " (Galatians 4:6). "For you did not receive the spirit of bondage again to fear, but you received the Spirit of adoption by whom we cry out, 'Abba, Father' " (Romans 8:15). Praying in the Spirit, we delight in God as a true Father, one who never has or will hurt us, desert us, abuse us, or fail us. You can actually enjoy Him right now. He is a loving God. Being filled with the Holy Spirit enables us to recognize the immediate presence, the imminence, of God residing in us (John 14:17, 23).

God is not distant. As we begin our day with this prayer, we can greet God and give Him renewed assurance of His open access to our hearts. Jesus taught us to begin to pray by recognizing the presence of God on the throne that the Holy Spirit has prepared in our hearts.

The Holy Spirit not only enables us to recognize God as our Father and give Him access to our lives, but also gives us access through the blood of Jesus into the very throne room of heaven. "For through Him we both have access by one Spirit to the Father" (Ephesians 2:18). A few years ago I wanted to get into the throne room in the presidential palace in Mexico City because I had heard that there were some very interesting murals around the walls giving the history of this great country. I went to the main gate and made my way toward the palace, only to find myself confronted by a half-dozen armed guards with submachine guns and bayonets pointing at me. I didn't understand what they were saying, but as they moved toward me with their guns and bayonets I took the hint and, after taking their picture, quickly walked away. I was quite surprised, however, when I walked around another corner of the building and discovered a small door that was unlocked. I tried the door, opened it, and walked into the palace. To my amazement, I had access right through to the throne room, where I was able to photograph the murals and enjoy myself immensely, walking alone in this beautiful place. I guess there are not many parts of the world where something like that could happen, and it certainly doesn't happen in heaven. We don't wander into the throne room of God, but find access only as the Holy Spirit uses the key made possible by the blood of Jesus (verse 18).

"Hallowed be your name." "Hallowed" is not an English word that is commonly used, although most modern translations of the Bible retain this word in Jesus' prayer because of its special meaning. The word can be confusing, and I know at least one child who went through many years of young life thinking that God's name was Harold. *The Living Bible* seems to convey a fairly accurate meaning of the word when it says, "Father, may your name be honored for its holiness." In this section of the prayer the Holy Spirit will lead you to honor God's name as the "Spirit Himself bears witness with our spirit that we are children of God" (Romans 8:16).

After recognition of God's presence there is joy in praising His name. Before we ask anything from God, we delight Him by blessing and honoring His name. This never fails to lift me up onto a higher level of fellowship with God. Praying through biblical names of God, you will exalt His wonderful character as you pray that, through the inner strength of the Holy Spirit, these names will become part of your life as a Christian (Ephesians 3:14-16). For instance, if you honor God as Yahweh Raphah, the Great Healer, you will also acknowledge Him as the one whose healing power can bring glory to God through you. In the next chapter I will give you 15 names of God that have aided modern Christians greatly in praying for hours in the Spirit in this way.

"*Your kingdom come. Your will be done.*" To be born of the Spirit means entrance into God's kingdom (John 3:5). When Jesus ministered in the Spirit, it signaled the coming of the kingdom (Matthew 12:28), and of course "the kingdom of God is . . . righteousness and peace and joy in the Holy Spirit" (Romans 14:17). So when you pray this prayer in the Spirit you will be signifying your willingness to be involved in the actions and attitudes of the kingdom. This means a total surrender to the will of God. This is a powerful way to pray, to begin a day.

Some people fear the will of God, thinking that it will involve putting up with pain or disease or perhaps setting out as a missionary to a distant germ-infested land. "I could never ask for God's will to be done in my life," a lady informed me. "I could never be sure what He would do to me." But God's will is good and best, and is always what we would choose ourself if we could see the end from the beginning. Enabling us to pray in God's will is the great work of the Holy Spirit.

A respected church leader, Robert Dale, wrote to encourage me with his prayers. He also reminded me of God's great promise in Romans 8:28: "And we know that all things work together for good to those who love God, to those who are the called according to His purpose." Only recently did the Holy Spirit help me understand the connection between this verse and the two that preceded it: "Likewise the Spirit also helps in our weaknesses. For we do not know what we should pray for as we ought, but the Spirit Himself makes intercession for us with groanings which cannot be uttered. Now He who searches the hearts knows what the mind of the Spirit is, because He makes intercession for the saints according to the will of God" (verses 26, 27). The Spirit does not intercede for us as Jesus does (Romans 8:34; Hebrews 7:25), but He prays through us in a way that brings us completely into the will of God.

Christian writer and pastor A. W. Pink has compared our two Intercessors in this way. "If it be asked, why has God provided two Intercessors for His people, the answer is: to bridge the entire gulf between Him and us. One to represent God to us, the other to represent us before God. The one to prompt our prayers, the other to present them to the Father. The one to ask blessings for us, the other to convey blessings into us."[6]

Without the Holy Spirit we do not know what to pray about. Are you surprised at that? It is the Holy Spirit that not only leads us to pray for forgiveness and victory but also to pray in openness to God's will in all situations in which we have no idea what is right. You know what I mean by that, don't you? You have no idea of where it would be best for you to live, work, go to school, whom to marry, or when it would be best to exit from some hard situation or even recover from a painful sickness. Right at a very busy time in my ministry I became very sick and had to be admitted to a hospital for about a week. Every day I prayed most earnestly for instant recovery until the Lord showed me the significance of Romans 8:26, 27 and convicted me that I must pray in the Spirit, not knowing if it was best for me to recover at that time. Perhaps God was bringing good out of the evil of my present situation by using it to protect me from some other terrible tragedy.

It is in this attitude of prayer in the Spirit according to the will of God that Romans 8:28 applies. When we pray according to the will of God we know then that all things will indeed work together for good. Notice how Bounds differentiates between prayers of the natural person and the one who is in the Spirit. "The natural man prays, but prays according to his own will, fancy, and desire. If he has ardent desires and groanings, they are the fire and agony of nature simply, and not that of the Spirit. What a world of natural praying there is, which is selfish, self-centered, self-inspired! The Spirit, when He prays through us or helps us to meet the mighty aughtness of right praying, trims our praying down to the will of God, and then we give heart and expression to His unutterable longings. Then we have the mind of Christ, and pray as He would pray. His thoughts, purposes, and desires are our desires, purposes, and thoughts." [7] Bounds' conclusion is even more graphic: "If our prayers are not according to the will of God, they die in the presence of the Holy Spirit. He gives such prayers no countenance, no help. Discountenanced and unhelped by Him, prayers not according to God's will soon die out of every heart where the Holy Spirit dwells." [8]

Not only can we request that our own lives be in God's will this day, but we can also ask God that our family, friends, work associates, neighbors, national leaders, and even whole countries be placed in God's will. Conference president Don Jacobsen on Sabbath morning prays especially for his pastors, asking that they be completely in God's will as they preach His Word to their congregations. Some pastors pray through a few pages of their church directory each day, asking that each person be completely in God's will. Other members have joined their pastors in doing this. No wonder there is Holy Spirit power in these congregations.

"Give us day by day our daily bread." The anointing of the Holy Spirit not only makes possible the supply of spiritual needs (Isaiah 61:1-3), setting captives free and supplying the oil of joy, but also enables Christians to

recognize God's concern for the practical necessities of life, such as finance, food, and shelter. Whatever your need is, you can talk to God about it. He already knows if the muffler is falling off your car, your horse is hurt, your roof is leaking, or your insurance will not pay, but you can bring all these practical problems and much more to God, showing that your trust is in Him. The Holy Spirit also led the early Christians to care for the practical needs of fellow believers. In a society without Social Security or government handouts the Holy Spirit made sure that none of God's children lacked in necessities of life (Acts 4:31-37). The Holy Spirit not only sensitizes Christians to the need to receive and share the "bread of life," but also to receive and share funds and possessions for the glory of God.

"Forgive us our sins, for we also forgive..." The Holy Spirit leads people constantly to repentance as He convinces them of the realities of "sin, and of righteousness, and of judgment" (John 16:8). The Holy Spirit also shows that every sin can be forgiven by the blood of Jesus, and provides the power so that the results of total forgiveness can be experienced by every person who prays this prayer. "And such were some of you. But you were washed, but you were sanctified, but you were justified in the name of the Lord Jesus and by the Spirit of our God" (1 Corinthians 6:11). I have had to pray for forgiveness many times. In fact, it is only the certainty of God's forgiveness that enables me to carry on in service for Him. I am also asking the Lord for the same forgiving spirit so that I can forgive others and myself for circumstances and actions that have caused hurt and harm.

"I can't understand why Jesus didn't place this request for forgiveness right at the beginning of His prayer," an elderly man said at one of my Trinity Power Prayer seminars. I asked the audience if someone could suggest a reason, and a young lady gave a very good answer. "The Holy Spirit wants us to think about God's nearness and His greatness first. When we do this, we are not brainwashing ourselves with our own weakness and failures, but impressing our minds with God's strength and love. Then when we pray for forgiveness we can have complete confidence in our wonderful Saviour. Also, it is His loving example and character that creates in us the desire to forgive others."

This lady was right. The Holy Spirit doesn't want us convicted more of our weakness than He does of His power. God doesn't want us more convicted of our sin than of His righteousness. Notice that He doesn't even supply us with daily bread on the basis of our repentance—He does it because of His great love. This is the way He also wants us to treat others.

"Do not lead us into temptation, but deliver us from the evil one." Here is where the victory power of the Holy Spirit comes into prominence like

Mount Fuji towering above the green tea plantations, the seemingly endless residential settlements, and the vast industrial complexes I saw along the bullet train route from Tokyo to Osaka in Japan. The Holy Spirit delights to answer this victory prayer. He towers over all the forces of evil. "You are of God, little children, and have overcome them, because He who is in you is greater than he who is in the world" (1 John 4:4). In a later chapter we will rejoice in the amazing evidence God has given us of the victory power of the Holy Spirit in us. It is against the forces of evil that the sword of the Spirit is used most effectively (Ephesians 6:17, 18) and the Christian is strengthened in the inner man (Ephesians 3:16). Whatever temptations you are facing now, I mean today, claim this victory power as yours as you pray in the Spirit, and you will not be disappointed. He will deliver you from the evil one.

Let me give you an example of how the Holy Spirit may lead you to pray through this prayer. Remember, of course, that you can spend many minutes in each section. "Father, I am praying to You today because I believe that You love me and that You are the real Father in my life. I ask for the Holy Spirit to fill me today, so that I can be fully aware that You are present with me, right through every minute of this day. Thank You, Lord, for doing this now. I want to praise Your name and glorify You as the great God, King of kings and Lord of lords. May Your name be magnified on all the earth. Father, I want to be totally submissive to Your will today. You know that there are a number of situations I am facing that I don't understand, and I'm not sure what is the right or best thing to do. Lord, I earnestly pray that You will help me and direct me according to Your will so that Your kingdom will be revealed. I pray for Your will to be done in the lives of some people who are special to me. Please give me today the bread I need. You understand my position, financially, spiritually, physically, emotionally, and I place this all in Your hands right now. I thank You that Jesus has provided forgiveness for me at the cross, and I confess to You my sinfulness and claim the blood of Jesus right now. Thank You that You have covered me with Jesus' blood. Please give me a forgiving spirit. Lord, You know the temptations I am struggling with right now. I pray through the power of the Holy Spirit that Satan will be bound up and have no authority over me. I claim victory power now through the promises of Your Word. Praise Your name. I give You the glory, through Jesus Christ my Lord. Amen."

Praying through the Lord's Prayer in this way will eventually enable you to spend an hour or more in very meaningful prayer each day. You can pray not only kneeling in prayer in the early morning, as a very important beginning to the day, but also as you walk, work, or drive. There will be little pockets of time throughout the day when you can lift your heart and mind to God in a special way. If you think that the potential of an hour or more with God each day is exaggerated, you will be amazed to discover that large numbers of Christians of many different denominations are praying for more than an hour in the Lord's Prayer every day. They are spending an hour in concentrated prayer each morning as well as praying spontaneously throughout the day. As a result of this type of praying, the Holy Spirit is leading large numbers of these people into truth and righteousness. Becky Tirabassi in her delightful book on prayer gives a personal testimony of the result of spending an hour with God each day: "Upon recognition that prayerlessness was sin in my life, I was deeply touched by God to make a commitment to pray for one hour a day. Six years (and many 'hours') later, God has changed my personality and character, increased my faith through unbelievable answer to prayer, called me to accountability in innumerable areas, and given me a vivid vision of possibilities for His will in my life. Having been a teenage alcoholic, I know that this disciplined prayer life is a work of the Holy Spirit within me, not a privileged performance that I have perfected." [9]

I read of the impact of the Lord's Prayer recently in an old *Review and Herald*, a Christian magazine. "In the Lord's prayer, we have an example of a perfect petition. How simple, yet how comprehensive it is! This prayer should be taught to the children. Let all study carefully the principles contained in it." [10] Yes, this prayer contains principles, not just pretty words. In other issues of this magazine the same author has said, "He who would pray should enter into the meaning of his prayer, putting heart and soul into his request. Let the Lord's prayer be the real expression of your needs. Often to repeat this form of prayer will not be termed vain repetition." [11] "If those who know the Lord's prayer would try to take its meaning and realize its depth and breadth, the church would be what God desires it to be—the light of the world. Men would have less desire for form and ceremony; for they would seek to plant in the heart those principles that sanctify the character." [12]

I had been teaching seminars on prayer to pastors in a number of countries when a pastor I knew and respected from my own city came to me with an exciting experience. "You remember when you taught us about praying for one hour each day in the Lord's Prayer that you warned us not to tell our congregations what we were doing for at least three months? Well, this is my third week praying this way, and already my people are coming to me and are saying, 'Pastor, what has happened? Something is different about you. You have changed. Even your sermons are different. Tell us how the Holy Spirit is working in your life.'" After a few more weeks the pastor shared the secret with his congregation, and soon the Holy Spirit was leading them also into a new experience of prayer power.

When Jesus in Luke 11 taught His disciples to pray, He was teaching them to pray in the Holy Spirit (Jude 20). In this way they could pray with Spirit and with the understanding also (1 Corinthians 14:15). They prayed *for* the Holy Spirit and *by* the Holy Spirit, and the Holy Spirit prayed *in* them and *through* them. The Holy Spirit also impressed the principles of the Lord's Prayer on the disciples so strongly that the essential elements of this prayer became the basis of all the actions, teaching, and theology of the rest of the New Testament. All subsequent Christianity grew out of the seedbed of this prayer instruction that Jesus gave.

Give the Holy Spirit a chance today to teach you to pray in a deeper and more satisfying way than ever before. It will mold not only your prayer life but your whole life. You will realize that the Holy Spirit is praying in you and through you as He leads you fully into the will of God, and you will know the fullness of power of the Holy Spirit in such a way that the results will be miraculous.

SMALL GROUP STUDY
Chapter Five

Cohesive Contrasts

As small groups develop, they pass through not only general stages of progress but also levels of communication. The first level will be that of cliché communication. This will be evident by a very shallow level of conversation. It will be entirely nonthreatening dealing simply with things that are superficial and safe, such as general public knowledge. The second stage introduces the sharing of information and facts, but not on a personal level—the communication of general knowledge. There is little risk in this, especially if one is sure about the right answer. In the next study guide we will notice three further levels of communication that involve opinions, feelings, and fellowship.

Begin your group meeting today by discussing this question. When and how did you get to know or understand one of your parents as a real person?

Concentrating on the Word
Study Text: Luke 11:1-13

How many illustrations of prayer or different words for prayer do you find in verses 1-13? List these here.

_____
_____

Why do think that Jesus waited until the disciples asked Him before He taught them about prayer?

_____
_____

Jesus comdemned the use of vain repetitions in prayer (Matthew 6:7). In what ways could using the Lord's Prayer each day as the basis for extended prayer time be safeguarded from falling into the category of vain repetition?

_____
_____

Is it wrong to pray for something again and again? Why or why not?

_____
_____

How does the idea of "demanding" the Holy Spirit from God make you feel?

Shocked _____	Humble _____
Nervous _____	Surprised _____
Proud _____	Grateful _____
Confused _____	Delighted _____
Other _____	

What does the word "persistent" in the story of the man seeking bread (verses 5-8) teach you about praying in the Holy Spirit?
_____
_____

What connection do you see between "daily bread" in the Lord's Prayer, the man seeking bread from his friend, and asking for the Holy Spirit in verse 13?
_____
_____

What connection do you see between Romans 8:26, 27 and the wonderful promise in verse 28? Is this connection important to you?
_____
_____

Conversation With the Lord

Conclude your group study meeting today with a time of conversational prayer, this time centering on the Lord's Prayer. Spend some time praying through the Lord's Prayer together, sharing praise and supplication in the various sections of this prayer. Also remember to pray for the "empty chair" as usual, asking the Lord to lead each group member to someone who can be invited to join the group next week.

Committing the Word to Memory

This week, write out a verse from Luke 11:1-13 and share it with someone as soon as possible.
_____
_____

Chapter Six
▼

Give the Holy Spirit a Chance
To Glorify God's Name

"Do you want the name-brand medication, or will you take the generic tablets?" the pharmacist asked the young lady who had brought in her prescription. In the late eighties we entered what some have called the generic age. Plain black-and-white boxes without brand-name protection appeared on supermarket shelves containing everything from cookies to soap powder at much lower prices than their brand-name counterparts. Would you like to buy a generic automobile? Really? Some people like to belong to a generic church. "I am a member of the Nondenominational Community Fellowship," they will tell you if you ask about their religious affiliation. What about having a generic God? "We don't talk about God; we just speak of a higher power or life force," I have heard people say.

If you give the Holy Spirit a chance today, He will reveal to you a very personal God whose names will have significance in your life. In fact, as the Holy Spirit teaches you and guides you as you pray through the names of God, you can develop a fellowship with God that will be very important in your life.

Many Christians today are coming back into a realization of the tremendous meaning there is in the biblical names of God. Each one of these names reveals a facet of God's character and a revelation of His power that is available to Christians through the Holy Spirit. God has always been willing to share His name with His people, risking misrepresentation at times when sin has allured them into evil. "If My people who are called by My name will humble themselves, and pray and seek My face, and turn from their wicked ways, then will I hear from heaven, and will forgive their sins and heal their land" (2 Chronicles 7:14).

In ancient times names were very significant to the Jewish people. In fact, a study of some of the 1,500 names in the Bible can be very informative, although I doubt that many people are going to sit down and work their way through from Abraham to Zedekiah with the excitement that is generated at an NBA final or an Indianapolis 500.

In Jesus' Name

Whose name excites you the most? No name is so sweet to Christians as that of Jesus. While "Christ" seems crisp and formal, "Jesus" has an aura of love, joy, and peace. The Holy Spirit testifies or witnesses about Jesus (John 15:26), and because of this the Holy Spirit leads people to pray in the name or authority of Jesus. "And whatever you ask in My name, that will I do, that the Father may be glorified in the Son. If you ask anything in My name, I will do it" (John 14:13, 14). "And in that day you will ask Me nothing. Most assuredly, I say to you, whatever you ask the Father in My name He will give you. Until now you have asked nothing in My name. Ask, and you will receive, that your joy may be full" (John 16:23, 24). Asking in the name of Jesus lays the foundation for true joy, which is the Holy Spirit's happy privilege to give all those He fills. Joy is one of the fruits of the Spirit (Galatians 5:22). "For the kingdom of God is not food and drink, but righteousness and peace and joy in the Holy Spirit" (Romans 14:17).

Jesus explained to His disciples that the Holy Spirit would "glorify Me" (John 16:14). The significance of this in relationship to God's name is very interesting. Understanding this was for me like opening a window in a computer program so that a whole new body of information could be displayed. Move the mouse so the arrow is on "glorify," double click, and see what you will discover in this "window" of truth.

Let me give you a very meaningful illustration of how the Holy Spirit uses this word "glorify" to exalt the name of Jesus. Pray through Psalm 86. It is a magnificent song of worship and praise. In this psalm you can find many attributes of the Holy Spirit, including praying in the Spirit (verses 6, 7; Ephesians 6:17, 18), teaching and truth (verse 11; John 16:13), strength (verse 16; Ephesians 3:16), signs (verse 17; Romans 15:19), and comfort (verse 17; Acts 9:31). In the midst of all of this we find the Holy Spirit's ministry of glorifying God's name. "All nations whom You have made shall come and worship before You, O Lord, and shall glorify Your name. . . . I will praise you, O Lord my God, with all my heart, and I will glorify Your name forever" (Psalm 86:9-12).

Jesus Himself prayed that He would glorify the Father's name.

" 'Father, glorify Your name.' Then a voice came from heaven, saying, 'I have both glorified it and will glorify it again' " (John 12:28). "And whatever you ask in My name, that I will do, that the Father may be glorified in the Son" (John 14:13). In His great prayer before Gethsemane Jesus again repeated the focus of His ministry: "I have glorified You on the earth. I have finished the work which You have given Me to do. . . . I have manifested Your name to the men whom You have given Me out of the world" (John 17:4-6).

If you have wondered why we would spend time praying through the "Old Testament" names of God as the Holy Spirit leads us to hallow the Father's name in the second part of the Lord's Prayer, remember that the emphasis of Jesus Himself was to glorify the Father's name. But notice this: by glorifying the Father, you also glorify the Son. The relationship between the Father, Son, and Holy Spirit is so close that Jesus can say, "Go therefore and make disciples of all the nations, baptizing them in the name of the Father and of the Son and of the Holy Spirit" (Matthew 28:19). The Father, Son, and Holy Spirit all have the one family name. As the Father is glorified in the Son (John 14:13), so, when the names of God are exalted, Jesus' name is glorified in a beautiful way. The Holy Spirit moved on the hearts and minds of the Roman Christians, and even these Gentiles began to glorify God's name and thus glorify Jesus. "And that the Gentiles might glorify God for His mercy, as it is written: 'For this reason I will confess to You among the Gentiles, and sing to Your name'" (Romans 15:9).

Can you think of some songs you have heard Christians sing about the name of Jesus? Perhaps you have sung them many times without thinking of their deep significance. But as the Holy Spirit fills your life these songs, like all beautiful Christian music, will have new meaning: "The name of Jesus is so sweet, I love its music to repeat." "Jesus, name above all names." "In the name of Jesus, in the name of Jesus, we have the victory." "'Jesus,' oh, how sweet the name! 'Jesus,' every day the same." "All hail the power of Jesus' name! Let angels prostrate fall." "There's no other name like Jesus, 'tis the dearest name we know."

Let me come back now to the "window" we opened by the power of the Holy Spirit and emphasize again the point that the Holy Spirit is helping us understand about Jesus. When John reported Jesus' statement that the Holy Spirit would glorify Jesus (John 16:14), John used the Greek word for "glorify," which would have immediately signaled to his Jewish readers that Jesus was, together with the Father and the Holy Spirit, the God whose name we glorify from the Old Testament. Here is an amazing text to pray about. It clarifies John's written word and Jesus' spoken word in John 16:14. "For unto us a Child is born, unto us a Son is given; and the government will be upon His shoulder. And His name will be called Wonderful, Counselor, Mighty God, Everlasting Father, Prince of Peace" (Isaiah 9:6). When Jesus taught His disciples, and us, to pray, "Our Father in heaven, hallowed be Your name," He was laying the foundation for His own glorification as the great God. "And now, O Father, glorify Me together with Yourself, with the glory which I had with You before the world was" (John 17:5).

As you pray through the names of God, you will be glorifying Jesus in the power of the Holy Spirit. Give the Holy Spirit a chance to show you what a joy that is today. When the disciples were filled with the Holy Spirit from the day of Pentecost onward, they exalted the name of Jesus. In fact, there is a very dramatic illustration of this in Acts 4, in which the Jewish leaders ask the disciples for their credentials of authority: "And when they had set them in the midst, they asked, 'By what power or by what name have you done this?' " (verse 7). Peter and John did not have a generic God. Their God was like the name-brand signs I saw in Electric City, Tokyo. Brands flashed in the night on huge neon signs, each one competing with another for more brilliance, clarity, and attention. Peter was now filled again with the Holy Spirit, and Jesus' name was glorified. "Let it be known to you all, and to all the people of Israel, that by the name of Jesus Christ of Nazareth, whom you crucified, whom God raised from the dead, by Him this man stands here before you whole. . . . Nor is there salvation in any other, for there is no other name under heaven given among men by which we must be saved" (verses 10-12). This will be your experience as you pray through God's names each day. You will exalt and glorify Jesus. No one will be able to stop you. Like Peter and John, you will say, "For we cannot but speak the things which we have seen and heard" (verse 20).

Safe in the Strong Tower

At the busy international airport in São Paulo I was saying farewell to a number of Brazilian church leaders, including Tercio Sarli, who every month for 12 years has written a one-page feature on prayer in the Portuguese language edition of the *Adventist Review*. Pastor Sarli is known as Brazil's man of prayer, and God has used him mightily in this way. So I was surprised when he said, "Tell me how it is possible for you to spend more than three hours in prayer each day as you travel by plane around the world." I explained to him about praying in the Spirit through the Lord's Prayer and then reminded him also of what I had been teaching in meetings with Brazilian pastors about praying in the names of God. "This type of prayer is not just repeating God's names," I told him, "but actually thoughtfully considering the meaning of each name as the Holy Spirit applies it to one's present relationship to God and circumstances of life."

I have found the acronym ACTS has helped me with this. Who originated the ACTS idea I am not sure, but I know many Christians have used it effectually. Listen to Bill Hybels, pastor of Willow Creek Community Church in Chicago, who preaches to more than 14,000 people each weekend. He explains it this way: "I'm going to offer you a pattern to follow. It's not the only pattern or the perfect pattern, but it's a good pattern that has been used for many years in Christian circles. It's balanced, and it's easy to use. All you have to remember is the word ACTS, an acrostic whose four letters stand for adoration, confession, thanksgiving, and supplication." [1]

Adoration is simply praising God for who He is. As Hybels explains, adoration sets the tone for the whole prayer, as it brings the mind's focus entirely onto God. **Confession** means recognizing sin in relationship to one of the names of God. For instance, if I am praying to God as El Shaddai I may confess that I have tried to do things in my own strength and have failed miserably. I am specific, and this allows the Holy Spirit to bring me to genuine surrender and true repentance. It also eliminates the effects of guilt on my mind and body and enables true healing to take place. **Thanksgiving** is just great. What a joy it is to praise God for all that He has done and is doing. Is it hard to praise God with thanksgiving? No! "Count your many blessings, name them one by one, and it will surprise you what the Lord has done." **Supplication,** as we have noticed in the previous chapter, is a concentration on specific needs, petitions, and urgent requests we bring to God in prayer. For many people the majority of prayers are in this category, so it is important to give the Holy Spirit a chance to fill our hearts with adoration, confession, and thanksgiving before supplication takes center stage.

I could see that Pastor Sarli appreciated the idea of praying in this way, and sometime later he told me how significant this has become in his life. I don't doubt that you will have the same joy in prayer if this type of praying in the Spirit is new to you.

Before we begin to pray through the names of God, we need to remind ourselves of how the Holy Spirit makes this possible. Our unconverted, sinful human hearts and minds do not want to do this. They shrink from the idea of fellowship with God, just as cats do not consider swimming one of their recreational delights.

"I was singing, but my heart wasn't in it," a young man confessed. When you pray, is your heart in it? The Holy Spirit creates a new heart in those who turn to God. This heart is alive and tender (Ezekiel 36:26, 27; 37:14). As a result of this new creation a person can glorify God's name (Psalm 104:30, 33, 34). The new creation finds time to think about the deep significance of God's name: "Then those who feared the Lord spoke to one another, and the Lord listened and heard them; so a book of remembrance was written before Him for those who fear the Lord and who meditate on His name" (Malachi 3:16).

The Holy Spirit leads God's people to victory as they reverence God's mighty name. "So shall they fear the name of the Lord from the west, and His glory from the rising of the sun; when the enemy comes in like a flood, the Spirit of the Lord will lift up a standard against him" (Isaiah 59:19). Often the effects of evil sweep into human lives like dirty floodwaters but in the name of God there is total security. "The name of the Lord is a strong tower; the righteous run to it and are safe" (Proverbs 18:10). "We cannot save ourselves from the tempter's power; he has conquered humanity, and when we try to stand in our own strength, we shall become a prey to his devices; but 'the name of the Lord is a strong tower: the righteous runneth into it, and is safe' (Proverbs 18:10, KJV). Satan trembles and flees before the weakest soul who finds refuge in that mighty name." [2]

Are you ready to run to the tower now? Give the Holy Spirit a chance, and He will enable you to shout hallelujah from the high place of safety.

The Spirit and the Names

Look now at the list (Figure 1) of the 15 names of God. You may like to choose other names to pray through, but these have been very helpful to me since (in October 1986) I asked the Holy Spirit to lead me to names of God I could pray through in this way. The 14 names of God I chose in the sequence you see in Figure 1 because they correspond twice to the seven sections of the Lord's Prayer. The last name I have since added to my list because it continues to have major significance in my life.

For a few months I carried these names with me written on a small card until I had memorized them and could pray through them in different ways a number of times each day with the aid of the Holy Spirit.

Let me give you now an example of praying through ACTS in each name of God. I am praying that the Holy Spirit will help me to do this effectively for you in the name of Jesus.

"Yahweh-Shammah, I **adore** You today because You are the God who is always present. There is no time when You are not near and concerned about my life. I praise You that You are not present to injure Your creation in any way but that You are a God of love. You are a tremendous God. I enjoy so much being in Your presence. I am opening my heart to You and am worshiping You right now. Yahweh-Shammah, I **confess** that even this morning I forgot about Your presence and was impatient and unkind, and I ask You to forgive me. I am so sorry, because I know this hurt You more than anyone else. I surrender my will to You right now and claim Your victory power. Lord, I know that if I remember Your presence every moment it will be much more difficult for me to sin in any way. I praise You right now that I am free from guilt because through the blood of Jesus I know You continue

> **PRAYING IN THE HOLY SPIRIT—JUDE 20**
> **EXALTING THE FATHER**
> Adoration—Confession—Thanksgiving—Supplication
>
> | | | |
> |---|---|---|
> | YAHWEH-SHAMMAH | Lord who is present | Eze. 48:35 |
> | EL-SHADDAI | Almighty God | Gen. 17:1-20 |
> | YAHWEH-RAAH | Lord is my shepherd | Ps. 23:1 |
> | YAHWEH-YIREH | Lord who provides | Gen. 22:14 |
> | YAHWEH-TSIDKENU | Lord my righteousness | Jer. 23:6 |
> | YAHWEH-NISSI | Lord my victory banner | Ex. 17:15 |
> | EL-ELYON | Supreme, powerful God | Gen. 14:19-22 |
> | EL-ROI | God who sees | Gen. 16:13 |
> | EL-OLAM | Everlasting God | Isa. 40:28 |
> | YAHWEH-SHALOM | Lord is peace | Judges 6:24 |
> | YAHWEH-EL-GMOLAH | Lord God of recompense | Jer. 51:56 |
> | YAHWEH-MACCADESHCEM | Lord my sanctifier | Ex. 31:13 |
> | YAHWEH-NAKEH | Lord who smites evil | Eze. 7:9 |
> | YAHWEH-SABBAOTH | Lord of hosts | 1 Sam. 1:3 |
> | YAHWEH-RAPHAH | Lord who heals | Ex. 15:26 |

Figure 1

to be present with me. Yahweh-Shammah, I want to **thank** You today that I recognized Your presence with me as I drove into the city, and to thank You for the encouraging phone call I received from a young pastor in California. Surely Your presence is with him right now as he works out the details for the spiritual retreat his church is planning for the fall. Father, right now I want to bring an urgent **supplication** to You that the family of Pastor Gayland Richardson, who died last night in Los Angeles, will know that You are Yahweh-Shammah, even in their time of grief and shock. Please be their strength as El-Shaddai. May they know that You will never leave them without help or the power to cope. Even when we walk through the valley of the shadow of death You are with Your people. Yahweh-Shammah, I pray that each of my family will recognize Your presence with them today and that they will know that You are a wonderful God of love."

Following this same ACTS sequence you can pray to God as El-Shaddai, praising His greatness and recognizing His indescribable power. You may be led by the Holy Spirit to confess your failure to accept His power and have fallen into sin because you relied on your own weakness. Be specific. God still considers you to be one of His children no matter what your sin is (2 Chronicles 7:14, 15). Thank God now for His almighty power. It is stronger than drugs, bad temper, immorality, lying, alcohol, moodiness, depression. Praise Him for what you have seen or heard of the working of His mighty power. Now come with your supplications for Him to use His power in specific situations or places that the Holy Spirit has impressed upon you to pray about right now.

It is obvious that praying in the Holy Spirit through the 15 names of God as we have described here is going to enable you to pray for extended periods each day.

You may choose to pray in the sequence of ACTS that takes you through every name in adoration, then through the whole list again in confession, and so on. This morning I was able to spend quite a number of minutes in adoration of God as revealed in each of the characteristics represented in His names. I am inviting you to join me in this prayer.

"Lord, I praise You that You are the God who is always present, the God of almighty power. Lord, I give You glory that You are Yahweh-Raah, my Shepherd. How tenderly You care for each of Your sheep and even this fallen world in which I live. I praise You that You are Yahweh-Yireh, the Great Provider. Your care and love is unfailing, and I appreciate so much the great God that You are. What a joy it is to know that You are my righteousness. You are righteous and holy. You are absolutely perfect. I come into Your presence with reverence, respect, and awe. I worship You as the gracious God of the universe."

After praying through the 15 names of God in this way, you may have time to give the Holy Spirit a chance to convince you of sin and come in confession in relationship to each name of God. For instance, when you come to Yahweh-Shalom, you might say, "Lord, I deeply regret that I have not reflected Your peace today. I have hurt a number of people, and I am really sorry. I hurt ——— and ———, and I recognize and admit exactly how this has happened. I accept Your forgiveness now and ask that You will give those that I have hurt this peace also and help me to do what I can to bring healing in their lives."

You may also have time now to pray through the thanksgiving and supplication sections of this prayer, or you may want to reserve this for later in the day. By the time you combine praying through the Lord's Prayer, praying in the Scriptures, and praying in ACTS through the names of God, I guarantee it will not be long before you will be spending at least an hour each day praying in the Holy Spirit (Jude 20). You may not always have a specific confession or supplication related to every one of the names of God, but the Holy Spirit will always lead you in adoration and thanksgiving.

Recently a truck driver told me that he is now able to spend more than an hour each day in concentrated prayer. I have been told the same thing by homemakers, physicians, secretaries, accountants, administrators, nurses, builders, dentists, farmers, and others, including pastors. Yes, there is a prayer revolution happening by the power of the Holy Spirit.

When I flew to Japan earlier this year, I had the opportunity to spend three or four hours praying through the names of God. It happened something like this. At the airport I was able to pray in the first two names of God on my list. Then the boarding announcement came. After settling into my seat, I was able to pray and meditate for a while on God as Yahweh-Raah and as Yahweh-Yireh. Then it was time for my meal. The airline vegetarian lunch seemed in stark contrast to the bountiful provision God makes for my life, so it was not long again before I could pray more about the generosity of Yahweh-Yireh. Then the "fasten seat belts and return tray table and seat backs to their upright and locked position" announcement was made, and we were ready to land in San Francisco.

Once I was on the ground there was ample time to work through ACTS in relationship to Yahweh-Tsidkenu because of a problem in getting the plane into the gate. Would I miss the connecting flight? "Yahweh-Nissi, Lord, I need a banner of victory now over worry and lack of faith."

Safely on the flight to Japan, I had the chance on and off to pray some more in the sequence of the names of God I have memorized and prayed through more than 4,000 times in the past five years. By the time the Boeing 747 had landed in Japan about nine hours after leaving San Francisco, I had not only enjoyed the opportunity to read a few magazines, have a pleasant conversation with the people sitting near me, and snatch a little sleep, but also to rejoice that since I left Portland, Oregon, 12 hours earlier I had been able to spend three or four hours in energizing prayer.

Here are two very beneficial variations of praying through the names of God that you may enjoy. Take the list in Figure 2 and pray through the names of God, allowing the Holy Spirit to apply each name to Jesus. Praise God for the way the real meaning of each name is revealed in Jesus' life and ministry. Now you can glorify Him in the power of the Holy Spirit. Give the Holy Spirit a chance to direct these characteristics of Jesus to your personal life. Follow ACTS through this list also.

The third step is a triple blessing. As you pray through the list in Figure 3, the Holy Spirit will reveal how each name of God applies to the Spirit Himself.

Talk to the Holy Spirit about each of these names. Have fellowship with

> **PRAYING IN THE HOLY SPIRIT—JUDE 20**
> **GLORIFYING JESUS**
> Adoration—Confession—Thanksgiving—Supplication
>
> | | | |
> |---|---|---|
> | YAHWEH-SHAMMAH | I am with you | Matt. 28:20 |
> | EL-SHADDAI | Alpha & Omega—Almighty | Rev. 1:8, 17, 18 |
> | YAHWEH-RAAH | The Good Shepherd | John 10:11 |
> | YAHWEH-YIREH | The Bread of Life | John 6:35 |
> | YAHWEH-TSIDKENU | Jesus the righteous | 1 John 2:1 |
> | YAHWEH-NISSI | Victory through Jesus | 1 Cor. 15:57 |
> | EL-ELYON | Head of all power | Col. 2:9, 10 |
> | EL-ROI | Jesus sees | John 1:48 |
> | EL-OLAM | From everlasting | Micah 5:2 |
> | YAHWEH-SHALOM | Prince of Peace | Isa. 9:6 |
> | YAHWEH-EL-GMOLAH | Reward of inheritance | Col. 3:24 |
> | YAHWEH-MACCADESHCEM | The Sanctifier | 1 Cor. 1:2 |
> | YAHWEH-NAKEH | Destroys works of devil | 1 John 3:8 |
> | YAHWEH-SABBAOTH | Lord of lords | Rev. 19:16 |
> | YAHWEH-RAPHAH | Healing ministry | Luke 4:18 |

Figure 2

Him in this way (Philippians 2:1; 2 Corinthians 13:14). He is your friend. You will get to know Him so well that you will not go anywhere without being very much aware that He is dwelling in you. You will notice that ACTS is not included in Figure 3, because our prayer relationship to the Holy Spirit is a little different from that which we have with the Father and Son. The acronym here is CHIEF, and we talk to the Holy Spirit as Convictor, Helper, Illuminator, Empowerer, and Friend. For instance, we do not ask the Holy Spirit to forgive our sins. When we have fellowship with the Holy Spirit, we are not asking Him to "give" us anything, but rather are acknowledging Him as the one who dwells in us. Praising Him, we tell Him that we love and appreciate His strength and gifts. We are giving Him permission to help us in our prayers to the Father through the name of Jesus. The Holy Spirit gives us the strength to reach out to the Father and to receive all that He conveys to us through the Holy Spirit.

Give the Holy Spirit a chance to glorify God's name today. Run to the strong tower and be safe.

Shirley is a Vermont grandmother who has a deep faith in God and is obedient to the call that God has given her to serve Him in prayer ministry.

> **PRAYING IN THE HOLY SPIRIT—JUDE 20**
> **FELLOWSHIPPING WITH THE SPIRIT**
> Convictor—Helper—Illuminator—Empowerer—Friend
>
> | | | |
> |---|---|---|
> | YAHWEH-SHAMMAH | Present everywhere | Ps. 139:7-12 |
> | EL-SHADDAI | Strengthens with might | Eph. 3:16 |
> | YAHWEH-RAAH | Led by the Spirit | Rom. 8:14 |
> | YAHWEH-YIREH | Helps the needy | Acts 4:31-35 |
> | YAHWEH-TSIDKENU | Righteousness by Spirit | Rom. 14:17 |
> | YAHWEH-NISSI | Overcomer of evil | 1 John 4:4 |
> | EL-ELYON | Power by the Spirit | Acts 1:8 |
> | EL-ROI | Revelation by the Spirit | 1 Cor. 2:10 |
> | EL-OLAM | Eternal Spirit | Heb. 9:14 |
> | YAHWEH-SHALOM | Peace is Spirit fruit | Gal. 5:22 |
> | YAHWEH-EL-GMOLAH | Gives abundantly | Eph. 3:20 |
> | YAHWEH-MACCADESHCEM | Sanctification of Spirit | 1 Peter 1:22 |
> | YAHWEH-NAKEH | Sword of Spirit | Eph. 6:17, 18 |
> | YAHWEH-SABBAOTH | Spirit of Lord of Hosts | Zech. 4:6 |
> | YAHWEH-RAPHAH | Gifts of healings | 1 Cor. 12:9 |

Figure 3

When she was widowed a few years ago it was prayer that enabled her to carry on managing the family dairy farm as well as interceding for many of her friends, church family, and local businesspeople with whom she dealt. At one of our seminars Shirley was thrilled to learn how she could pray through the names of God and find great strength in praise and petition. A week ago Shirley called to tell my wife and me of a motorbike accident that had injured her minister nephew. After our conversation I asked her if I could pray, and the Spirit led us to pray in the names of God.

"Yahweh-Shammah, I pray that you will be present with Shirley's nephew, David, who is in the hospital at this time. May his family recognize Your presence with them. I know that You are Yahweh-Raphah, the Great Healer, and I ask, Lord, that Your healing power will be revealed in David's life, especially in the injuries that he has received on his face. Father, we know that You are El-Shaddai. We recognize You reverently and humbly as the Almighty. We thank You that You give Your strength not only to David and his family, but also to Shirley and others who are concerned about David at this time. We know that You are Yahweh-Raah, the Good Shepherd, and Lord, we pray that You will shepherd this family and lead them by the still waters. May they sense, Lord, and know that You are their peace, that You are the God who will provide for them in this time of crisis. Dear Father, we know that You will not be doing this for these people because of their righteousness, but because of Your righteousness. We thank You, Lord, that the blood of Jesus has made that righteousness possible so that we can come to You through Jesus and request Your help at this time. I pray, Lord, that You will wave Your banner of victory over Shirley as she cares for her farm and all the responsibilities that she has, and may David's family and the people in the hospital where he is at this time understand the victory power of Your presence and that Your Holy Spirit is blessing and leading. We ask this in the name of Jesus."

I recently read that on average, six months after their birth more than 300 babies in Oregon still have no name. Generic children, many are not only unnamed but unwanted. But through the power of the Holy Spirit you and I can know that we have a new name given to us by God—in fact, we are the children of God, for the Holy Spirit convicts us of that (Romans 8:16). And the God we serve also has many wonderful and unique names. I have read that there are more than 45,000 John Smiths in England. Now, that is a common name! If you were to call out to "John Smith," you would not be sure who would answer, but only the Father, Son, and Holy Spirit will answer when you call out the names of God. If you pray in these names today, allowing the Holy Spirit to glorify God in you and through you, you will find that these names are a strong tower. You can run to them and will always be safe.

SMALL GROUP STUDY
Chapter Six

Cohesive Contrasts

In our small group last week we noticed two levels of communication, "cliché" and "factual information." Once the level of trust develops and deepens in the group, the people will be more comfortable coming to the next communication level, where they can share ideas and opinions. Differences will become obvious, and people will take the risk of expressing their views on various topics. The fourth level of communication is reached when people are willing to share their own feelings. There is an openness not just to facts and opinions, but hurts and joys that are very significant in a person's life.

On whatever level your group is on, spend a few minutes discussing and sharing the following: How do you like your first name? If you were to choose another first name for yourself, what would it be?

Concentrating on the Word
Study Text: Psalm 86

Although Psalm 86 does not mention the Holy Spirit, can you find and list eight qualities or ministries of the Holy Spirit that David refers to in this psalm?

_____   _____
_____   _____
_____   _____
_____   _____

The Holy Spirit leads people to pray in "Jesus' name." Why do you think that it is important to present Jesus' name as a validation for your prayers?

_____
_____

It seems in Psalm 86 that the Holy Spirit leads especially into praise of the Lord (YAHWEH). Which of the 15 names of God do you hear David praising in this psalm?

_____
_____

To which of the names of the Lord is David coming for supplication in Psalm 86?

_____
_____

Following the ACTS acronym, write out a brief prayer to Yahweh-Yireh, the Lord who provides.

_____
_____

The Holy Spirit exalts God's name. How can meditating on God's names (Malachi 3:16), memorizing God's names, and praying in God's names be like a strong tower Christians can run to and be safe?

_____
_____

Which name or names of God is most important to you today? Why is this? How can the Holy Spirit help you pray in this name?

_____
_____

Conversation With the Lord

Ask those in the group who would be willing to pray aloud through two or three verses of Psalm 86 until the whole psalm is completed. Now pray prayers of praise, prayers for the needs in the group and those outside the group, concentrating on the name Yahweh-Shammah, the God who is present. Conclude by praying for the "empty chair" and then the Lord's Prayer together.

Committing the Word to Memory

This week, write out a verse from Psalm 86 and share it with someone as soon as possible.

_____
_____
_____

CHAPTER SEVEN
▼

Give the Holy Spirit a Chance
To Give You Victory Power

In a small logging town in the northern Idaho panhandle I became acquainted with a young Christian man whose zeal for the Lord and joy in serving Him were impressive and contagious. When Craig was 20 he served as a radio carrier for a commander in Vietnam. One month before the day when he would return home to the United States an enemy bullet hit his spine, and suddenly Craig was a paraplegic. Back home Craig's life became a nightmare of drug addiction as he tried to hide his pain in a counterculture, hippie lifestyle. It seemed impossible that the gospel could ever reach a mind so stoned with potent chemicals, but through a chain of miraculous events Craig's life was changed by the power of the Holy Spirit. He went on to captain a winning wheelchair basketball team, cross the finish line in the Spokane Bloomsday race, and become a lay leader of a Christian congregation.

The Holy Spirit witnessed through Craig to bring many people to a saving knowledge of Jesus Christ. Craig was on the losing side in the Vietnamese conflict, but today he is on the victory side with the Holy Spirit. There are still battles he has to face every day with an enemy who tries to cripple and destroy, "yet in all these things we are more than conquerors through Him who loved us" (Romans 8:37).

Conquering External Evil

Paul wrote to the Ephesians about the battle a Christian faces against external evil forces and, after dealing with defensive armor, clearly identifies the Bible and prayer as the Holy Spirit's offensive weapons of victory. "For we do not wrestle against flesh and blood, but against principalities, against powers, against the rulers of the darkness of this age, against spiritual hosts of wickedness in the heavenly places. . . . And take the helmet of salvation, and the sword of the Spirit which is the word of God; praying always with all prayer and supplication in the Spirit, being watchful to this end with all perseverance and supplication for all the saints" (Ephesians 6:12-18).

John brands the enemy as antichrist and says that he even works through many "little" antichrists who have gone out from being part of the Christian family (1 John 2:18, 19). Once again the source of victory is pinpointed: "But you have an anointing from the Holy One, and you know all things" (verse 20). The anointing is the Holy Spirit (Acts 10:38), and this "anointing teaches you concerning all things, and is true" (1 John 2:27), because the Holy Spirit is the Spirit of truth, and is the one who teaches all things (John 14:26; 16:13). He is the most powerful factor of victory in the battle against evil. The Holy Spirit glorifies Jesus, and no evil can conquer in the presence of Jesus.

John again identifies the conflict when he points his finger at the spirit of antichrist, who is the power behind an army of false prophets (1 John 4:1-3). I like the way he exalts the victory power of the Holy Spirit in verse 4. In fact, this has been one of my favorite battle verses for a number of years. "You are of God, little children, and have overcome them, because He who is in you is greater than he who is in the world." Claim that verse right now if you are aware of a special need. "Lord, I know there are a lot of enemies trying to destroy me, but You are the Almighty, and I praise You today because greater is He who is in me than he who is in the world. Right now I claim the victory power of the Holy Spirit against these worldly forces of evil. May Jesus be exalted as the conquering king today."

Reach out and put your arms around that power prayer right now. It is a prayer that clearly reveals why it is extremely important to know that you are filled with the Holy Spirit. When you claim the Holy Spirit by faith as a gift from God (Luke 11:13) and you have the witness of the Spirit in you (Romans 8:16), this will enable you to stand in an invincible position against the enemy. As General Douglas MacArthur said at a joint meeting of the United States Congress, April 19, 1951: "In war there is no substitute for victory." So it is in the Christian life. While God will forgive those who are overcome by the evil one there are always battle scars that remain.

Forgiveness is wonderful, but victory is glorious. As an old Arab proverb says: "On the day of victory no one is tired." Victory brings rejoicing, gladness, festivity, peace. At the Olympic Games it seems that the athletes who win the gold always have enough energy remaining to stand proudly as their country's flag is raised and anthem played. The athletes who lose may barely have enough strength to move another millimeter, while the winner can jump with joy.

Overcoming the Flesh

"Flesh" is not a word that is used very often in the twentieth century.

When it is, we think of meat—the soft tissue of a body. Paul writes about flesh more than 90 times, and often he uses the word in the neutral sense of bodily existence (Galatians 2:20; Philippians 1:22, 24). On the other hand, there are many times Paul speaks of the flesh as evil. There are sins of the flesh (Colossians 2:11), lusts of the flesh (Ephesians 2:3), filthiness of the flesh (2 Corinthians 7:1), and corruptions of the flesh (Galatians 6:8). Now, you must admit this sounds frightening. Is it actually the material substance of the body that is bad? Is the "meat," or cells, of the body evil?

On top of these questions we find that the Holy Spirit and the flesh are in direct conflict (Galatians 5:17). They cannot coexist peacefully. They are in deadly battle. This conflict is happening within you and me. It is here that we must and can gain the victory. Failure in this battle taking place within our minds, hearts, and lives means that a sin is committed. Victory means that a sin or desire to sin, a temptation, is overcome. Each sin overcome is evidence of the Holy Spirit's great power.

During Operation Desert Storm, as the Gulf war of 1991 was known, television screens across many countries showed enemy targets in the gun or bomb sights of attacking jets. The suspected weapon storage building, for instance, centered in the sights. The bomb was released, and the next picture on the television screen showed the building exploding in violent destruction. Right now we are going to target sin and smash it to pieces by the power of the Holy Spirit. Only the Holy Spirit can break the power of sin in a person's life. As it says in the *Abingdon Bible Dictionary*: "Flesh with its downward pull can only be overcome by the Holy Spirit who, in Paul, is the power that leads men and women to God."

The television picture of sin is very confusing. "Sin is exciting; sin is fun. Life is boring without a little bit of sin." But every sin pictured as entertainment on television is a tragedy in real life. It's like saying poison is fun, poison is exciting, when in reality poison, like sin, is sickening and fatal.

A few years ago CBS spent $14 million producing a television mini-series entitled *Sins*. One day our daughter Lyndell came home from the supermarket and, knowing I was a preacher who often expounded on the dangers of sin, said to me with a cheeky smile, "Dad, there's a *People* magazine at the supermarket that you should buy; you'll really enjoy reading it."

"What's it about?" I replied cautiously.

"Sin," she informed me.

People reviewed the CBS television mini-series and ran surveys to discover the answers to such questions as Which of the Ten Commandments is the hardest to keep? (not taking the name of the Lord in vain) and Which of the Ten Commandments is easiest to keep? (not killing). Murder, rape, incest, child abuse, spying, and drug dealing were listed as the worst sins (in that order), while taping off radio and television, nude sunbathing, drinking alcohol, masturbation, not voting, and white lies were listed as the least evil, with about 40 sins between the two extremes. People surveyed listed parking in a handicapped zone as much worse than divorce or premarital sex. Churchgoers who responded to the survey felt they committed an average of 6.80 sins per month, which was a lot more than nonchurchgoers, who stated that they committed only an average of 2.76 sins per month. The magazine went on to examine the "moral turpitude" of *Sins* hostess Joan Collins, and asked sacrilegiously from Scripture, "Who would cast the first stone? Go, Joan, and sin *some* more." [1]

It is stunning to notice that Jesus' words, spoken to the woman caught in adultery, are exactly the opposite to *People*'s words to Joan Collins. "And Jesus said to her, 'Neither do I condemn you; go and sin *no* more'" (John 8:11). Jesus could have said, "Go and sin as little as possible," or "Go and sin only when temptation is too much for you." Instead He said, "Go and sin no more." Was He teasing, joking, asking the impossible? No; of all people, Jesus knew the victory power of the Holy Spirit. There is not one verse in the Bible that gives any excuse for sin, but the Bible does tell of forgiveness and victory through the Holy Spirit. In fact, the Bible writers are clear that sins can be overcome, one by one, every time.

Does talking about overcoming sin make you a little apprehensive? "Does that mean that we are going to be perfect or sinless?" people ask. A man came to me and claimed quite proudly, "I have not sinned for more than one week now." I looked at him with surprise, never having seen a person in such a state of purity before. "Have you loved the Lord your God with all your heart and soul and mind and your neighbor as yourself?" I asked quite seriously, knowing something of his community reputation. He became rather annoyed with my doubt and questioned my readiness for the second coming of Jesus.

Because of the negative connotation some people have about saying we can stop sinning by the power of the Holy Spirit, let us say that through the power of the Holy Spirit we can have victory over temptation. If sin is going to be defeated in us by the Holy Spirit, we must let Him do it at the temptation level. The battlefield with temptation is in the mind. Temptation need never be transferred into outward actions of evil. Temptation is one step before sin. Once sin happens, all the Holy Spirit can do is lead us to repentance, confession to God, and assurance of forgiveness.

Hit sin on the temptation level. To defeat sin before it happens, we must allow the Holy Spirit to give us victory over temptation. Temptation is not sin. Even Jesus was tempted, yet He did not sin in any way (Hebrews 4:15). Temptation is temptation because it makes sin appear desirable to the "flesh." Because of sin's appeal, temptation is dangerous even though it is definitely not sin in itself. That is why in the Lord's Prayer Jesus taught Christians to ask God each day not to allow them to be led into the place where temptation seems irresistible, like the small boy whose mother caught him with his hand in the cookie jar. "What are you doing?" she asked, to which he innocently replied, "Resisting temptation!" If that was true, this little boy was certainly making it harder for himself to resist the temptation to take a cookie than if he had had his hands in the kitchen sink washing the dishes.

The Three Laws

In the greatest Holy Spirit chapter of the Bible, Romans 8, Paul discusses in detail the conflict between the flesh and the Spirit. Let us take time for some concentrated study with Paul now so that this topic will become so unmistakable that we can sing a hallelujah chorus of victory as we face every temptation. Romans 8 is the chapter that mentions the Holy Spirit more than any other in the Bible. This chapter begins with "no condemnation" and ends with "no separation," and in the middle "all things work together for good to those who love God." What a chapter! I hope you can open your Bible and ask the Holy Spirit to lead you into all truth as you study the victory power of the Holy Spirit in this chapter right now.

The first important discovery is that you and I are not saved on the basis of our victory over sin. Victory over sin is a result of surrender to the complete control of the indwelling presence of the Holy Spirit, who comes into a person's life at conversion. And remember, it is at conversion that a sinner is saved from the penalty of sin. "For by grace you have been saved through faith, and that not of yourselves; it is the gift of God, not of works, lest anyone should boast" (Ephesians 2:8, 9). "Not by works of righteousness which we have done, but according to His mercy He saved us, through the washing of regeneration and renewing of the Holy Spirit, whom He poured out on us abundantly through Jesus Christ our Savior" (Titus 3:5, 6).

What is the purpose of victory over sin if it is not to save us from the penalty of sin? The answer is as clear as a beautiful crystal vase my wife and I were given after I had spoken at a camp meeting in England. Victory over sin glorifies God, defeats the devil, witnesses to other Christians and non-Christians of the power of God, and gives relief and satisfaction within the life of a born-again person. On top of this, failure to overcome sin not only can bring disgrace to the Christian and his or her God, but also can reverse a Christian's sanctification, plus deny one's justification and salvation. So let me emphasize this again. While you are saved totally on the basis of the blood of Jesus and the power of the Holy Spirit, not by your own works, victory over temptation will become the third most important factor in the Christian life—third only to conversion and daily surrender to the indwelling presence of the Holy Spirit.

With this in mind, let us come back to Romans 8. "There is therefore now no condemnation to those who are in Christ Jesus, who do not walk according to the flesh, but according to the Spirit" (verse 1). Those people who are not under condemnation find themselves walking—that is, living daily—not according to the flesh, but according to the Spirit. This is a promise for us to claim today. Flesh here is referring to the natural desires of the human organism, which have become corrupted by the generational effects of sin. This is why some versions of the Bible translate "flesh" as "sinful nature" or "sinful desires" or "carnal desires." For instance, appetite is good and was created by God as an indication of the body's need for more fuel. But because of sin, appetite can desire excess food and unhealthy food and in fact can become a god (Philippians 3:19). While the wrong desire for food can be relatively harmless to anyone other than the intemperate person, the same cannot be said for the wrong desire for possessions, sex, authority, drink, pleasure, or anger.

There are three laws that Paul discusses in Romans 8. The result of the corrupted desires of the human flesh is spoken of as the "law of sin and death" (verse 2). This type of law has been described as a "generalization examined until it is proven that there are no exceptions." In other words, it is seen that the same thing happens in the same way again and again. For instance, each time I am not victorious over my sinful nature's desire to be totally selfish, the result in me is always the same. That is the law of sin. If I do not repent of this sin, the result is also always the same—Jesus is denied, sin rules, and the wages of sin is death. So this law is called by Paul the law of sin and death.

Now, there is another law that makes people sensitive to the dangers of the sinful nature of the flesh. "Because the carnal mind is enmity against God; for it is not subject to the law of God, nor indeed can be" (verse 7). This second law, which Paul calls the law of God, can be summarized as the Ten Commandments. This law of God lists the things that God says to do or not to do. It is this law that the Holy Spirit uses to convict us that we are sinners in need of God's grace. This law is expanded and elucidated in the teachings of Jesus. Every commandment in the law of God sounds rather simple and relatively easy to keep, but it is not many years into childhood before most people discover that what Paul says about this law is true—it is weak because sinful human nature cannot of itself live up to it (verse 3). In the battlefield of the unconverted human mind the law of God always loses to the desires of the flesh. "So then, those who are in the flesh cannot please God" (verse 8).

Another pastor and I always visited together to study the Bible with a young lady involved in prostitution. "I can't leave this lifestyle; I like it, it is exciting, I make a lot of money," she explained. "Someday I may become a Christian, but not now. I know God would want me to change."

"Yes, I do lose my temper often," a man admitted. "But I don't care; my family needs to know I am not going to be pushed around by them."

"I am going to make all the money I can," the stockbroker boasted, "even if people who don't have a clue about investments lose a few thousand dollars because of their foolishness."

These may seem to be extreme cases, but I am sure we all understand how easy it is to reject the law of God in favor of the law of sin and death. Listen to Reformed Church pastor Andrew Murray: "If a Christian is to make progress and become fully convinced of the necessity of being filled with the Spirit, his eyes must be opened to the extent that sin dominates within him. Everything in him is tainted with sin, his will, his power, his heart; and therefore the omnipotence of God must take in hand the renewal of everything by the Holy Spirit." [2]

As Murray indicates, there is good news for the Christian. There is what Paul calls the third law. "For the law of the Spirit of life in Christ Jesus has made me free from the law of sin and death" (verse 2). The third law proclaims that the Holy Spirit can enable us to walk in victory. What a law of liberty! R. A. Torrey was a great Christian leader who followed in the steps of D. L. Moody. I like the way Torrey explains the third law of Romans 8. "In other words, when we come to the end of ourselves, when we fully realize our own inability to keep the law of God and in utter helplessness look up to the Holy Spirit in Christ Jesus to do for us that which we cannot do for ourselves, when we surrender our every thought, purpose, desire, and affection to His absolute control and thus walk after the Spirit, the Spirit does take control; He sets us free from the power of sin that dwells in us and brings our whole life into the conformity of the will of God. It is the privilege of the children of God in the power of the Holy Spirit to have victory over sin every day and every hour and every moment." [3]

All this emphasis on total victory may seem to be intimidating and discouraging to some Christians if it is perceived in the wrong way. "I am a born-again Christian, and I believe I am filled with the Holy Spirit," a young man told me recently. "Yet I still battle with temptation and sometimes fall into sin. Why can't I be free of it altogether?" I reminded him of God's unfailing forgiveness and also of the fact that the "flesh" will remain with Christians until the resurrection day. But while the flesh will remain, it need not reign. We need not be "in the flesh" as far as being dominated by it, but "in the Spirit" by willful choice and total surrender. Listen to Torrey again: "Here we have a life where not merely the commandment comes, but the Spirit comes and works obedience to the commandment and brings us complete victory over the law of sin and death. . . . The desires of the body are still there, desires which, if made the rule of our life, would lead us into sin; but day by day by the power of the Spirit we put to death the deeds to which the desires of the body would lead us. We walk by the Spirit and therefore do not fulfill the lusts of the flesh (Galatians 5:16, RV). 'We have crucified the flesh with the passions and the lusts thereof' (verse 24, RV)."[4]

Like a TV advertisement for a weight loss clinic, there are "before" and "after" pictures we can look at. Before conversion sin is easy and even fun, although the consequences may appear to be painful. After conversion we hate sin, and crucify it by the Holy Spirit (Romans 8:13). We fight against sin in the power of the Holy Spirit. We give into temptation and fall into trouble only when we forget Yahweh-Shammah, the God who is present in us by the power of the Holy Spirit. I have found myself in trouble a number of times in life because I did not remember for a few critical moments that I was still in the presence of the Holy Spirit.

Now, here is a law that is absolutely certain. With this law comes a 100 percent guarantee. **The power of temptation can be broken by the recognition of the presence of an external power that is loved or respected.** For instance, the little boy with his hand in the cookie jar found that the temptation evaporated when his mother appeared. The woman with the irresistible urge to steal from a store finds that the urge vanishes quickly when she recognizes a store security guard watching her. Even a pathological liar will resist the temptation in the presence of someone who knows the absolute truth. While the Holy Spirit is not a security guard or police officer, nevertheless recognizing the presence of the Holy Spirit bringing Jesus into our heart and mind gives power that will enable sin to be overcome every time.

Sometimes we say, "What I need is more willpower." Perhaps the opposite is true. Through the presence of the Holy Spirit, He gives more "won't" power. I am tempted to lose my temper, but through the power of the Holy Spirit I won't. I am tempted to tell a lie, but through the power of the Holy Spirit I won't. I am tempted to go to this place of evil, but through the power of the Holy Spirit I won't. I am tempted to watch this program that I know will not exalt Jesus, but I won't. I am tempted to eat or drink this substance that is bad for me, but I won't. The devil says, "You've given in before; once more won't hurt you. It will give you a lot of pleasure." But through the power of the Holy Spirit we cry out to Jesus and say, "Lord, I claim Your promise today, knowing that You are present with me, and through the Holy Spirit I will not give in to sin. I won't." Let me repeat that in my own life I recognize that when I have fallen into sin it is because for a few moments I have neglected to be fully aware of the presence of my friend the Holy Spirit. I am glad to say, though, that when we do sin the Holy Spirit leads us to repent immediately and to know the heartfelt sorrow that comes through recognizing how much we have hurt our God.

Not Threat but Promise

I used to be fearful of such statements as "that the righteous requirements of the law might be fulfilled in us who do not walk according to the flesh but according to the Spirit" (Romans 8:4). I used to think this meant my perfect keeping of God's law and thus being righteous in myself was a condition of salvation. Now, I know that this is not a threat but a promise of the Holy Spirit. A few years ago my family were camping with some friends at a beautiful lake in New South Wales. The water was warm, and after lunch I decided to swim across the lake to a boat mooring buoy. My daughter Carolyn and her friend Adrielle were swimming some distance from me when suddenly I was gripped by a terrible stomach cramp. It was impossible to swim on, and I quickly began to sink. When I came up the first time I yelled for help. The girls just laughed. They knew I could swim well. I had taught my daughter to swim, so they thought I was just joking. But this was no fooling matter. When I came up for the third and last time they knew I was serious, so they swam to help me with the speed of Olympic champions. Both had lifesaving medallions, so they were soon able to rescue me from drowning.

I guess I am one of the few fathers whose life was saved by his daughter. She didn't say, "Dad, I will save and love you only if you can swim to the buoy." Instead Carolyn and her friend held me up until a boat could be brought to carry me to safety. In the same way, when I have been sinking spiritually I have had friends whom the Holy Spirit has brought alongside not to push me under but to hold me up and get me to the spiritual destination of life and peace. In the same way God does not say, "You had better be able to keep the rules of the Bible perfectly or you will not be saved." Rather, His promise is "Because you have accepted Me as your Saviour I not only count you as being righteous in Jesus, but I have made it possible for you to live a righteous, holy life by the power of the Holy Spirit. I am doing this for you because you are one of My children, saved by grace. If you surrender to the power of the Holy Spirit every day, you will no longer be under the power of bad temper, intemperance, lust, greed, selfishness, or whatever your problems may be, but you will be able to live and move in the victory power of the Holy Spirit. By this other people will know what sort of God I am and what the practical value of Christianity is."

This is what Jesus was talking about when He said to the woman caught in adultery, "Go and sin no more." He was giving her a promise, telling her of a possibility of what would happen as the Holy Spirit dwelt in her. If you give the Holy Spirit a chance, He will make you aware of the victory power that can enable you to go and sin no more.

The victory power of the Holy Spirit is not some mysterious supernatural force. It is your friend the Holy Spirit working through fellow Christians and in your mind through the principles of prayer and scripture meditation as we have studied in the past three chapters. "Temptations often appear irresistible because, through neglect of prayer and study of the Bible, the tempted one cannot readily remember God's promises and meet them with the Scripture references."[5] The Holy Spirit will not allow temptation to appear that powerful to any person who prays in the Word, prays through the Lord's Prayer, prays in the names of God and makes them his or her strong tower of safety.

Brandon had grown up hearing the name of God blasphemed every day. His work with a construction team reinforced this until he was a prolific swearer, slipping foul and obscene adjectives between the syllables in other words. When he began to study the Bible and learned about Christianity, he was so excited about what he had learned that he would emphasize his interest in God's Word to people he was sharing with by swearing about it. Soon, without any person condemning this terrible practice, the Holy Spirit convinced him that what he was doing did not honor God in any way.

After Brandon was converted, the Holy Spirit helped him refrain from swearing audibly, but there were still times when the words came into his mind ready to be used. Each time this happened Brandon would ask the Lord to give him victory, and he would think of Bible verses and Christian songs and soon the urge would go away. He could never swear in front of Jesus or even think of swearwords knowing Jesus was with him through the Holy Spirit. Then came the time when Brandon realized that for many months he had not even had to struggle with the temptation to use bad language.

If the Holy Spirit can bring victory over swearing, He can do it with other temptations or sins. There is no doubt about it. I like the way Paul ends Romans 8: "Yet in all these things we are more than conquerors through Him who loved us" (verse 37). This is a powerful promise you can claim today. *Gold in the Making* is a wonderful little book a friend gave to me at a time when I was wrestling with a number of complex problems. I like the way the author, Ron Lee Davis, explains "more than conquerors" in Romans 8:37. "That phrase is . . . but one word in the original Greek: *hypernikomen*. *Hyper* means 'super'; *nikomen* means 'we conqueror.' What Paul said, in effect, was this: 'In all things we are super-conquerors through Him who loved us!' " [6] Give the Holy Spirit a chance today. He will help you be a super-conqueror.

Let me end this chapter with a warning that I always need to remember myself. After quite a number of years as a Christian, Brandon became careless and began to neglect prayer and Bible study in the power of the Holy Spirit. He slipped into the habit of watching movies that used bad language to punctuate the action. Some of the books and magazines he read did the same thing. It wasn't long before Brandon was fighting the battle in his mind again. Occasionally a word even slipped out, shocking those who heard. "How could a good churchgoing man talk that way?" they exclaimed in surprise.

Now Brandon was very discouraged, and began thinking about giving up attending church and forgetting about being a Christian. But the Holy Spirit wasn't going to let Brandon slip away that easily. Surprisingly, the battle was much harder this time than it had been at the beginning. There was extra guilt, self-condemnation, and even a sense of hopelessness as the bad language became connected to thoughts of evil. Brandon began to contemplate suicide. He lost his job and almost destroyed his marriage. Now the Holy Spirit led Brandon's family and some friends and fellow church members into times of intense prayer for him. They asked that satanic forces would be bound and this man would be set free. They claimed many great promises and asked that Brandon would recognize the mighty love and power of El-Shaddai. Today Brandon has again accepted the victory power of the Holy Spirit. Although there will be battle scars that will remain, he is once again a super-conqueror. The Word of God and prayer are weapons of the Holy Spirit that Brandon will never let go of again.

SMALL GROUP STUDY
Chapter Seven

Cohesive Contrasts

We have noticed that levels of communication in a group correspond to the levels of trust that participants sense among the members of the group. This means that nothing personal shared within the group must go out of that room—not even to a spouse or close friend. New people joining the group should be made aware of this immediately. Even so, when new members join it may be a couple weeks before the group can be as spontaneous as before. If new people are coming into the group every week, the trust may stay on a fairly superficial level. Choose one of the parts of the following question for discussion in your group meeting. "What has been one of the greatest victories in your life?" or "What victory in history do you think has had the most impact on our modern society?"

Concentrating on the Word
Study Text: Romans 8:1-14

How many times in Romans 8:1-14 do you find Paul contrasting the flesh of the Spirit? What do you consider his strongest words concerning the contrast between these two opposing forces within a Christian?

_____
_____

In such passages as 1 John 3:24-4:4 and Ephesians 6:12 the Bible writers identify external evil forces that a Christian must battle. What evidences have you seen of the working of these powers of darkness?

_____
_____

The forces of evil apparently use many worldly means to try to discourage Christians and turn them from faith in God. How do you think the following could be used either by evil powers or by the power of the Holy Spirit?

Billboard _____

Movies/Television _____

Magazines/Books _____

Music _____

Sporting events _____

Parties _____

Remember that many different opinions may emerge in the group as the above questions are answered. It will be very important that group members do not become judgmental of the views or standards of others, but try to look for the common ground on which principles can apply.

Romans 8:1-14 seems to concentrate on the internal battle each person fights against evil. Which do you consider the more difficult—internal or external conflict? Why?

_____
_____

In your own words, how would you describe Paul's three laws in Romans 8:1-7?

_____
_____

Describe a method you have found successful in dealing with an unexpected evil thought.

_____
_____

Is there some way you could be used by the Holy Spirit to help another person to be a super-conqueror today? How would you do it?

_____
_____

Conversation With the Lord

Pray victory prayers in your group to conclude your meeting today. First, praise God for victories that have taken place. Now pray for victories needed by people in the group. Finally, pray for other situations outside the group. Pray also for the "empty chair," and conclude with the Lord's Prayer.

Committing the Word to Memory

This week, write out a verse from Romans 8:1-14 and share it with someone as soon as possible.

CHAPTER
EIGHT
▼

Give the Holy Spirit a Chance
To Shatter Self-control

Powells New and Used Bookstore in Portland, Oregon, is one of the largest in the world. A friend had recommended a book to me that was not available in bookstores in my part of the city, so I visited Powells and asked at the desk what section of shelves to search. They directed me to the self-help section, where, although I did not find what I was looking for, I discovered a vast array of books on self-control. Through the right mental attitude, determination of the will, and various other techniques most problems can be overcome, the books seem to say. Compulsive behavior, addictions, depression, results of childhood abuse, personality disorders, financial chaos, marital conflict, and many more negative situations and lifestyles can be dealt with, I was informed, by the right methods of self-control. Control is power. Control is what we want. It is what we like. We want to control others, events, decisions, ourselves.

At a school concert the first- and second-grade teacher was running around behind the scenes trying to keep track of a few dozen little children. "Don't panic; everything will be all right," I said, trying to calm her down a little. With fiery eyes she replied: "I *am* in control, thank you!"

The ministry of the Holy Spirit is in total contrast to the secular concepts of control. In fact, if you give the Holy Spirit a chance, He will shatter self-control in a way that will expose the potential powers that can miraculously transform any life that is filled with the Spirit. Control is his topic when Paul writes to the Galatians about the Holy Spirit. Two of the best-known texts concerning the Holy Spirit are found in Galatians 5:22, 23: "But the fruit of the Spirit is love, joy, peace, longsuffering, kindness, goodness, faithfulness, gentleness, self-control. Against such there is no law."

Actually, if you notice that "fruit" is singular you will discover, as many others have, that the fruit of the Spirit is LOVE and that the other eight are facets of love that flourish in lives that are filled with the Holy Spirit. Through the Holy Spirit joy is love exalting, peace is love at rest, longsuffering is love enduring, kindness is love relating to others, goodness is love in action, faithfulness is love in confidence, gentleness is love handling delicate situations, self-control is love in command. The love of God is poured into our hearts by the Holy Spirit (Romans 5:5), and when love is in command of a human life all the other fruit will be evident.

Self-control is the root of the fruit. It is on the strength of self-control that all the other fruit grows. At a wedding ceremony that I was officiating, the young bridegroom lost his temper at the photographer, who was terribly slow. As the bridegroom lashed out verbally, joy, peace, longsuffering, kindness, goodness, faithfulness, and gentleness all evaporated, leaving the bride and the rest of the wedding party hurt and embarrassed. We forgave the bridegroom for this momentary lapse, but certainly the fruit had been torn out at the root because of a breakdown of self-control.

"Lord, how can I have self-control even in the most difficult situations?" I often asked as a young man. Was the answer in willpower, culture, or education? One of the most revolutionary moments of my life came when I discovered that self-control is possible only when my life is completely out of the control of self. That is the answer—allow yourself to be out of control. If that sounds dangerous, remember that only when your life is in the total control of the Holy Spirit will the rest of the fruit of the Spirit be safe.

In reality there is no such thing as self-control. Every life is either in the control of the Holy Spirit or the control of the flesh. "For the flesh lusts against the Spirit, and the Spirit against the flesh; and these are contrary to one another, so that you do not do the things that you wish" (Galatians 5:17). If people are not doing the things they wish, as Paul says, they are certainly not in control. When a life is out of the control of the Holy Spirit, the works of the flesh begin to surface and dominate. When a life is filled with the Holy Spirit, the fruit of the Spirit begins to flourish, and this is not what the flesh desires to see activated. The flesh desires self-gratification rather than kindness or goodness. Notice how the works of the flesh are in complete contradistinction to the fruit of the Spirit in Galatians 5:19-23.

Fruit of the Spirit	*Works of the Flesh*
Love	Adultery, fornication, uncleanness
Joy	Licentiousness, idolatry, sorcery
Peace	Hatred, contentions
Longsuffering	Jealousies
Kindness	Outbursts of wrath
Goodness	Selfish ambitions
Faithfulness	Dissensions, heresies
Gentleness	Envy, murder
Self-control	Drunkenness, revelries

So according to Paul's two lists the opposite of true self-control, in the power of the Holy Spirit, is drunkenness and revelry. When a person is controlled by alcohol, he or she does things that they do not want to do. On the other hand, when people are filled with the Holy Spirit, they will do things that the sinful self, the flesh, does not want them to do, such as praising God, sharing His love, and witnessing joyfully about His salvation. Strange things happen when a mind is affected by an outside power. This could be the reason Paul says, "And do not be drunk with wine, in which is dissipation; but be filled with the Spirit" (Ephesians 5:18). Alcohol affects the brains and lives of more than 60 percent of Americans today. The results are devastating. The *American Journal of Public Health* reported that 65 of every 100 people will be involved in an accident with an alcohol-affected driver. What would happen if 65 percent of the population were truly under the command and control of the Holy Spirit?

In the 1800s one of the greatest woman speakers in the temperance movement was Adventist pioneer Ellen White. She was acclaimed by newspapers and civic leaders not only in the United States but in Australia and New Zealand. I was interested to read how in many of her lectures and writings she dealt with the control issue. To those struggling with addiction and evil she outlined the basis of victory: "Your part is to put your will on the side of Christ. When you yield your will to His, He immediately takes possession of you, and works in you to will and to do of His good pleasure. Your nature is brought under the control of His Spirit." [1] On several other occasions she wrote from Australia, "When men [and women] are not under the control of the Word and the Spirit of God, they are captives of Satan, and we know not to what length he may lead them in sin." [2] *"Satan takes the control of every mind that is not decidedly under the control of the Spirit of God."* [3]

"You can do it," the self-control books say to people struggling with a vast array of problems. "Just realize the full potential of your mind." But it appears that if we claim autonomy and say, "I will exercise full self-control on my own behalf," we will find ourselves under the satanic control of the sinful flesh. Some may say, "I will be a kind and loving person, but I do not want to have anything to do with Jesus Christ." Through culture and education some refinement of the life may be possible, but it is not possible to have the true fruit of the Spirit without the Holy Spirit any more than it is possible to have an apple orchard without apple trees.

Recently a professor went berserk on the campus of his university and shot a number of people. It was reported that he had become depressed about the possibility of losing his job. He was highly educated but out of control. In its pure heavenly form love and all that grows out of it are available only to those who are controlled by the Holy Spirit. This is the love that, in the middle of His discussion of spiritual gifts in 1 Corinthians 12-14, Paul elevates as the most important ingredient of the Spirit-filled life. To have true love while under control of the sinful nature is about as possible as finding strawberries growing on cacti.

Have you noticed in the Gospels how many times Jesus came in contact with people possessed by evil spirits? The small group in our home recently prayed through the story of the man living in the Gadara cemetery (Mark 5:1-20). No chains could bind him but he was shackled to a power that controlled his life. No one could tame him. He was out of human control; out of self-control. He was doing, as Paul said in Galatians 5:17, the things that he did not wish to do, because he was possessed by evil forces. When the healing power of Jesus set this man free from the powers of evil, the immediate change in his life revealed the beginning of the growth of the fruit of the Spirit, especially the fruit of peace. "Then they came to Jesus, and saw the one who had been demon-possessed and had the legion, sitting and clothed and in his right mind. And they were afraid" (Mark 5:15). Now the Holy Spirit in him took possession of this man's life and, contrary to the fact of the man wanting to be with Jesus (verse 18), the Holy Spirit led him home to be a mighty witness for God. "However, Jesus did not permit him, but said to him, 'Go home to your friends, and tell them what great things the Lord has done for you, and how He has had compassion on you.' And he departed and began to proclaim in Decapolis all that Jesus had done for him; and all marveled" (Mark 5:19, 20).

While the Holy Spirit will certainly never violate free will, as He is invited into a person's life He will begin to make radical changes that would otherwise be impossible. The result of these changes is a wonderful witness for Jesus.

Peggy Paine had been brought up in a mainline Christian church, but at 16 turned to atheism as a result of school science classes and because she didn't understand how a God of love could allow all the suffering of the world. Eventually Peggy graduated with a master's degree in social work, and by the time she was 31 her life was out of control to such an extent that she came to the edge of a nervous breakdown and found herself battling the urge to commit suicide. In this state of mind Peggy could no longer carry on her social work, so she turned to cleaning houses, and it was there that she met a woman who had been crippled by polio since she was 3. Peggy cooked and cleaned and cared for this lady, who was a born-again Christian.

The beautiful prayers of this Christian reached the heart of Peggy even though for three weeks she refused to study the Bible. To please and help her employer, Peggy eventually agreed to study the Bible for one hour per week. As soon as she started to read the Scriptures, all the broken, mismatched pieces began to come together, and Peggy found herself understanding why she had been possessed by darkness and death.

Recently I met Peggy and her husband and listened to some of the songs the Holy Spirit had given her to write when she had committed her life to Jesus and become possessed by His Spirit. The very first song, which she had written and sung to the crippled lady that the Holy Spirit had used to lead her to Jesus, said, "Carry me back home, Lord, to the rejoicing of Your heart. Let Your angels sing and give praise to Thee. . . . You searched and You called, refusing to give up on me. . . . My heart broke as You spoke soft and low. . . . I turn around now, and there You are. . . . Carry me back home, Lord; I want to go home to the rejoicing of Your heart." Peggy has come out of the control of spiritual death and is alive in the power of the Holy Spirit. " 'I will put My Spirit in you, and you shall live, and I will place you in your own land. Then you shall know that I, the Lord, have spoken it and performed it,' says the Lord" (Ezekiel 37:14).

When the Spirit possesses a life, He "causes" remarkable changes to take place. "I will give you a new heart and put a new spirit within you; I will take the heart of stone out of your flesh and give you a heart of flesh. I will put My Spirit within you and cause you to walk in My statutes, and you will keep My judgments and do them" (Ezekiel 36:26, 27). The story of the dry bones is an unusual illustration of Holy Spirit possession. Without the Spirit the bones had the Word of the Lord and organization, but no life. When the Holy Spirit filled those bodies, they became a great living army (Ezekiel 36:10). The Spirit "caused" resurrection life and victory when He filled His people (Ezekiel 37:12).

"I can't believe the change in Martin's life since he became a Christian." Have you ever heard words like that? Whenever the Holy Spirit takes possession of a life, He causes transformation. For instance, God promised Saul that the Holy Spirit would cause a radical change in his life. "Then the Spirit of the Lord will come upon you, and you will prophesy with them and be turned into another man" (1 Samuel 10:6). Peter explained to the leaders of the early Christian church that the Holy Spirit, when in possession of a life, would cause purification to take place. "So God, who knows the heart, acknowledged them, by giving them the Holy Spirit just as He did to us, and made no distinction between us and them, purifying their hearts by faith" (Acts 15:8, 9).

This is why the Holy Spirit is called the Spirit of holiness (Romans 1:4), and it is through the Holy Spirit, in the name of Jesus, that Christians are washed, sanctified, and justified as they are released from the control of the works of the flesh. "Do you not know that the unrighteous will not inherit the kingdom of God? Do not be deceived. Neither fornicators, nor idolaters, nor adulterers, nor homosexuals, nor sodomites, nor thieves, nor covetous, nor drunkards, nor revilers, nor extortioners will inherit the kingdom of God. And such were some of you. But you were washed, but you were sanctified, but you were justified in the name of the Lord Jesus and by the Spirit of our God" (1 Corinthians 6:9-11).

Listen to this beautiful statement. "When the Spirit of God takes possession of the heart, it transforms the life. Sinful thoughts are put away, evil deeds are renounced; love, humility, and peace take the place of anger, envy, and strife. Joy takes the place of sadness, and the countenance reflects the light of heaven. No one sees the hand that lifts the burden, or beholds the light descend from the courts above. The blessing comes when by faith the soul surrenders itself to God. Then that power which no human eye can see creates a new being in the image of God." [4]

My wife has always had a fear of drunks. If she sees one approaching on a city sidewalk, she will cross the street rather than have to pass close by the person. Of course, she becomes fearful only when the drunk is in an advanced state of intoxication, and can only stagger, rather than walk with a straight, firm step. Paul uses walking to illustrate the matter of control: "I say then: Walk in the Spirit, and you shall not fulfill the lust of the flesh" (Galatians 5:16). "If we live in the Spirit, let us also walk in the Spirit" (verse 25). "There is therefore now no condemnation to those who are in Christ Jesus, who do not walk according to the flesh, but according to the Spirit. . . . He condemned sin in the flesh, that the righteous requirement of the law might be fulfilled in us who do not walk according to the flesh but according to the Spirit" (Romans 8:1-4).

Just as the mind controlled by alcohol is not in command of its walking or driving, so the unconverted self cannot fully control its actions. The desire may be present, but the ability is lacking. There are insufficient funds in the bank of human power to cash the check of total self-control. This leads to frustration in the secular world. As Dr. William A. Miller says: "Particularly here in America the development of control in the developing personality is highly regarded and seen as a very positive sign of growth toward maturity. Being able to control oneself and behave rationally is considered to be a significant indicator of maturity. In our society it is rewarded and positively reinforced whenever it is manifested. On the other hand, its opposite—being out of control and behaving irrationally—is regarded as a very negative thing in American culture and society. People who are out of control are actually socially unacceptable. They may be tolerated, but even then it is with disdain. At worst they are fined or hospitalized or imprisoned." [5]

Strangely enough, though, the vast majority of Hollywood productions are dominated by people who are out of control—yelling, fighting, killing, committing immorality, lying, stealing, etc. These movies picture people walking not according to the Spirit, but according to the flesh. They walk according to their own ungodly lusts (Jude 18). They walk in darkness (1 John 1:6). They walk according to the flesh (2 Peter 2:10).

When the Holy Spirit leads a person to repentance and conversion, He then enables that person to have a new, strong, straight walk, not in darkness, but in the light of Jesus' love. "But if we walk in the light as He is in the light, we have fellowship with one another, and the blood of Jesus Christ His Son cleanses us from all sin" (1 John 1:7). The Holy Spirit-possessed Christian walks in newness of life (Romans 6:4), walks honestly (Romans 13:13), walks by faith (2 Corinthians 5:6, 7), walks worthily (Ephesians 4:1), walks in love (Ephesians 5:2), walks circumspectly (Ephesians 5:15), walks in wisdom (Colossians 4:5), walks according to the commandments (2 John 6), walks in truth (3 John 4). Eventually this person will walk in white (Revelation 3:4). He or she will walk in the light of the glory of the New Jerusalem (Revelation 21:24).

Now, all of this walking may sound like hard work and a little intimidating if we forget some basic facts. These statements regarding the walk of a Spirit-controlled person are not threats, but promises. They are not the means of salvation, but the fruit of salvation. They are perfectly fulfilled only in the life of Jesus. But through the Holy Spirit each of these walks are not only reckoned or imputed to the life of a born-again Christian, but are made possible in the Christian life by allowing the Holy Spirit to control. Remember Galatians 5:16, "I say then: Walk in the Spirit, and you shall not fulfill the lust of the flesh." That is a promise. There are sufficient funds in your account in heaven by the blood of Jesus for you to cash that check every day. In Rome I noticed many branches of the Bank of the Holy Spirit. That, I thought, would be a great place to have an account, but my bank of the Holy Spirit is not in Rome, but in heaven, and the Holy Spirit sets up a branch in my life when I become His dwelling place. I draw from that account anytime. I can always cash there the promised checks from God's Word.

As I look at my own life I see many times when I have grieved the Holy Spirit by trying to exercise self-control in my own strength. The result has always been failure and the reemerging in my life of one or more of the works of the flesh. I saw the most amazing sight one day as the airport bus in which I was riding pulled into the parking lot of the Pasadena Hilton. The hood was open on a lovely white Cadillac, and there was a man hitting the engine with a golf club. Everyone in the bus witnessed the scene, and our amazement soon turned to laughter. Whatever the Cadillac's problem, I doubt whether that sort of treatment was beneficial. Our carnal minds can also be hit and harassed with things evil or good, and the results will not be much different than hitting the Cadillac engine with a golf club. We can hit the mind with drugs or good intentions, but self-control will still be elusive. "Because the carnal mind is enmity against God; for it is not subject to the law of God, nor indeed can be. So then, those who are in the flesh cannot please God" (Romans 8:7, 8). Only when the Holy Spirit is given possession is the possibility of change and new life a reality.

Many times people surrender to the control of the flesh because they feel that it is the strongest power in them and is impossible to overcome. Years ago as a schoolboy I spent some time learning boxing and was involved in this "sport" for a number of years. One thing I learned is that you never enter into a fight with someone whom you are certain will beat you. If you are going to fight, you must have a certainty that the other person is weaker or less skilled than you are. It is murder or suicide to fight unless you are convinced that you can win. As the Holy Spirit fills the life of a Christian, He will give that person an absolute assurance that he or she can win against the forces of evil, against the demands of the sinful flesh. Give the Holy Spirit a chance, and He will give you this confidence today. Not self-confidence, but Spirit confidence.

In looking at this subject of control from another direction, I must give you a warning. When a mind is possessed by alcohol or evil spirits, strange things can happen. This is also the case when the Holy Spirit possesses a person's life. After comparing the effects of alcohol and Holy Spirit possession in Ephesians 5:18, Paul goes on to give an interesting illustration of what can happen when the Holy Spirit fills a Christian. "And do not be drunk with wine, in which is dissipation; but be filled with the Spirit, speaking to one another in psalms and hymns and spiritual songs, singing and making melody in your heart to the Lord, giving thanks always for all things to God the Father in the name of our Lord Jesus Christ" (verses 18-20).

I have always enjoyed the story of the elderly gentleman who began singing hymns on a crowded bus. Other passengers were amazed and asked him the reason for his sudden late entry into the world of gospel vocalists. He explained, "I am so excited and happy; Jesus has died for my sins and loves me more than I can ever understand." Someone called out, "Yes, but Jesus died 2,000 years ago." To which the old man replied, "I know, but I have only just found out."

When Charles Wesley was filled with the Holy Spirit at the Moravian Chapel on Fetter Lane in London, January 1, 1739, he immediately found himself filled with Christian music. Many of the thousands of hymns he wrote while controlled by the Holy Spirit have the 1739 date on them. In one of those great songs he said, "O for a thousand tongues, to sing my great Redeemer's praise! The glories of my God and King, the triumphs of His grace! . . . He breaks the power of canceled sin, He sets the prisoner free; His blood can make the foulest clean, His blood avails for me." The great hymnwriter Isaac Watts is reported to have said that he would have traded all the hymns he had written just to have composed that one song.

Early Methodists, led by Charles's brother John, were persecuted, mocked, attacked, and derided in many parts of Great Britain. But they sang their great songs of praise, preached the Word, and led many people to new life in Jesus as they were possessed by the power of the Holy Spirit. Instead of being controlled by bitterness, criticism, strife, or evil, the Spirit-filled Methodists praised God. In the life of a Holy Spirit-possessed person the power of canceled sin is broken, as Wesley said, and in the joy of that realization people who are set free will shout "Hallelujah"; they will admonish one another in the beautiful music of the Holy Spirit. Some may be able to sing audibly. Some may make music in their hearts to God.

I was speaking at revival meetings in Tokyo, where youth director Stephano Tsukomoto had inspired many Japanese young people and helped them form a youth choir. One Saturday evening this choir was to sing during my meeting, so I met with them beforehand for worship and prayer. "Let us say hallelujah and praise God," I suggested. They said it very quietly in the dignified Japanese manner. After three or four practices I was at last able to get them to shout "Hallelujah" with the exuberance of Spirit-filled youth. During the revival meeting I asked the audience to praise God with a hearty "Hallelujah," but they would only whisper the word. Then the youth choir, which had sung so beautifully, stood up and praised God with a hallelujah that made the angels sing. The audience caught the spirit and joined their youth with an enthusiasm that was greater than that of any sumo wrestling crowd.

Although those under the control of the Holy Spirit will not become insensitive to others and will want all things done decently and in order, they will no longer be held back by the inhibitions of self-consciousness, unworthiness, timidity, or pride. As an inspired commentary on the book of

Acts says: "So mightily can God work when men and women give themselves up to the control of His Spirit." [6]

On the day of Pentecost the disciples were filled with the Holy Spirit, and the results were so dramatic that the unconverted thought the disciples were possessed by the wrong spirits. "Others mocking said, 'They are full of new wine.' But Peter, standing up with the eleven, raised his voice and said to them, 'Men of Judea and all who dwell in Jerusalem, let this be known to you, and heed my words. For these are not drunk, as you suppose, since it is only the third hour of the day. But this is what was spoken by the prophet Joel' " (Acts 2:13-16). Possessed by the Holy Spirit, Christians will have such a joy in sharing and worshiping Jesus and be so willing to face danger or ridicule that some people may consider them drunk. When people are possessed by the sinful flesh, they will reveal the character of evil. But when possessed by the Holy Spirit, people reveal the character of Jesus as is summarized in the fruit of the Spirit: "Love, joy, peace, longsuffering, kindness, goodness, faithfulness, gentleness, self-control."

Give the Holy Spirit a chance to shatter self-control today. Then you can be out of control. Your life can be out of the control of sin. Your church can be out of the control of lukewarm formalism. Your denomination can be out of the control of limited human restrictions.

A number of times over the past 50 years Roger's life went out of control. Roger grew up in a Christian home but became rebellious at an early age. It seemed that home, school, and church had taught him, "Salvation by obedience and only by obedience." One church school teacher told him that because of his rebellion it would be impossible for him to be saved.

The last Saturday evening of a great camp meeting, at the close of my sermon, I asked Roger to come onto the platform before the crowd of thousands of people and tell his story of the battle between the flesh and the Spirit. I could soon see that many people in that large audience were identifying with Roger's testimony. After leaving school, Roger operated heavy equipment and learned carpentry, and was so successful in his work that he became, at the age of 25, construction manager for one of the largest construction companies in the world. "I was drinking heavily, smoking two and a half packs of cigarettes a day, and couldn't live without my 15 cups of coffee a day. I was an alcoholic at the age of 26. By the age of 28 I was smoking three and a half packs of cigarettes a day (that's about one cigarette every 20 minutes), and drinking a minimum of 20 cups of coffee a day. I was making excellent money, but the nightclubs got most of it. I was losing my wife and five children, but 'I had arrived.' I was enjoying what Satan had to offer—at least I thought I was enjoying it," Roger admitted as he told his story. His life was in the control of the satanic desires of the sinful flesh.

But when Roger was 30 God led him to a series of evangelistic meetings. "I did not go willingly, but agreed to go to just one meeting to get my wife and children off my case." It was at those meetings that the Holy Spirit began to work on Roger's heart again. At the conclusion of the series Roger was baptized. "But I came back into the church the same way I had left it," Roger admitted to the camp meeting audience that night. "I came back believing in salvation by obedience. I struggled and failed. God had given me the victory over alcohol, cigarettes. and coffee. But I still had my violent temper and major problems."

Roger was on his way back out of the church when he first heard the beautiful truths of salvation and righteousness by faith in Jesus. Now for the first time he was truly converted and knew the joy of being filled with the Holy Spirit. Immediately Roger and his wife, Donna, wanted to share the wonderful message of the gospel, and they prayed that the Lord would open the way for them to study the Bible with people who wanted to learn more about Jesus and His Word. Listen to Roger's enthusiasm: "I continued to pray for more Bible studies, and God continued to lead people to me. I never went out searching for people; God led them to me. One evening as I was preparing to leave the house to give two Bible studies, my wife asked me if I was still praying for more studies. I replied, 'Yes; why?' 'Well, I think you should stop praying' was her reply. We paused for a moment and counted. I was giving Bible studies to 23 people a week."

Roger told the audience of the many Bible seminars he has taught and stop-smoking clinics he has held. He knows of more than 100 people who are committed Christians today because of his and Donna's ministry.

I like the way that Roger concluded his testimony that camp meeting Saturday evening. "Where I once was led by Satan and controlled by the power of alcohol I now am led by my Saviour, Jesus, and am controlled by the power of the Holy Spirit. Nothing that we have done for the Lord has been in our own power except yielding our will and our time."

Give the Holy Spirit a chance today, and you will praise His name as your life is controlled by your wonderful Friend.

SMALL GROUP STUDY
Chapter Eight

Cohesive Contrasts

While some people in your group may enjoy taking a rather low-key role, others may seem quite domineering, opinionated, determined to get control of the group. Any of these characteristics will be major hurdles for the group to overcome if it is going to survive. It may be necessary for the leader to reemphasize that a successful group is based on a democratic approach to leadership. People must be willing to listen to and accept one another. No person's opinion is more important than that of another. Mutual trust, respect, and empathy are paramount.

It is especially important to pray that the Holy Spirit will enable the fruit of the Spirit to be revealed in each group member's life. If someone in the group refuses to submit to the control of the Holy Spirit, that person should then become the object of special care and prayer by the other group members. Domineering group members may be directed into other areas of ministry where, if they are filled by the Holy Spirit, their spiritual gifts and energy can be used to maximum benefit of God's service.

Here is a sharing question for the group to begin with now. Assume you are in a management position. What methods do you think would be most effective in getting employees to do what you want them to do?

Concentrating on the Word
Study Text: Galatians 5:16-26; 6:1

Identify the controlling powers that Paul mentions in Galatians 5:16-26; 6:1. Which of these powers seem the most successful?

_____
_____

Why do you think Paul used "walk" as an illustration of life under the control of the Holy Spirit or evil?

_____
_____

In this chapter at least 10 different "walks" of the Christian life are listed.

Which do you find easiest and which the hardest? Why?
_____
_____

Is there some other fruit of the Spirit you could add to Paul's list in Galatians 5:22, 23? If so, what are they?
_____
_____

From your study of this chapter, how would you describe self-control?

Determination _____	Willpower _____
Surrender _____	Education _____
Culture _____	Self-affliction _____
Hopelessness _____	Difficult _____
God's power _____	Other _____

Describe either a positive or negative situation in which you did not or could not do as you wished.
_____
_____

In what ways do you see Spirit control as like or unlike drunkenness?

LIKE	UNLIKE
_____	_____
_____	_____
_____	_____

Have you had an experience in which music played a special part in a very Spirit-filled time in your life? What happened?
_____
_____
_____

In what ways can the Holy Spirit use hymns, psalms, and spiritual songs to enable one Christian to speak to one another?

Can you give an illustration of how the Holy Spirit worked in you to "cause" to obey God's Word in some particular way? Were you happy that this happened, or did you at the time feel annoyed that the Holy Spirit had led you into this truth? If you feel comfortable doing so, please share this with the group.

If you are acquainted with someone who has been overtaken by the controlling power of evil, what steps could you take to restore the person in gentleness (Galatians 6:1), according to the fruit of the Spirit?

Conversation With the Lord

Conclude your small group meeting with a time of conversational prayer, centering on praise, needs within the group, and intercession for others outside the group. Finish your prayer time with the Lord's Prayer and also pray for the "empty chair," asking the Lord to lead each group member to someone who can be invited to join the group next week.

Committing the Word to Memory

This week, write out a verse from Galatians 5:16-26; 6:1 and share it with someone as soon as possible.

Chapter Nine

Give the Holy Spirit a Chance
To Give You a Household of Faith

"And the Lord God said, 'It is not good that man should be alone; I will make him a helper comparable to him'" (Genesis 2:18). Have you ever felt alone spiritually? God never intended that Christians should exist in that way. Just as He made a helper comparable or compatible for Adam, so He has planned for you to be part of a household of faith. I bought a pair of binoculars in Hong Kong a few years ago. They have excellent magnification and can be very helpful in identifying distant objects such as whales migrating up the Oregon coast. The work of the Holy Spirit through the Word of God and prayer is powerful, but can still seem distant. Through a household of faith the Holy Spirit's ministry may be magnified many times, helping you to identify more clearly the factors that can enable you to be a victorious Christian. Today these households of faith are often called small groups, cell groups, or basic Christian communities. Like an ideal household, they are nurturing, caring, expanding centers of relational life. Households of faith grow naturally out of Spirit-filled Christian lives because the Holy Spirit exalts Jesus, who, through the Spirit, draws people in relationships that center on nurture and ministry.

Within a spiritual household are fellowship and love—both of which are dominant qualities of Spirit life. Notice Romans 5:5: "Now hope does not disappoint, because the love of God has been poured out in our hearts by the Holy Spirit who was given to us." Compare that verse with Philippians 2:1, 2: "Therefore if there is any consolation in Christ, if any comfort of love, if any fellowship of the Spirit, if any affection and mercy, fulfill my joy by being like-minded, having the same love, being of one accord, of one mind." Look at the "togetherness" words in Philippians 2:1, 2—"fellowship," "like-minded," "one accord." Christianity is not a religion of loners fighting solo battles with the internal and external forces of evil. Christianity is people joined together by the Holy Spirit in households of faith, strengthening, supporting, upholding one another in the Lord.

Jesus laid the foundation of the households of faith, not only by modeling

His own ministry with the disciples, but also by the promises He made to Christians of all ages. "Again I say to you that if two of you agree on earth concerning anything that they ask, it will be done for them by My Father in heaven. For where two or three are gathered together in my name, I am there in the midst of them" (Matthew 18:19, 20).

Always, when Jesus promised His presence with all of His followers everywhere, He was actually foretelling the omnipresent ministry of the Holy Spirit. Jesus was limited by voluntarily taking upon Himself humanity, so He gave the Holy Spirit to represent Him always among His people. "I will pray the Father, and He will give you another Helper, that He may abide with you forever" (John 14:16). "Nevertheless I tell you the truth. It is to your advantage that I go away; for if I do not go away, the Helper will not come to you; but if I depart, I will send Him to you" (John 16:7). Although the Holy Spirit always fills people individually, He delights to work in groups, where He can combine a diversity of spiritual gifts into a powerhouse of ministry and nurture. It is in the unity of a small group of Christians that the Holy Spirit can magnify His victory power in the experience of each individual. This is the principle of Ecclesiastes 4:12: "Though one may be overpowered by another, two can withstand him. And a threefold cord is not quickly broken."

Do you have the support of a small group, a household of faith? On a flight to Tucson, Arizona, I met a gemstone dealer who had been an active church attender but had fallen away and no longer lived a life of victory in the Holy Spirit. "Tell me what happened," I asked, hoping to discover some way to help this man back into a new relationship with the Lord.

"I prayed, read my Bible, and attended church each week," he replied with a sadness in his voice that was not hard to detect. "However, I seemed so lonely. I sat in the church and tried to participate with the large congregation, but it was impersonal. I started to develop a few friends outside the church, and enjoyed some entertainment and sports with them. When I finally left the church, nobody contacted me, nobody cared. Oh yes, after about a year a deacon visited me and said that the church was raising money for a new building, and wondered if I would like to contribute. When I had explained that I had not attended the church for a long time, he replied that there are many who do not attend, but at least I could still support the church with my tithes and offerings."

I wish this was a rare case, but there are very definite indications that this type of scenario has been reenacted millions of times in the past few years. When I suggested that the gem dealer return to church, he was understandably very negative. "How would you like to be part of a neighborhood fellowship group?" I then asked.

"What do they do?" he replied cautiously.

"They share together, care for each other, study the Bible, pray, and reach out to others in the community," I explained, giving him additional details of the basic New Testament unit of Christianity.

The man became quite excited. "That is what I want to be part of; that sounds like real Christianity to me." He was right—that is real Christianity.

In the New Testament the basic unit of society was called the *oikos*, which is translated as "house" or "household." This word refers not so much to a building or blood relatives as to the personal community that exists around each individual. Although there are connections and interrelationships between various households, each person has their primary *oikos*. "Each of us has a primary group which includes some of our relatives, and some of our friends, who relate to us through work, recreation, hobbies, and neighbors. These are the people we talk to, relate to, and share with, for at least a total of one hour per week." [1]

Jesus' ministry concentrated on penetrating households with the gospel, and as a result a new and dynamic system of households was set up. "Therefore, as we have opportunity, let us do good to all, especially to those who are of the household of faith" (Galatians 6:10). "Now, therefore, you are no longer strangers and foreigners, but fellow citizens with the saints and members of the household of God" (Ephesians 2:19). The household of God or the household of faith was in reality the New Testament church, gathering in houses as small groups of people who supported each other, cared for and nurtured each other, and reached out to draw others into these living fellowships. When the 3,000 were baptized on the day of Pentecost, having received the gift of the Holy Spirit, they were immediately welded into household fellowships by the Holy Spirit. "And they continued steadfastly in the apostles' doctrine and fellowship, in the breaking of bread, and in prayers" (Acts 2:42).

The Holy Spirit led the disciples not only in public Temple teaching but also in household ministry (Acts 5:42). When Saul set out to smash the ministry of the Holy Spirit in the New Testament Christian church, he had to try to flatten the households of faith (Acts 8:3). Although the apostles utilized synagogues and public meeting places until persecution eliminated these as teaching and preaching sites, the small group meetings in houses were always the basic unity of Christianity. As Ralph W. Neighbour, Jr., says: "The heart of the Christian life is not related to a word 'temple' or 'synagogue' or 'church building.' As the basic fabric of human life is imbedded in the oikos, even so the life of the body of Christ is to be oikos-based." [2] "And how I kept back nothing that was helpful, but proclaimed it to you, and taught you publicly and from house to house" (Acts 20:20).

Even persecution could not obliterate these house churches. It was in the house of Cornelius that the Holy Spirit was poured out (Acts 10:11). Paul wrote of the church in the house of Aquila and Priscilla (1 Corinthians 16:19), he sent greetings to the church in the household of Nymphas (Colossians 4:15), and also to the church in the house of Archippus (Philemon 2). In fact, there were virtually no church buildings anywhere in the Roman Empire until the time of Constantine. The church was literally and spiritually a household.

A few years ago I began to collect miniature churches, and always look out for another to add to my collection wherever I travel around the world. Among many others I have a marble miniature of Saint Paul's Cathedral, in London; a church made of coal from my grandfather's village in Wales; a wooden church with onion domes from Russia; ceramic churches from South America; stone churches from England; bamboo churches from China.

But in reality these beautiful little models do not represent the New Testament church at all. They are the legacy of the Roman emperor Constantine, not of New Testament Christianity. The church of the Holy Spirit was households of people meeting together to share, study, pray, and reach out to others. The small group of people was the church building, not a structure of wood or stone. "You also, as living stones, are being built up a spiritual house, a holy priesthood, to offer up spiritual sacrifices acceptable to God through Jesus Christ" (1 Peter 2:5). "But if I am delayed, I write so that you may know how you ought to conduct yourself in the house of God, which is the church of the living God, the pillar and ground of the truth" (1 Timothy 3:15). Give the Holy Spirit a chance today, and He will give you joy and strength in a household of faith.

Pray now through Romans 15 and let the Holy Spirit show you the dynamics of Spirit-filled small group Christianity. If you are going to not only survive but grow and flourish as a Christian today, there are some principles in this chapter that are essential for understanding how you can be part of a household of faith.

Household Christians

The issue at the beginning of Romans 15 is how the Christian who is strong can be understanding and supportive of the weaker Christian. "We then that are strong ought to bear the infirmities of the weak, and not to please ourselves" (Romans 15:1, KJV). The strong Christian is one who is consciously used by God in the power of the Holy Spirit. In fact, the word for "strong" here in Romans 15:1 is the same word that Paul places a double emphasis on in Ephesians 3:16: "I pray that, according to the riches of his glory, he may grant that you may be strengthened in your inner being with power through his Spirit" (NRSV).

As Spirit-filled Christians minister in the household of faith, the result is the building up of the *oikos* or household fellowship. "Let each of us please his neighbor for his good, leading to edification" (Romans 15:2). In the New Testament a person who edifies is an *oikodomeo*, a house builder. In the next chapter we will notice how the Holy Spirit uses spiritual gifts in the household or small group to make this edifying or building up take place. Spirit-filled Christians will seek to excel in building up the church. "Even so you, since you are zealous for spiritual gifts, let it be for the edification of the church that you seek to excel" (1 Corinthians 14:12). This building up of the *oikos* is done by strong Spirit-filled Christians ministering to group members, not in pride, not because of superior knowledge, but in the spirit of the fruit of the Spirit, which is love.

Household Comfort

As Christians minister to their neighbors in the household of faith, they will also bring them an awareness of the Comforter. The Holy Spirit stands beside those who need encouragement, not in some invisible, mystical presence, but in the person of fellow household members who share the Scriptures and represent the character of Jesus. "For whatever things were written before were written for our learning, that we through the patience and comfort of the Scriptures might have hope. Now may the God of patience and comfort grant you to be like-minded toward one another, according to Christ Jesus" (Romans 15:4, 5).

I like the word "comfort," don't you? It was my grandmother's middle name. She was Mary Comfort Fisher. Our youngest daughter, Sharon, was born on her great-grandmother's eightieth birthday, so we gave her Mary as her middle name. Sharon has always been grateful that we did not choose Comfort. My grandmother used to say that she was made for comfort, not for speed, and as I grew up she was a great comfort and strength to me in many ways. The Holy Spirit's ministry of comfort, along with edification, was a special factor in the growth of the Christian church. "Then the churches throughout all Judea, Galilee, and Samaria had peace and were edified. And walking in the fear of the Lord and in the comfort of the Holy Spirit, they were multiplied" (Acts 9:31). No wonder these churches grew not by addition but by multiplication. They did not depend on the construction of costly buildings; they were households of faith and were as plentiful as were the houses in which families lived.

If you need comfort or edification right now, the Holy Spirit's place to do it with maximum magnification is in a household of faith. If you don't have a place like that, pray that God will quickly lead you into a small group fellowship. If you feel that you are not in need of comfort or edification and are strong in the Spirit, then a household of faith needs you to minister to others. In small groups, ministry is a verb, not a noun.

I haven't talked to Jim for more than 20 years, but will always remember him because he taught me a lesson early in my ministry about the value of small groups as basic Christian communities. Just out of college, I felt called to be an evangelist, so it was not long before I was able to rent a public hall in a Sydney suburb and advertise some meetings. I announced there would be "two identical sessions to accommodate the crowds" on the opening Sunday. When Sunday came, we waited and prayed with eager anticipation. At 3:00 p.m. a few people arrived and seemed to enjoy the meeting, but at the 7:30 p.m. session the hall was empty; not one person came. Soon after 7:45, just as the helpers were packing up the chairs, one gentleman entered the hall and was surprised to discover that the program was over before it had even started. I didn't have the heart to preach to one man, so after learning his name I said, "Jim, we are going to meet in a home near here; we will study the Bible and pray. Would you like to join us?" Jim readily agreed, and remained a regular attender at our small group meeting for many months.

About a year later, when we were living 700 miles away in Queensland, we received a call from Jim asking if he could come and visit with us. "Garrie," he announced as soon as he arrived, "I want to thank you for saving my life."

"What do you mean, Jim?" I asked in surprise.

"Remember the small group I attended with you in Sydney? Well, during that time my marriage was breaking up, and a number of times I was tempted to take my own life. Each time, however, the prayers, support, and ministry of the group enabled me to carry on even though the group did not know how deeply I was hurting."

Yes, that is the comforting and edifying power of the Holy Spirit in a household of faith.

"Therefore receive one another, just as Christ also received us, to the glory of God" (Romans 15:7). Households of faith transcend racial, religious, ethnic, cultural, and economic barriers because Spirit-filled Christians are open to receiving others in comfort, love, and edification, just as Jesus has received each one of them. I have seen Jews and Palestinians together in Christian groups in Jerusalem. In other places I have seen Blacks and Whites, Serbs and Croatians, Koreans and Japanese, millionaires and low-income earners, scholars with doctorates and uneducated laborers, men and women, young people and older people together in households of faith.

Today neighborhoods are divided, and people are separated into islands of loneliness. Writers like Vance Packard speak of "a nation of strangers," people on the move, robbed of community togetherness by the electronic isolationism of a television-saturated society. But through the Holy Spirit men and women are brought into the unity of the faith. "Now, therefore, you are no longer strangers and foreigners, but fellow citizens with the saints and members of the household of God" (Ephesians 2:19).

Household Help and Happiness

While there are many types of community gatherings, including social parties, community college classes, home sales meetings, etc., households of faith differ in some very significant ways. I like the concise way Paul lists the key characteristics of the households of faith. "Now may the God of hope fill you with all joy and peace in believing, that you may abound in hope by the power of the Holy Spirit. Now I myself am confident concerning you, my brethren, that you also are full of goodness, filled with all knowledge, able also to admonish one another" (Romans 15:13, 14).

The Holy Spirit's fruit of joy, peace, and goodness flourish in these basic Christian communities. They are centers of hope, Homes of Hope, by the Holy Spirit's power. Satan's counterfeit for this type of gathering has often been called the "party." I remember a party I attended years ago. There was very little action until the alcohol began to take effect. Then joy, peace, and goodness were rapidly replaced by hilarity, trouble, and evil. Two men started fighting at the back of the house; three people crowded into the toilet in deep distress because the alcohol and other substances had sent their internal organs into violent spasms of rejection. One lady was crying bitterly because her husband kept dancing with another woman. "This party will be fun," I had been told. Instead the result was tragedy, topped off with head-splitting hangovers the next day.

In contrast, the household of faith is a healing community in which comfort and love shout for joy and rest in peace. The Holy Spirit knows that you and I need such a place. Give the Holy Spirit a chance to help you grow in a household of faith today. In the household of faith there are people who will pray for you, with you, people you can trust as brothers and sisters in God's family.

Paul is also confident that the Christians of the Roman households of faith were able to admonish one another (verse 14). He uses a very strong word for "able" that comes from the same word as "power" of the Holy Spirit in verse 13. When you are Spirit-filled, He will equip you and empower you with words of knowledge to admonish or instruct others in the faith. While there is a time for personal, one-on-one admonition, the Holy Spirit most often uses the household of faith for this reason. In fact, in the small group even music can be used most effectively for admonition. "And do not be drunk with wine, in which is dissipation; but be filled with the Spirit, speaking to one another in psalms and hymns and spiritual songs, singing and making melody in your heart to the Lord" (Ephesians 5:18, 19). "And let the peace of God rule in your hearts, to which also you were called in one body; and be thankful. Let the word of God dwell in you richly in all wisdom, teaching and admonishing one another in psalms and hymns and spiritual songs, singing with grace in your hearts to the Lord" (Colossians 3:15, 16).

Janet has led a ladies' small group Bible study in her home for more than 12 years, and during that time many people have been edified, comforted, and admonished. Beth came into this household of faith when the group was studying and praying about the Holy Spirit, using *How to Be Filled With the Holy Spirit and Know It* as a guide. Soon the Spirit was able to speak clearly to Beth's heart, and as a result she was led to write some beautiful songs that God has used to admonish many people. I attended the group one Tuesday morning when Beth played the piano and sang a number of the songs the Spirit had given her, and the Lord certainly used them to speak to me that day. I was especially admonished by one that questioned me concerning the Holy Spirit. "When a day goes by that you don't invite Him in, you will lose the unity with Christ that God has promised men. He promised His power and He promised His joy; did you ask for the Spirit today? Did you ask for the Spirit today, did you ask for His guidance along the way? Did you ask for His power, did you ask for His peace? Did you ask for the Spirit today?"[3]

Paul concludes Roman 15:14 by saying, "Admonish one another." In the households of faith this admonition is always given by the Holy Spirit, through a Spirit-filled Christian, in love. Dr. Carl George lists 59 "one anothers" he has found in the New Testament. It is exciting to see how many of these the Holy Spirit applies to the small group fellowships, but I especially appreciate George's conclusion: "Twenty-one of the 59, or fully one third, call for Christians to love!"[4] Yes, 21 times the New Testament admonishes Christians to love one another. That is real Christianity.

The Holy Spirit Leads

It can be readily seen that the ministry focus of a small group can be right today only when the Holy Spirit is recognized as the key facilitator of the group, as He was in New Testament times. I like the way Dr. Neal F. McBride, of George Fox College in Oregon, outlines to small group leaders the role of the Holy Spirit in a household of faith: "An important foundation undergirding your role as a small group leader is the place of the Holy Spirit within the group. Simply put, He is the unseen but present group member and leader. You serve as His co-leader, the human instrument of His guidance and direction. Your primary role is to facilitate the Holy Spirit's ministry in the members' lives through planning and guiding the group activities. Please weld this reality into your thinking and actions, because it is vital to your success as a leader and to the group's success.

"In condensed form, here are seven ministries the Holy Spirit performs in your group.

"**He indwells** (Romans 8:9-11). The Scriptures are clear that the Holy Spirit dwells in every person who has accepted Jesus Christ as Saviour. The Holy Spirit is present whenever Christians gather together. This means that He is present at every group meeting. We must acknowledge this fact and act accordingly.

"**He guides** (John 16:13). As with individual believers, the Holy Spirit also provides guidance within small groups. Whether the issue is making scheduling decisions, selecting a format, responding to the Word, dealing with an obstinate member, rejoicing over one person's personal success, or anything else, we must remain sensitive to His guidance and direction. This process isn't always easy. Yet every effort must be exerted to practice following His leadership and discerning the will of God.

"**He teaches** (John 14:26). The Holy Spirit is our teacher. Through His illumination of the biblical text, we can come to know and understand spiritual truth. In teaching us, He may use a fellow group member to explain or illustrate from that person's life the spiritual truth being considered.

"**He convicts** (John 16:8). When we are confronted with the demands of Scripture, it is the Holy Spirit who bears witness with our spirits and convicts us of our wrong attitudes and actions. The Spirit may convict all the group members simultaneously. It is possible that an entire group needs to turn away from some attitude and/or action that is displeasing to God.

"**He intercedes** (Romans 8:26). The Holy Spirit intercedes with God the Father on our behalf. Our corporate prayers reinforce individual prayers. In our spiritual weakness, the Spirit helps us in pleading our case before God. Individually and corporately, we have One who indwells us, knows our deepest needs, and makes intercession within us while Jesus Christ makes intercession for us at the right hand of God.

"**He enables** (1 Corinthians 12:11). Spiritual gifts are God-given abilities to serve the Body of Christ wherever and however He may direct. The Holy Spirit is the source of our spiritual gifts. Through His gifting us we have the ability to serve one another, specifically our fellow group members.

"**He unifies** (Ephesians 4:3). As God's children we are one people. The same Spirit makes us one and does all the things previously mentioned. Our practical unity as a group is possible on the basis of our spiritual unity through the Holy Spirit." [5]

As you pray through McBride's seven ministries of the Holy Spirit in small groups I am sure it will become increasingly clear why every great revival of the Holy Spirit in Christian history has led to the formation of small group households of faith or has been built on households of faith that have already begun to meet together. As Howard Snyder says in *Signs of the Spirit*: "Renewal is less likely to come and more likely to die in a tradition-bound group where everything happens routinely in the church building and there is little freedom to innovate. Renewal is more likely when believers begin to share their faith together in homes, when traditional forms are periodically reevaluated, and when the structural vitality and flexibility of the early church are rediscovered." [6]

"Pietism had its *collegia pietatis*; the Moravians had their bands; Methodism had its classes and other groups. Vital renewal movements, it seems, not only rediscover community but develop practical structures to build the *koinonia* of the Spirit. A pragmatic renewal strategy will use some form of small groups as basic structure in congregational life. The precise form of such groups may vary and will need to fit the particular setting. Usually renewal movements have found the practical value of meeting in homes as a more informal and 'family' setting for experiencing Christian community. Often it is practical to supplement such meetings with cell groups which meet wherever is most convenient." [7]

What happened on the estate of Count Zinzendorf in Saxony in 1727 is a powerful illustration of the connection between the Holy Spirit and small groups. You may say that 1727 was a long time ago, and that is true; however, a large part of modern Christianity was influenced by those events. The Herrnhut community of about 300 people had come from many different religious backgrounds, but when the Holy Spirit filled the congregation with mighty power on August 13, 1727, the results were truly miraculous. "Zinzendorf described this day as 'day of the outpouring of the Holy Spirit upon the congregation' and 'its Pentecost.' Spangenberg said, 'Then were we baptized by the Holy Spirit Himself to one love.' Christian David commented, 'It is truly a miracle of God that out of so many kinds and sects as Catholics, Lutheran, Reformed, Separatist, Gichtelian, and the like, we could have been melted together into one.' " [8]

That day of the outpouring of the Holy Spirit had been preceded by a number of important factors, including a division of the whole community into small group prayer bands. These bands met every few days from July 19. On August 5 Zinzendorf and 14 others spent the whole night in Bible conversation and prayer. On August 12 Zinzendorf visited every home in the settlement praying with the people of each household. That night two young girls who were to be confirmed the next day spent the whole night in prayer. Little wonder that the Spirit moved with such power in the Communion service the next morning.

From that time on, the small group movement took a new step. "At the same time, Pietism's genius for creating small groups within the established churches was systematized at Herrnhut. To strengthen the spiritual life . . . , 'choirs' were formed—first among the single brethren, then the single sisters, married couples, and the widowed. These lay men and women traveled to other parts of Saxony and beyond, encouraging cells of believers in personal Bible study and pious living. 'Out of this grew a network of societies within the churches to which eventually the term "Diaspora" was applied,' says Weinlick. Herrnhuters roved to and fro on the continent, to Moravia, the Baltic States, Holland, Denmark, and even to Britain." [9]

Small groups became the foundation of the Methodist movement, spreading their influence across the Atlantic into America and helping Methodism become the largest Protestant denomination in this country in the nineteenth century. United Methodist bishop Richard B. Wilke, analyzing the loss of more than 2 million Methodists in the past few decades, pinpoints a very important factor: "When Wesley was preaching, he would invite people to join a class, and would sometimes form a new class that very evening. . . . The most powerful hidden resource for our church in winning new people to faith and fellowship is our homes. We have become so acculturated to our sophisticated American society that we want our homes to be places of privacy and refuge. We resent any intrusion. If we opened up 10 percent of the homes of United Methodist people for one night a week of Bible study and prayer and invited newcomers into the fellowship, it would revolutionize the church." [10]

Wilke tells a story to show that the solution for Methodists can be the basis for growth of any Christian group because it follows the original New Testament principles. "An Assembly of God preacher moved to one of our

Midwestern cities about six years ago. His church of 50 members was in a trailer park in a low-rent part of town. Today the church has 600 worshipers on Sunday morning. When I interviewed this pastor, I asked him how in the world he had built up this great congregation. He said that his congregation was just old-fashioned 'Methodists.' They just had their laypeople invite folks into their homes one evening each week. I went on to ask what was done in the meetings. He said that they studied the Bible and talked about problems people have, or problems in the community or in the world, and that they prayed for one another. He said that the people invited folks who lived in the trailers next to them, or their acquaintances at work, or friends at school. When asked how many groups the fellowship had, he responded, 'We've started a group every few weeks. I guess we have about 50 or 60 groups now that meet in the homes. Each one has about 8, 10, 12, or 14 persons in it. That is about all the houses will hold.' Then he said, 'Of course, I teach the leaders one night a week, just like Wesley did.' " [11]

Clay Peck is a spirit-filled Adventist pastor who has been very successful in helping his church family become involved in households of faith. The Davenport, Iowa, church calls their small groups Friendship Circles. This pastor says that small groups have totally changed the climate of his church. "Members' attitudes to evangelism have also changed," Peck says as he outlines the changes small groups have made in his congregation. "We now view evangelism as a process of building relationships, not an event." Two and a half years ago a maximum of 12 people attended a weekly prayer meeting in this church; now more than 100 members are involved in about a dozen small groups, with an average of four or five people in each group who have come to know the Lord and have been baptized as a result of the nurture and ministry of small group members.

A Household of Prayer

Paul makes this very personal. Let's come back to Romans 15 and observe Paul beginning to express his own need of a household of faith. "Whenever I journey to Spain, I shall come to you. For I hope to see you on my journey, and to be helped on my way there by you, if first I may enjoy your company for a while" (verse 24). If we think that Paul was just being polite to the Romans, that idea is quickly shattered in verse 30: "Now I beg you, brethren, through the Lord Jesus Christ, and through the love of the Spirit, that you strive together with me in your prayers to God for me."

Paul begs; he earnestly cries out to these people, on the basis of the love of Jesus that is poured into their hearts by the Holy Spirit, that they come together in earnest, fervent prayer for him. They could have replied, "Paul, you can pray for yourself; you know more about prayer than we do. We have enough problems as it is. You take your problems to the Lord, and He will hear you just as well as He would hear us." But that was not the spirit of early Christianity. These Christians were members of households of faith (Romans 16:5, 10, 11, 15). They knew the strength of agreeing in prayer where two or three are gathered together (Matthew 18:19, 20). So Paul could trust himself to these people and their prayer ministry, knowing that they would not let him down.

This is so important that I want to ask you again, Do you have a household of faith? Do you have a Holy Spirit support team that you can trust? Are you meeting with them each week, or are you trying to survive alone, or as a member of a large impersonal congregation? I have had the joy of seeing Trinity Power Fellowships, Homes of Hope, Tender Loving Care groups, or whatever they are called moving ahead as cell group churches around the world. The results are always amazing. If you do not know of a household of faith near you, invite some neighbors, work or school associates, or friends or relatives to study this book and the small group study guides connected to it with you. That will be a good start and the beginning of a household of faith right where you are.

We all like stories with a happy ending, but Ron's story is one that helps us understand why the Holy Spirit leads Christians into small groups of nurture, love, and ministry. I first met Ron when I was a teenage carpentry apprentice. I was a fairly new Christian, and was the subject of his mockery and swearing whenever he came on the job with a team of local plumbers. I avoided Ron as far as possible, not wanting to hear his taunts of "Bible basher" punctuated with various blasphemies and obscenities.

To my surprise, Ron appeared in church one day. I tried to hide, thinking he had come to taunt me some more, but eventually met him in the foyer when the worship service was over. "What are you doing here?" I asked him in a rather undiplomatic and unfriendly way.

Ron told me how he had been looking for a room he could rent, and eventually found one in the home of an elderly Christian lady who was a member of our local congregation. "She sang hymns and prayed and had a small group meeting in her home each week," he explained. "I have accepted Jesus and would like to become a member of this church."

The miracle of Ron's transformed life amazed everyone. I regretted my lack of faith, and praised God that Ron's life and speech were so different now.

Somehow, though, it seemed that Ron never did quite fit into the culture of that congregation. Although he served the Lord faithfully as a member in a number of official positions, he was never really integrated as part of the family. The small group in the home where Ron boarded concluded when old Mrs. Warren died, and no other took its place. There was no young lady in the church interested in marrying Ron, so he met a woman outside the church family with whom he shared his faith. Soon she became a church member and Ron's wife. The Lord blessed Ron and his family with some lovely children, but years later, when the children had become teenagers, it seemed that Ron was still finding difficulty integrating into the church body. Sometimes he did not attend for long periods, and it appeared there was no one who understood him.

One day one of Ron's daughters came home and looked around the house for her father. His car was there; she was sure he was home somewhere. It was not long before she made the tragic discovery of Ron's body hanging in a shed at the back of the house. Ron was dead. If only he had belonged to a household of faith. If only he had known a small group of people who had cared. They may have heard a cry of help. They could have edified, comforted, and admonished Ron. They could have been used by the Holy Spirit to bring Ron hope. But now it is too late. This is why Paul said, "That I may come to you with joy by the will of God, and may be refreshed together with you" (Romans 15:32). That's where God wants His people to be, together in the Spirit.

Give the Holy Spirit a chance today; then you will come each week with joy to your household of faith and will be refreshed, strengthened for victory and ministry together with each person in the basic Christian community of love.

SMALL GROUP STUDY
Chapter Nine

Cohesive Contrasts

In the chapter four study guide we noticed two of the four stages or seasons of small group development—honeymoon and disillusionment. Hopefully, by now your group is well into the third stage—that of synthesis. People who have been together in a group for six or eight weeks begin to grow together, recognizing each other's strengths and weaknesses. There has been a move from "What can I get out of this?" to "What can I give? How can I help these other people? What can I do to contribute to the spiritual nurture, love, edification, and comfort in this group?"

If money were no problem, what gift would you like to give to each member of your group? Write it on a piece of paper and give it to that person. When each person has a piece of paper from each group member, then he or she can read their list to the group. Why do people often give to others what they would like to receive themselves?

Concentrating on the Word
Study Text: Romans 15:1-33

Underline and list the key words in this chapter (Romans 15) that indicate that Paul was writing about people coming together in Christian fellowship.

_____

_____

Do you have an illustration that you can share with the group showing how the victory principle of two or three working together (Ecclesiastes 4:12) has been or could have been successful for you?

_____

_____

What are some ways a person's secular household of friends and relatives is similar and different from the Christian household of faith?

Similar	Different

_____   _____
_____   _____
_____   _____

How can a small group minister in a neighborhood in ways that a large congregation or formal church service cannot do?
_____
_____

List the fruits of the Holy Spirit that you see in Romans 15. In what way can each of them flourish in a household of faith?
_____
_____

What are some ways the Holy Spirit can use group members to edify one another in love?
_____
_____

Admonish means to instruct, or even correct, as well as to inform. When are you most open to this? How can music help make this possible (Colossians 3:16)?
_____
_____

What part of the Holy Spirit's role in small groups (pp. 122ff.) is most encouraging for you? Why?
_____
_____

How would you feel about urgently requesting people to pray for you and with you for a specific reason, as Paul did in Romans 15:30, 31?

Embarrassed _____   Comfortable _____
Relieved _____   Tense _____
A failure _____   Dependent _____
Strong _____   Disadvantaged _____
Weak _____   Happy _____
Submissive _____   Other _____

What is the most comforting thing someone could do for you right now? If you are able, share this with your group. Alternatively, you may want to tell what in the past comforted you most in a time of special need.

_____
_____

Paul twice mentions joy in Romans 15 (verses 13, 32). How can your group best express its joy in Jesus through the power of the Holy Spirit?

_____
_____

Conversation With the Lord

Perhaps today your meeting can conclude by praying that each member of the group will receive a word of edification or admonition that the Holy Spirit would like shared in prayer before the meeting concludes. First, pray prayers of praise, especially for the nurture and love you have experienced in specific ways in this group. Now pray regarding edification and admonition, and if the Lord leads you to pray or begin a song for the group as a whole or an individual member, please do this in love. Conclude by interceding for other situations outside the group. Always pray for the "empty chair," keeping the focus on ministry, and conclude your group as usual with the Lord's Prayer together.

Committing the Word to Memory

This week, write out a verse from Romans 15:1-33 and share it with someone as soon as possible.

_____
_____

Chapter Ten
▼

Give the Holy Spirit a Chance
To Gift You for Healing Ministry

"Have you ever been anointed?" I asked Rene as we stood around her hospital bed. I had come with some members of a small group to pray with Rene, who had spent four of the past six years in the hospital. In 1985 Rene had an operation to correct a kneecap problem, and it was during this procedure that she received an infection in her legbone that could not be healed. After 45 operations Rene's leg was amputated at the knee in December 1987. Following the amputation Rene began to attend church, and became a born-again Christian. She says, "I believe there is a story about the shepherd who brought wandering sheep back to the fold by breaking one leg, then carrying them back home and keeping them close to him while they healed. I believe this was true in my case. It took a personal disaster to bring me home."

Because of her illness, Rene's son and husband have also come to know the Lord. By November 1991, as the bone infection continued, the remainder of Rene's leg was removed from her hip. Her suffering should have been over, but, as she told me the day we stood around her bed, "I still have an ongoing infection and have just had my seventy-second operation." A little later, in answer to my question about anointing, she replied, as her eyes reflected the pain and heartache of those years of suffering away from her home and family, "I have many people praying for me. My small group meets here each week and prays for me, but I have never been anointed."

The small group members who joined me that day for prayer included two Baptists, three Seventh-day Adventists, one Roman Catholic, and one Jewish lady. They love Rene, they are part of her healing community. We shared some promises together, we read some Bible verses about God's healing love, and then we anointed Rene with oil, asking that the Holy Spirit bring her peace as she put her life fully into God's hands.

Writing later about her experience that day, Rene says, "The night before Garrie was to come I was very sick, so when the group came I was not feeling very well at all. The group began with some prayers of affirmation; then

Garrie explained what anointing was, and I was anointed. There were some songs and some more conversation, and the group of comfort left. . . . I found the experience to be very wonderful, and I was feeling better and at great peace when they left. I felt, though, I had missed something or that I had not received the full healing yet. It took about a week, and then I knew what it was. With a serious illness you see many doctors. By the time I was where I was, I had been filled with all their opinions and a ton of my own doubts. After the healing service I was emptied of all of these negative feelings and left with a hunger for the Lord. Now all I can do is praise the Lord and the Holy Spirit because what He brought to me was what I needed more than my leg." Rene's healing household of faith continues to meet with her each week, and God is certainly using each one of the small group members in healing ministry.

All Christian ministry, in the power of the Holy Spirit, is healing ministry. Not only can body, mind, and spirit be healed; so can relationships, memories, painful circumstances, poverty, ignorance, selfishness, satanic harassment, wrong values and principles, and a multitude of other problems that are potentially more dangerous than Rene's dreadful leg infection. As the Holy Spirit works through the combination of spiritual gifts found in households of faith or small groups, then healing ministry can flourish.

Have you ever thought about the full extent of Jesus' healing ministry as He was anointed with the Holy Spirit? Usually we equate Jesus' healing with crippled arms or leprous bodies, but it went much deeper than that. "The Spirit of the Lord God is upon Me, because the Lord has anointed Me to preach good tidings to the poor [spiritual healing]; He has sent Me to heal the brokenhearted [emotional healing], to proclaim liberty to the captives [healing of circumstances of bondage], and the opening of the prison to those who are bound [healing from evil oppression]; to proclaim the acceptable year of the Lord, and the day of vengeance of our God [healing of erroneous teachings and expectations]; to comfort all who mourn, to console those who mourn in Zion [to heal all the effects of sin and spiritual death], to give them beauty for ashes, the oil of joy for mourning [the healing of hurts], the garment of praise for the spirit of heaviness [healing of depression]; that they may be called trees of righteousness [healing of insecurity], the planting of the Lord, that He may be glorified [healing of instability]" (Isaiah 61:1-3). Yes, Jesus' healing ministry certainly encompassed every need of human lives. As with Rene, the greatest need for healing is not always physical, no matter how desirable that is, but rather spiritual, so that people can have, as Rene testified, "great peace."

Healed Healers

Speaking to His people through the ancient prophet Jeremiah, God said, "For thus says the Lord: 'Your affliction is incurable, your wound is severe. There is no one to plead your cause, that you may be bound up; you have no healing medicines'" (Jeremiah 30:12, 13). Still there is hope, "'for I will restore health to you and heal you of your wounds,' says the Lord" (verse 17). In view of God's promise Jeremiah has prayed, "Heal me, O Lord, and I shall be healed; save me, and I shall be saved, for You are my praise" (Jeremiah 17:14).

The need for all types of healing can be traced back to the oppression of people, circumstances, and world conditions by satanic forces. So Peter explains the healing ministry of Jesus through the anointing of the Holy Spirit in this way: "How God anointed Jesus of Nazareth with the Holy Spirit and with power, who went about doing good and healing all who were oppressed by the devil, for God was with Him" (Acts 10:38). As we today cry out for healing, just as Jeremiah did, then the Holy Spirit is ready to meet our needs through the ministry of other Spirit-filled people.

In the household meeting with Cornelius and his relatives and friends in Caesarea God, by the outpouring of the Holy Spirit in this group, healed the racial and religious barriers between the Jewish Christians and the despised Gentiles. The Christian leaders in Jerusalem were amazed when they heard what happened, just as administrators within traditional Christian organizations are often amazed and gratified to hear of the Holy Spirit's healing ministries in households of faith today. "'And as I began to speak, the Holy Spirit fell upon them, as upon us at the beginning. . . . If therefore God gave them the same gift as He gave us when we believed on the Lord Jesus Christ, who was I that I could withstand God?' When they heard these things they became silent; and they glorified God, saying, 'Then God has also granted to the Gentiles repentance to life'" (Acts 11:15-18).

Initially the Holy Spirit leads many people to small group fellowships because of their need for personal healing. According to Ralph Neighbour, "every one of us arrives in the kingdom 'crippled inside.' Living apart from God for years creates inner brokenness which must be mended. In addition, simply living in a fallen world of fallen men continues to damage us as we seek to live under His Lordship. The cell group exists as a community where the healing power of God is to be manifest. . . . When we begin a life together in which we are all equipped for ministry, the most effective growth takes place in an environment where we are called upon to give as well as to receive, to heal as to be healed. How does Christ desire for us to be healed? Are we to find our healing independently, going to Him alone? While that happens, it's not His primary plan for us. Instead, He gives gifts of healings to His body. Spiritual gifts are related to the body and its needs." [1]

Following the mighty outpouring of the Holy Spirit at Herrnhut on the estate of Count Zinzendorf on August 13, 1727, the Moravian Christians, as we noted in the previous chapter, were divided into small groups or bands. These small groups, in the power of the Holy Spirit, were healing communities. John Wesley, who visited Herrnhut following his conversion in 1738, records in his journal that he found "about ninety bands, each of which meets twice at least, but most of them three times a week, to 'confess their faults one to another, and pray for one another, that they may be healed.'" [2]

Ron Lee Davis tells the story of Ruth, who had become severely depressed after many years in active local church leadership. Ruth's psychiatrist told her pastor that Ruth, in his opinion, would remain in deep depression for the rest of her life. But Ruth's pastor believed that the Holy Spirit could use Christians as healing agents through the prayerful use of spiritual gifts, so he decided to refer her to one of a number of house churches within his congregation. "Three months after joining that house church, Ruth was completely off prescribed drugs. Within six months, she had returned to work. Though she had been written off as a hopeless emotional cripple by her psychiatrist, today she experiences a wholeness that can come through a vital personal relationship with Jesus Christ and with other Christian brothers and sisters." [3]

Those whom the Holy Spirit uses most effectively for healing ministries are Christians who have been broken, hurt, sick, and even failures spiritually themselves, but have come, like Peter, in deep humility to Jesus and have found that there is a "balm in Gilead, to make the wounded whole; there is a balm in Gilead to heal the sin-sick soul." Listen to Davis again: "What are your wounds? Where is your brokenness? How can the trials of your life be transformed into healing power, a brand-new ministry to others? It's one of the great, glorious ironies of the Christian life that only through our wounds can we be used as channels of God's healing. Only through our brokenness can we bring others to wholeness in the midst of a broken world." [4]

Healing Gifts

Have you recently looked at the list of spiritual gifts and noticed how they relate to various aspects of healing? Pray through these lists and ask God to show you a need that will allow a healing gift to flow through you. In 1 Corinthians 12:1-11 you notice how each of the spiritual gifts can relate to healing ministry. A "word of wisdom" can bring a healing from bad decisions and a lack of spiritual insight. A "word of knowledge" may be healing from bad information or a lack of true information. "Faith" is a healing from a lack of confidence and trust. "Gifts of healing" can involve physical, mental, or spiritual restoration. "The working of miracles" is a healing that creates something from nothing and supersedes the ordinary forces of nature. "Prophecy" can bring healing of relationships and damaged emotions, because "he who prophesies speaks edification and exhortation and comfort" (1 Corinthians 14:3). "Discerning of spirits" brings healing from satanic deceptions. "Tongues" and "interpretation of tongues" may bring healing from problems of communication.

At the end of 1 Corinthians 12 Paul adds another four gifts. "Apostleship" coordinates healing ministries in a region or country. "Teaching" brings healing truths, including the gospel and biblical doctrines in clear, understandable focus. "Helps" can bring healing from urgent needs, emergencies, and catastrophes. "Administration" brings healing from disorganization in the lives of individuals or the corporate body of Jesus, which may be the union of a number of households of faith for ministry and missionary purposes.

As he outlines spiritual gifts in Ephesians, Paul adds a couple more to his list (Ephesians 4:7-11). "Evangelists" are the agents of healing through the proclamation of the Word of God. "Pastors" bring healing through a combination of gifts, especially as they guide the households of faith into healing relationships with each other and the Good Shepherd.

In Romans 12:6-8 Paul includes "ministry," which is healing through serving others where they are hurting with unmet needs. "Giving" brings healing resources to those who are in situations of material or financial sickness. "Mercy" can bring healing through compassion and empathy.

Gifts of Ministry in Groups

If you pray through the lists of gifts very carefully, you will notice the Holy Spirit has designed that no gift can encompass all the essential details of Christianity on its own. The gifts are indications of team ministry in each household of faith, the body of Jesus. Neighbour is on target about spiritual gifts as he discusses the cell group church. "There is no better place for spiritual gifts to be developed than in cell groups. All necessary conditions are present for the gifts to be received and used for edification. Needs present in the lives of believers and the small size of the group make it possible for all present to exercise gifts for building up one another in the Spirit. The modeling of the proper use of gifts can protect new believers from absurd access. Members should be taught to appreciate, desire, exercise, and receive the benefits of spiritual gifts. Through using them, they can learn how to become channels of God's power. This makes the activity of the Holy Spirit very personal to members of cells. Members must experience both the power of gifts flowing through them to edify others, and the personal edification received from others who exercise them. There is a grave danger present when a cell is unplugged from the work of the Holy Spirit and the use of spiritual gifts. It has no alternative except to become a social religious club, which soon ossifies and diverts its activity to other tasks." [5]

My own experience with small groups has confirmed Neighbour's analysis of the connection between spiritual gifts and cell group ministry. A cell group is the premium place for the Holy Spirit's spiritual gift ministry. In a large congregation people who believe that they have a spiritual gift will often try to pressure the whole congregation into doing exactly what they feel is important. "We should all be out visiting from door to door with gospel tracts," one may say. Another may suggest that all church members should be feeding the hungry. "The man with the gift of teaching encourages everyone to be a teacher. The evangelist says the key to living the Christian life is winning people to Christ daily. I've even had people with the gift of helps lay the trip on me that unless I spend more time helping my fellow man, I am displeasing to God." [6] Most people under this sort of attack will sit back and do nothing, feeling they are not public speakers, Dorcases, or door knockers.

The Holy Spirit's design was that church members be released for team ministry in the small households of faith. "Now there are diversities of gifts, but the same Spirit. There are differences of ministries, but the same Lord. And there are diversities of activities, but it is the same God who works all in all. But the manifestation of the Spirit is given to each one for the profit of all" (1 Corinthians 12:4-7). William McRae, of the Dallas Theological Seminary, who discusses spiritual gifts from an evangelical viewpoint, comes to a surprising conclusion. "Yet, in the traditional church, what opportunity is there for the practice, the discovery, and the development of gifts? Too often, very little. Not so in the New Testament meeting of the church. A study of Scripture will reveal several significant elements of the meeting of the early church. . . .

- "It was a meeting without any professional ministry. 'Each one [of you]' (1 Corinthians 14:26, RSV) suggests free participation by members of the body.
- "It was a meeting without any settled format at all (1 Corinthians 14:26-33).
- "It was a meeting for the free exercise of spiritual gifts (1 Corinthians

14:26-33). The guiding rule is 'Let all things be done for edification.'
- "It was a meeting with a threefold purpose: edification of believers, worship of the Lord, and evangelism of unbelievers. This is obvious from the variety of ingredients in the meeting.
- "Song, doctrine, tongues, prophecy, interpretation (1 Corinthians 14:26).
- "The Lord's Supper (1 Corinthians 11:26).
- "Prayer for the unsaved and government (1 Timothy 2:1-8).
- "Testimony and missionary report (Acts 14:27).
- "Offering (1 Corinthians 16:1, 2).
- "These are activities directed toward the Lord, saints, and unbelievers.

"Must we meet this way today? Should we? Could we? Of course we could. Some do. Perhaps we should as well. This was the manner of meeting established by the apostles. Apostolic practice is apostolic precept (1 Corinthians 4:17).

"What better way to give expression to the headship of Christ than for the church to meet and allow His representative, the Holy Spirit, to preside? What better way to demonstrate the priesthood of all believers than to meet as priests with no officialdom? What better way to practice the doctrine of gifts than to have a meeting where men are free to exercise their utterance gifts in the presence of discerning elders under the impulses of the Holy Spirit?" [7]

In a men's small group there was one who was obviously very sick. His friends knew he needed physical healing, but they did not think this was a gift they possessed. But they did have the gift of helps and service, so they lifted their friend and carried him to where Jesus was ministering. Seeing the crowd around Jesus, they connected their gifts to human effort and were able to place him, through the roof, right down at the feet of Jesus, where their sick friend received the healing he needed (Mark 2:1-12). Did you notice in the story whose faith Jesus recognized and rewarded? "When Jesus saw their faith, He said to the paralytic, 'Son, your sins are forgiven you' " (verse 5). As the small group who meet weekly in our home prayed through this passage, Joe responded, "Lord, help me to be a friend like the man who brought the paralytic to Jesus." Someone else prayed, "Father, can my faith bring healing to another person? Please show me what to do."

There was a time when I thought that spiritual gifts were given primarily to win the unconverted to Jesus. However, now I see that there is another emphasis that is just as important. "Even so you, since you are zealous for spiritual gifts, let it be for the edification of the church that you seek to excel" (1 Corinthians 14:12). The gifts begin to grow as they are used to build up the households of faith, the body of Jesus, the church.

Let's be practical about the ministry of spiritual gifts. How does this ministry happen in small groups? The meeting together of Christians in the time of the New Testament involved them all in sharing and ministry. "How is it then, brethren? Whenever you come together, each of you has a psalm, has a teaching, has a tongue, has a revelation, has an interpretation. Let all things be done for edification" (verse 26). If there are, for example, 10 people in a group today, God will reveal gifts among the people that will meet the needs expressed or even unexpressed. For instance, all group members will need shepherding, so there will be at least two people who will exercise the pastoral gift.

Count Zinzendorf saw how important spiritual gifts were and noticed how these could coincide with the natural human temperaments of people within the groups by the wisdom of the Holy Spirit. "That we aught not to lay all the duties of the church on one person no more needs proof than we need to demonstrate that the foot is not to eat . . . or the eyes to hear. . . . If, for example, we were to set a man naturally mild and gentle in his character, to watch over and detect the various deceits of the human heart, he would be distressed, and a thousand times deceived. If, on the other hand, a man of keen mind and hard disposition were charged with the duty of exhortation, there would be no end of disputes, and his exhortation would either have no effect, or a very bad one. But if the former is set to exhort and the latter to apply himself to the discernment of spirits, truth and love are maintained together."[8]

Someone in the group may express a deep need for spiritual healing, and while all the group will pray and agree in prayer, binding Satan and refuting his authority over the person, one or two in the group will meet the need by using a special gift of healing. The Lord may see that there is need for admonition, exhortation, and comfort, so He will give a gift of prophecy to meet that need. In this way the household of faith will be built up (1 Corinthians 14:3, 4), and the people will experience spiritual, emotional, and possibly even physical healing.

During the past five years Ginny Allen has led a women's prayer group and has assisted her husband, David, with another small group Bible fellowship. As a result, spiritual gifts have been used to build up and bring healing to many people. "Spiritually, small groups have helped me to know that God undoubtedly answers prayer," Allen said in an interview for the *Trinity Power Newsletter*. "It has been a most beautiful experience to see other people growing spiritually and to know that God is using me and whatever abilities I give Him. It is just beautiful and I just keep praising Him because I keep thinking, *Lord, this isn't me talking, but it is You who is using me. Lord, I want to be the kind of person You can just use as You choose.* And the Lord has done that, and I just keep thanking Him.

"But seeing answers to prayer is really exciting. One family was having a hard time in their marriage, and God has now brought healing to that marriage. It is just too beautiful for words.

"One girl had a lot of pain in her jaw. She was struggling both spiritually and physically, but the Lord brought her through that. He has strengthened her through the loving fellowship of that group who uphold her constantly in prayer. She says she becomes so encouraged knowing that the folks in the group are praying for her. It has really made a difference in her life. We have had so many exciting things happen and so many answers to prayer that it is really difficult to remember them all."

Sometimes today, healings and miracles are turned into a spectator sport by some TV evangelists. Contrast this to the attitude of the Moravian Christians who saw by 1731 many miraculous cures taking place. "[Zinzendorf] did not wish that the brethren and sisters should regard such things as extraordinary, and thus attach themselves to them; but whenever they occurred, as, for instance, when anyone experienced an instantaneous cure, . . . he regarded it as a thing that was known, and spoke little about it. He also frequently asserted . . . that wonder-working faith was a gift, which did not make its possessor a better child of God, but that he might even be inferior to others who did not possess such gifts, . . . that the love of Christ be resigned to him in all things." [9]

Gifts Reach Out

Where there are needs outside the small group that the Holy Spirit brings to the attention of small group members, then spiritual gifts will also flow in that direction, bringing unconditional love, practical Christianity, and evangelism. Group members will be the support team the Holy Spirit uses to encourage those in the group who are reaching out to the surrounding community. If some gifts of the Holy Spirit can be used in midsize seminars or large combined meetings of many households of faith, then the small group members will also be upholding their fellow group members in prayer as they teach, preach, or administer.

Look at the incredible illustration of this in Acts 4. Peter and John have been severely threatened by the Jewish leaders (verse 17), but they did not run away; instead they went exactly where we would expect them to go for the support they needed. "As soon as Peter and John were set free, they returned to their group and told them what the chief priest and the elders had said" (verse 23, TEV). Immediately the group came into a time of concentrated prayer, agreeing with each other in prayer (Matthew 18:19, 20), as they were in one accord. They based their prayers on the Word of God, asking for spiritual gifts of evangelism, teaching, healing, and miracles. "Now, Lord, look on their threats, and grant to Your servants that with all boldness they may speak Your Word, by stretching out Your hand to heal, and that signs and wonders may be done through the name of Your holy Servant Jesus" (Acts 4:29, 30).

The results were absolutely dramatic as the Holy Spirit shook the household, brought them into ministry for one another, and enabled them to reach out to unbelievers and proclaim the power of His resurrection. "And when they had prayed, the place where they were assembled together was shaken; and they were all filled with the Holy Spirit, and they spoke the word of God with boldness. Now the multitude of those who believed were of one heart and one soul; neither did anyone say that any of the things he possessed was his own, but they had all things in common. And with great power the apostles gave witness to the resurrection of the Lord Jesus. And great grace was upon them all" (Acts 4:31-33).

Carolyn Hamilton leads a group of ladies who meet in her home each week for prayer and fellowship. A few months ago they began to pray for two young people who had drifted away from the family of God and were being deceived by the multiplicity of evils that flourish in the Los Angeles area. A group of middle-aged ladies praying for young people—what would the result be? Miraculously, the Spirit of God began to move in the lives of these two young people, and soon they began to talk about having Bible studies. In fact, they told one of the ladies they would like to bring a friend to join them in learning about the Word of God. Soon these three young people were so moved by the Holy Spirit that they began to invite other young people to join them in their Bible study group.

Eventually there was a small group of about 12 young men and women ranging in age from 14 to 24. Some had been involved in drug addiction, eating disorders, and a multiplicity of evil practices. But through the resurrection power of the Holy Spirit they came to know what it meant to be healed by Jesus and given new life in Him. On the day they were baptized they came up out of the water shouting, "Hallelujah, praise God."

Because they wanted to serve God in ministry, this group of young people took the name Firebrands. It was not long before the Firebrands had many other young people join them as they went out into the streets, parks, and nightclubs inviting young people to come to Jesus and join them in celebrating new life in Him. One weekend soon after their baptism the

Firebrands joined some of the people who had been praying for them before their conversion and they came for a weekend of prayer and Bible study at a ranch high in the San Bernardino Mountains. They prayed especially that they might know what spiritual gifts God could reveal through them. They noticed what the Bible said about spiritual gifts: "Earnestly desire the best gifts" (1 Corinthians 12:31). "Desire spiritual gifts" (1 Corinthians 14:1). In the midst of that time of intense prayer as they sang and prayed in the Word, God revealed to each of them gifts that He would choose to work through them to meet subtle deception. God has worked in a miraculous way through these young people to bring many others out of satanic deception into the beautiful light of Jesus' truth.

Gifts of Grace

How is it possible to discover the spiritual gifts that God has made available for the ministry of every Christian? I used to think of spiritual gifts as secret abilities that God has hidden within us that can be discovered only by knowing some special spiritual code. That is not the case. It is also dangerous to separate spiritual gifts from the needs they are designed to meet and to try to enjoy them for their own sake, like some sort of spiritual toy. Neighbour makes a couple very helpful points: "How are spiritual gifts discovered by the believer? Has God latently stored up supernatural power within us as a flashlight battery stores up electric energy? No! Spiritual gifts are not stored up, ready for a special occasion to be taken out and utilized. Instead, they are like an electric current that must flow from a source to a need. If the believer is not attached to both Christ, the source, and another person with a need, there's little likelihood the gift will be manifested. Spiritual gifts are the 'energizing' that service the work of God where a need exists. Thus, in the cell group each need of a body member is a valid reason for the gifts to flow. As a result, the needs in the life of a person will call forth the spiritual gifts that are necessary for Christ to meet the problem area. In references to gifts throughout the New Testament, the emphasis is on their activity, not the gifts themselves." [10]

Once again I suggest that you pray through the lists of spiritual gifts in 1 Corinthians 12, Romans 12, and Ephesians 4 and ask that God will present you with needs that will bring out the healing gifts God can energize for service through you.

In *The Desire of Ages*, that classic commentary on the life of Jesus, the point of spiritual gifts meeting needs is also emphasized. "When the Saviour said, 'Go, . . . teach all nations,' He said also, 'These signs shall follow them that believe; In my name shall they cast out devils; they shall speak with new tongues; they shall take up serpents; and if they drink any deadly thing, it shall not hurt them; they shall lay hands on the sick, and they shall recover' (Mark 16:17, 18, KJV). The promise is as far-reaching as the commission. Not that all the gifts are imparted to each believer. The Spirit divides 'to every man severally as he will' (1 Corinthians 12:11, KJV). But the gifts of the Spirit are promised to every believer according to his need for the Lord's work. The promise is just as strong and trustworthy now as in the days of the apostles. 'These signs shall follow them that believe.' This is the privilege of God's children, and faith should lay hold on all that it is possible to have as an indorsement of faith." [11]

Occasionally I have had people say to me, "I want to be a Christian and be part of a small group, but I don't expect God to work through me in any special way."

"Why do you say that?" I ask them.

They usually reply, "I'm not good enough. My past has been so bad. I have made many mistakes even while I have been a member of the church."

At a camp meeting in New England a man handed me a piece of paper on which he had written a short Bible study on the gifts of the Holy Spirit. In this Bible study he noticed correctly and convincingly that spiritual gifts are all gifts of grace. That means that you do not merit them or deserve them—they are given on the basis of the love of God. "I thank my God always concerning you for the grace of God which was given to you by Christ Jesus, that you were enriched in everything by Him in all utterance and all knowledge, even as the testimony of Christ was confirmed in you, so that you come short in no gift, eagerly waiting for the revelation of our Lord Jesus Christ" (1 Corinthians 1:4-7). "Having then gifts differing according to the grace that is given to us, let us use them: if prophecy, let us prophesy in proportion to our faith" (Romans 12:6). "But to each one of us grace was given according to the measure of Christ's gift" (Ephesians 4:7). "And God is able to make all grace abound toward you, that you always having all sufficiency in all things, have an abundance for every good work" (2 Corinthians 9:8).

On top of this it is even more encouraging to remember that the New Testament looked on grace not only as God's favor, but also as the Holy Spirit's power. This is the power that energizes the gifts. When Peter and John and their prayer group were filled with the Holy Spirit, "great grace was upon them all" (Acts 4:33). John Wesley recognized grace in this way, as the power that will enable you to be a gifted minister for God. "By 'the grace of God' is sometimes to be understood that free love, that unmerited mercy, by which I a sinner, through the merits of Christ, am now reconciled to God. But in this place it rather means that power of God the Holy Ghost, which 'worketh in us both to will and to do of his good pleasure.' As soon as ever the grace of God in the former sense, his pardoning love, is manifested to our souls, the grace of God in the latter sense, the power of His Spirit, takes place therein. And now we can perform, through God, what to man was impossible. Now we can order our conversation aright. We can do all things in the light and power of that love, through Christ which strengtheneth us." [12]

Many Christians are frustrated today because they are sitting in churches inactive and unfulfilled in Christian service. Many have the gift of pastoring, but it is not flowing through them between God and a need because the professional ministry of the church or organization has not released them for service. When households of faith are opened and members are together in the Spirit in small groups, then many church members can be channels for pastoral ministry. The same is true for all the healing gifts of the Spirit. Give the Holy Spirit a chance to show you what New Testament Christianity is like, and then you will know what your healing gifts are. You will have energy and health to use these gifts to the glory of God. If you have been filled with the Holy Spirit, you have the anointing of God. It dwells in you (1 John 2:20, 27), and you can have new supplies of physical and mental power to be an agent of God's healing grace.

Not only have auto mechanic shop supervisor Bill McCord and his wife, Nancy, attended the small group in our home each week, but they have also led two groups of their own for almost four years. For them this is a pastoral ministry that has helped dozens of people find healing in times of personal crisis. Nancy tells of people who have found new self-worth and confidence in their groups so that they have been able to go out and serve God as spiritual gifts have flowed through them to meet specific needs in the church or community. "There have also been miraculous physical healings from the ministry of groups," Nancy told me recently as she praised God for what He has been able to do through them and the intercessory prayers of the groups who meet in their apartment block. "I think Bill and I have received the most blessing out of this, though," Nancy concluded. "We have gotten to know so many people. This is ministry, absolutely!"

Give the Holy Spirit a chance. He can gift you for healing ministry today.

SMALL GROUP STUDY
Chapter Ten

Cohesive Contrasts

Sometimes conflict will develop in a group. Conflict is bad when it becomes divisive and people are hurt by their own or others' unwillingness to accept differing feelings and opinions. Sometimes there may be theological differences about a scriptural teaching or a religious tradition. Conflict is good if it enables people to hear different viewpoints and to recognize the genuine struggles some people have with what may be considered orthodox Christianity. Four steps help deal with conflict.

1. **Recognize** that a person has a problem and may be upset.

2. **Personalize**. Remember that people are not to be made to feel bad, inferior, or superior because they have differences. Discuss the issue and differ as friends.

3. **Clarify**. This is very important. Sometimes people who believe the same way are misunderstanding each other. Spend time defining and making the problem as simple as possible.

4. **Resolve**. The problem may be solved in the group. People may see another viewpoint or agree to disagree. Perhaps the problem can be dealt with outside the group or by asking expert help or advice.

Begin your group today by discussing this question: If you would be able to work just one miraculous healing right now, who or what would you heal? Why?

Concentrating on the Word
Study Text: 1 Corinthians 12

List the evidences you find in 1 Corinthians 12 that spiritual gifts are designed by God to be activated in a group setting.

_____

_____

Is there one gift that is designed to enable a person to serve God in total

isolation from other people? Why?
_____
_____

Paul says we should earnestly desire the best gifts (verse 31). Which of the gifts would you consider to be the best? Why?
_____
_____

If you could choose spiritual healing or physical healing for a loved one, what factors would you consider in making your decision between the two? How hard would it be?
_____
_____

How are evangelism, teaching, and pastoring, for example, all part of a healing ministry? What example of this do you see in Jesus' ministry?
_____
_____

In what ways can a small group be more effective than an individual in bringing healing to a person or need?
_____
_____

What do you think about the idea that spiritual gifts are given on the basis of needs that must be dealt with rather than elevating the person possessing the gifts? For instance, is the gift of supernatural wisdom given so people can say "What a wise person," or so that needs for wise counsel can be met? Why?
_____
_____

If you were told you definitely have a gift of healing, how would you react?

Who said? _____ Not me _____
Wow! _____ How do you know? _____
Let me try _____ I know _____
I have been healed myself _____
Can I pray for you? _____

Healing through which gift? _____
Am I different from other Christians? _____
I'm frightened _____ Other _____

Why is it the Holy Spirit (not Christians) who decides which gift is needed at a certain time and place (1 Corinthians 12:11)?

_____
_____

Paul says that gifts are "distributed" to individuals, but "appointed" in the church (verse 28). What does that mean to you as you understand the significance of households of faith?

_____
_____

If someone suggests that there is one certain gift that all Christians "must" have, how does that compare with Paul's teaching in 1 Corinthians 12?

_____
_____

What encouragement does it give you that the gifts of the Holy Spirit are spoken of as gifts of grace?

_____
_____

Conversation With the Lord

Center your prayers today on healing. First, praise God for healings you have experienced or know about. Now pray for healing, for needs in the group and outside the group. Continue to pray for the "empty chair," so that others can be brought into your healing fellowship. Conclude as usual with the Lord's Prayer together.

Committing the Word to Memory

This week, write out a verse from 1 Corinthians 12 and share it with someone as soon as possible.

_____
_____

CHAPTER
ELEVEN
▼

Give the Holy Spirit a Chance
To Make Worship Meaningful

The candles twinkle in the grandeur of the great cathedral. You look up past the stained-glass windows and the stonework lattice to the beautiful mosaics on the ceiling high above. You notice a man bowing before a statue of Jesus and see a woman reverently dipping her finger in the holy water and making the sign of the cross. Walking out of this building, you make your way down the road to another architectural masterpiece. Inside, the choir sings an ancient anthem. People sit and stand repeatedly as prayers are read and scriptures recited. The atmosphere is heavy with a gloomy solemnity, and the service seems about as interesting as watching paint dry. A few blocks away you find yourself in a rather inornate building where people are wearing a type of military uniform. The band is playing a rousing tune as the people sing "Onward, Christian Soldiers!" Your next "church hopping" destination this beautiful spring morning takes you into a large fan-shaped sanctuary. Even before you pass through the doors you can hear the beat of the music and the clapping of the people. In this church the worshipers are excited, some jumping up and down with joy. A woman shouts "Hallelujah" while her large pendulum earrings swing in the air as she dances round and round. You have had enough variety of worship for one morning, so you walk to the beautiful park nearby and sit quietly beside the river. There are blossoms breaking out everywhere, the birds are singing, and the air is full of the scent of a thousand flowers. You take out your Bible and read for a while and then quietly pray. Suddenly you feel an incredible closeness to God, and you praise His holy name.

What is worship? Is it a solo or group activity? Has God accepted everything we have seen on our morning tour? Does it make any difference to Him? Of course, we do not really know. According to our own traditions, biases, culture, and taste we will judge worship formats, eliminating as unworthy those that do not suit us. It is not my purpose to become an arbitrator or final authority on various external worship forms, but rather to give the Holy Spirit a chance to lead us into an understanding of worship principles that will explode with meaning, shattering the lethargy of lifeless formalism and the excitement of empty emotionalism.

The Holy Spirit is intimately involved in our worship. In fact, He is the one who makes it possible. "It is we, not they, who have received the true circumcision, for we worship God by means of His Spirit and rejoice in our life in union with Christ Jesus. We do not put any trust in external ceremonies" (Philippians 3:3, TEV). Jesus was very definite about the Holy Spirit's role in true worship. "God is Spirit, and those who worship Him must worship in spirit and truth" (John 4:24). Pray about that verse. The Holy Spirit will lead you to see it in a context that will bring true worship into clear focus.

Look at the three clear points that Jesus makes in John 4:23: "But the hour is coming, and now is, when the true worshipers will worship the Father in spirit and truth; for the Father is seeking such to worship Him." Here Jesus clarifies some very basic issues. First, there are people who will be recognized as true worshipers. Second, the true worshipers will worship the Father. Third, the Father is seeking such worshipers. Isn't this amazing? God is actually looking for people who will worship in Spirit and truth. He is not passively sitting around in heaven hoping that a true worshiper will find Him there. He is searching for them, leading them to Him. That is the work of the Holy Spirit.

It is the children of the Father who worship Him in Spirit and in truth. That is why every time we are filled with the Holy Spirit, He gives us the inner witness with the absolute assurance of who we are. "For as many as are led by the Spirit of God, these are sons of God. For you did not receive the spirit of bondage again to fear, but you received the Spirit of adoption by whom we cry out 'Abba, Father.' The Spirit Himself bears witness with our spirit that we are children of God" (Romans 8:14-16).

As children we come in adoration of God, and there is an intimacy in this that mixes awe and excitement. "And because you are sons, God has sent forth the Spirit of His Son into your hearts, crying out, 'Abba, Father' " (Galatians 4:6). All this true worship is possible only because of the Holy Spirit dwelling in us. Dutch Reformed pastor Andrew Murray rejoices in this way: "Blessed be God! the hour is come, and now is, we are living in it this very moment, that true worshipers shall worship the Father in spirit and in truth. Let us believe it; the Spirit has been given, and dwells within us, for this one reason, because the Father seeks such worshipers. Let us rejoice in the confidence that we can obtain to it, we can be true worshipers, because the Holy Spirit has been given." [1]

The "Must" of New Birth

Jesus does not give a vague hint or innuendo when He speaks of worship. He uses a very emphatic imperative when He says that we "must worship in spirit and in truth" (John 4:24). Some translators use "It is necessary." We can paraphrase this by saying, "If you are filled with the Holy Spirit, you are absolutely bound to or tied to worshiping God in spirit and in truth." This is not force but fact. It is like saying, "If you are filled with alcohol you are absolutely bound to lose control of your judgment and coordination." Or to use another illustration: "If you are committed to physical fitness, you absolutely must exercise."

The "must" in John 4:24 is the third such imperative Jesus uses in His sequence of teaching on the Holy Spirit (as recorded by John). The first "must" appears in John 3:5-7. "Jesus answered, 'Most assuredly, I say to you, unless one is born of water and the Spirit, he cannot enter the kingdom of God. That which is born of the flesh is flesh, and that which is born of the Spirit is spirit. Do not marvel that I said to you, "You must be born again." ' " In these verses Jesus begins two parallel themes, water and family relationship with God, which reveal the work of the Holy Spirit in an interesting way. The Holy Spirit is the agent of the new birth, which is likened to being cleansed with water. "Not by works of righteousness which we have done, but according to His mercy He saved us, through the washing of regeneration and renewing of the Holy Spirit, whom He poured out on us abundantly through Jesus Christ our Savior" (Titus 3:5, 6). It is this new birth, by the Holy Spirit, that brings us into the family of God and enables us to worship the Father "in spirit and in truth." So we adore Him as "Abba, Father."

All humanity is designed to worship just as surely as we are designed to eat and drink. In the flesh, without the Spirit, people will worship false gods, such as self, fashion, material possessions, pleasure, or position. All these things can be good, but apart from the Holy Spirit, they are objects of false worship. Cain worshiped God, but according to his own desires. His was false worship and was followed by murder (Genesis 4). Since Adam all humans have been born into a family line of false worship (Romans 5:12). This heritage can even affect the worship of cultural Christians unless they are born of the Spirit. I led a weekly Bible study group in the home of Chris and Carol. They were members of a large prominent church. They sang in the choir and liked the sophisticated ritual of the worship service. "I can see that there are many parts of our worship service that are not biblical," Chris confided in me one day. "I enjoy it, though, and don't think it makes much difference to God." A few weeks later Carol asked me to visit with her, and it was then that she shared with me a rather sad story. "Chris has no real attachment to the things of God," she said. "In fact, he cares for nothing but himself and his own pleasure. Recently his young brother died and Chris didn't show any feeling at all, but last night the new engine in his speedboat blew up, wasting thousands of dollars, and what do you think happened? He cried and cried because his pleasure god had let him down." I don't want to judge Chris by Carol's opinion of the situation, but this evidence of false worship is repeated many times over in many different ways. The Holy Spirit can answer this problem only as He reveals Jesus to us as the second Adam, the beginning of a new family line (1 Corinthians 15:45). That is why Jesus said, "You must be born again." "Born of water and the Spirit." We can be born again into the family line of true worship.

What does Jesus mean when He says "God is Spirit" (John 4:24)? He is not defining God, but describing the way God deals with humanity. "It means that God is Spirit toward men because He gives them the Spirit . . . which begets them anew." [2] He reveals Himself to us by the Spirit. In the same way John says God is light (1 John 1:5) and God is love (1 John 4:8). Just as darkness cannot co-exist with light and hatred cannot coexist with love, so unconverted flesh cannot coexist with Spirit. It is simply impossible for sinful human flesh to truly worship God.

Think about this with me. As the Holy Spirit inaugurates the new birth experience, there is placed in a person's life the desire to come into unity with God. This is the true worship that "Abba, Father" is seeking. It is not dependent on outward forms, ceremonies, orders of service, prescribed rituals, or certain locations or buildings. It is the direct drawing together of God and people who have the Holy Spirit dwelling in them. In Australia, Aborigine children have sometimes been adopted at an early age by Europeans. They have been brought up in a European environment with all the refinements of European culture. But it seems that at a certain age the children will always feel the inner call to go back to the bush, back to their own people. At a camp meeting in central Canada a Jamaican brother admitted to me that even though he enjoyed the town in which he lived, he was the only West Indian, and felt the call back to his own people. That is what true worship in the Spirit is like. It is the call of the born-again person to be united in mind and heart with the Father in heaven. Until this happens, there will be no personal worship, and public worship will *seem* empty and even boring. If the leaders of public worship are not filled with the Holy Spirit, worship *can be* empty and boring. A pastor noticed an old sea captain in church as he preached his sermon, so after the service was over, as the people were shaking hands with the pastor, he asked, "Captain, how did you enjoy the sermon?" The captain replied, "Sorry, I was thinking about whales."

Sing a New Song

In Egypt, Israel could only sigh and cry and groan (Exodus 2:23, 24), but after going through the Red Sea experience they could now sing and praise God. "The Lord is my strength and song, and He has become my salvation; He is my God, and I will praise Him; my father's God, and I will exalt Him." "Who is like You, O Lord, among the gods? Who is like You, glorious in holiness, fearful in praises, doing wonders? You stretched out Your right hand; the earth swallowed them. You in Your mercy have led forth the people whom You have redeemed; You have guided them in Your strength to Your holy habitation" (Exodus 15:2, 11-13). This is the first time "redeemed" appears in the Bible and with it comes a song of true worship to God.

Remember Ephesians 5:18, 19? As soon as the Holy Spirit fills a life, He gives to that person songs that make melody to God. At each step of experience with the Holy Spirit there are new songs, songs of experience. Much formal worship consists of old songs that are often sung without any thought. But not so in the experience of the born-again, Spirit-filled person. When David was lifted out of the pit he said that the Lord "has put a new song in my mouth" (Psalm 40:3). Repeatedly the psalmist admonishes God's people to sing a new song (e.g., Psalm 98:1). New songs are sung in the great throne room of heaven (Revelation 5:9). The redeemed people who rejoice with Jesus on Mount Zion sing a new song before the throne of God (Revelation 14:3). Give the Holy Spirit a chance to put a song of experience, surrender, joy, or praise in your heart today as you worship God.

When Howel Harris, a burning flame of Welsh Methodist Christianity, was converted and filled with the Holy Spirit at the Talgarth Anglican Church in 1738, the experience brought him into immediate worship of God. "I felt suddenly my heart melting within me, like wax before the fire, with love to God my Saviour. . . . I could not help calling God my Father. I knew that I was His child and that He loved me and heard me. My soul, being satiated, cried, 'It is enough, I am satisfied. Give me strength and I will follow Thee through fire and water. I could say that I was happy indeed.' " [3] A little later Harris, preaching in the open air on his parents' grave outside the Talgarth church (since he was not allowed to speak in the building), noticed a young man on horseback listening to his preaching from the other side of the church fence. I stood recently by that grave and pictured the scene of more than 250 years ago. William Williams, as he sat on his horse, was converted that day as Harris preached, and soon afterward God placed a new song in his heart. I love to hear the Welsh people sing that hymn today. It is their national song. When they sing, "Guide Me, O Thou Great Jehovah!" to the tune "CWM Rhondda," it lifts you out of this world into the throne room of heaven. One day, as a congregation was singing this hymn in one of my meetings in Wales, I stopped them and asked, "This is not a new song for any of you, you can sing without even thinking of the words, so does it really have any meaning to you to sing, 'I am weak, but Thou are mighty; hold me with Thy powerful hand'?" Some could say "Amen" because this is a song that is renewed in their hearts by a born-again and Spirit-filled experience each day.

Surprising as it may seem, to worship in spirit and in truth one must be born by water and the Spirit as Jesus said, because those who are not born of the Spirit are counted as dead by God (1 Timothy 5:6). The dead cannot worship God. As the psalmist explains: "The dead do not praise the Lord, nor any who go down into silence" (Psalm 115:17). (Please forgive my homiletic use of this text!) The emphasis of the New Testament is life through the power of the Holy Spirit. Jesus clearly teaches this: "It is the Spirit who gives life; the flesh profits nothing. The words that I speak to you are spirit, and they are life" (John 6:63). Paul confirms his belief in this great truth of life through the Holy Spirit. "But if the Spirit of Him who raised Jesus from the dead dwells in you, He who raised Christ from the dead will also give life to your mortal bodies through His Spirit who dwells in you" (Romans 8:11). Those who are alive in the Spirit can praise the Lord.

I like the way Adventist pioneer Ellen White links the Holy Spirit, worship, and song as powerful weapons against the enemy. "Pray for the impartation of the Holy Spirit. When this Spirit fills the heart, the praise of God will be in the congregation, and it will be reflected from your faces. Love for God will be shown by your love for one another, and this will give you power for service."[4] "God is worshiped with song and music in the courts above. As we thus express our gratitude we are approximating the worship of the heavenly hosts. 'Whoso offereth praise glorifieth' God (Psalm 50:23, KJV). Let us with reverent joy come before our Creator with 'thanksgiving, and the voice of melody' (Isaiah 51:3, KJV)."[5] "I saw that we must be daily rising and keep the ascendancy above the powers of darkness. Our God is mighty. I saw singing to the glory of God often drove the enemy [away], and praising God would beat him back and give us the victory."[6] "As lessons of the wondrous works of God are repeated, and as the heart's gratitude is expressed in prayer and song, angels from God take up the strain and unite in praise and thanksgiving to God. These exercises drive back the power of Satan. They expel murmurings and complainings, and Satan loses ground." [7]

The enemy cannot stand in the presence of true worship, so he has tied much Christianity to empty rituals and emotionalism. But when a person is born of the Spirit and worships the Father in true humility and praise, the results are miraculous and victorious.

Looking Up to God

Jesus' second "must" in His series of imperatives leading to worship in spirit and in truth is also very significant. When, as a carpentry apprentice, I was learning how to construct complicated hip and valley roofs, my supervisor said to me, "Garrie, there are a number of important points you must remember if you are going to have the correct angles on each of the rafters." On one occasion I skipped one of the supervisor's "musts" and found that the roof did not look right at all—in fact, the ridge board that was supposed to run level ended up with about a 10-degree slope, and I almost ended up without a job. Our worship will also be out of level unless we give the Holy Spirit a chance to exalt Jesus. "And as Moses lifted up the serpent in the wilderness, even so must the Son of Man be lifted up" (John 3:14). A group I visited was praying in worship recently when the Holy Spirit led us to sing a number of times that beautiful chorus "Turn your eyes upon Jesus, look full in His wonderful face; and the things of earth will grow strangely dim in the light of His glory and grace." This is the ministry of the Holy Spirit; the Holy Spirit glorifies Jesus and turns our eyes on Him (John 16:14, 15).

The serpent on the pole did not represent Satan, but Jesus bearing the sins of the whole world. Read the story in Numbers 21:4-9. In the time of the Exodus the children of Israel, bitten by a serpent (sin), could be saved only by looking at the serpent (the One who became sin for us) on the pole. These people were not told to fight the serpents. To try to overcome the effects of sin, without the Holy Spirit, is impossible. They were not told to look at Moses—looking at leaders, pastors, or denominations will not save any soul or enable true worship to take place. They were not to look at their wounds. The Holy Spirit does not lead us to magnify the effects of sin, but to glorify the sin bearer. True worship is looking up in faith. Look up and live. The Holy Spirit enables us to look up above the world, away from past failures and mistakes, beyond self-satisfaction and pride, past friends or enemies.

Initially true worship will lead to sorrow for sin and deep repentance for hurting Jesus. "I will pour on the house of David and on the inhabitants of Jerusalem the Spirit of grace and supplication; then they will look on Me whom they have pierced; they will mourn for Him as one mourns for his only son, and grieve for Him as one grieves for a firstborn" (Zechariah 12:10). But the Holy Spirit will not leave true worshipers in sorrow, because the anointing of the Holy Spirit brings the oil of joy for mourning, the garment of praise for the spirit of heaviness (Isaiah 61:3). A fruit of the Spirit is joy (Galatians 5:22). The kingdom of God is righteousness, peace, and joy through the Holy Spirit (Romans 14:17). Those who are born of the Spirit are filled with all joy (Romans 15:13). In looking to Jesus there will be joy through the Holy Spirit, even in the face of personal affliction and external evil (1 Thessalonians 1:2-6).

When the Holy Spirit leads you to look to Jesus as you worship, you see nothing else. Not buildings, architecture, performers, speakers, musicians, rituals. Only Jesus. For true worship a cave is as grand as a cathedral, a humble cottage is as beautiful as an ornate church, because all eyes are turned onto Jesus, and "Abba, Father" is exalted and magnified. Nothing else is important. I was visiting Edmonton with my family when I saw on the news that Princess Diana was in town that day with her husband, Prince Charles. My family had seen Charles a number of times, and our daughter Lyndell had shaken hands with him in New Zealand, but we had never seen Diana. We rushed to a good location where we could be near the couple, and arrived just in time to see them close up a number of times. As Diana walked by, our eyes were on only her. We didn't look at the crowd, the buildings, or the weather, only Diana. I even forgot to take a photo. For a few moments there was nothing else in the world but Princess Di. In true worship the Holy Spirit will glorify Jesus and reveal the Father through Him, so there will be a total, all-absorbing awareness of His presence. In true worship every spoken word, prayer, song, and even offering will turn our eyes upon Jesus so that the things of earth will grow strangely dim in the light of His glory and grace.

Worship in the Water

Jesus' third "must" finds its context in a discussion about water. Jesus was near Jacob's well, still a sacred site for the Jews and Samaritans. On one of my visits to the well I had to dodge bullets that flew in an angry Israeli-Palestinian conflict. But the conflict between the Jews and Samaritans was even more volatile. Sitting in the ruins of the Samaritan temple, on top of Mount Gerizim, I have thought about Jesus' words to the woman He met at the well. He explained to her that the location of worship was now no longer important (John 4:19-21). No, it was not the place of worship that was now significant; it was the Spirit of worship that was important. This true worship would actually be in springs of living water.

Water is one of Jesus' key symbols of the Holy Spirit. He spoke of living water (verse 10) and explained the meaning of this in John 7:38, 39: "He who believes in Me, as the Scripture has said, out of his heart will flow rivers of living water. But this He spoke concerning the Spirit, whom those believing in Him would receive; for the Holy Spirit was not yet given, because Jesus was not yet glorified." The Holy Spirit is a fountain of life springing up or leaping up in the experience of a born-again Christian (John 4:14). The Spirit as the water of life will flow out in the ministry of spiritual gifts from a person who worships in spirit and in truth to those who are in need.

Long ago Thomas Aquinas said that the Holy Spirit is the very font or spring of grace. The water symbolism of the Holy Spirit takes many forms. There is the baptism of the Holy Spirit (Acts 1:5). The Spirit is poured out (Acts 10:45). People were able to drink of the Spirit (1 Corinthians 12:13). There is the washing of regeneration through the Holy Spirit (Titus 3:5, 6). So worshiping in spirit and in truth could be called worshiping in the water and the word. "That He might sanctify and cleanse it [the church] with the washing of water by the word" (Ephesians 5:26). The Word of God is the Scripture, which the Holy Spirit uses to cleanse and purify each human life that has the Holy Spirit dwelling within.

Is doctrinal accuracy an essential as God works out who are His true worshipers? "God is Spirit, and those who worship Him must worship in spirit and truth" (John 4:24). There is a temptation to believe that worship in truth means in true doctrine, teachings, or understanding of the Bible. But the meaning is different. Spirit-filled people who have not known all truth or have been wrong in some biblical understandings have still been able to truly worship if they are not deliberately rebelling against God's Word. Notice how Andrew Murray explains this: "Just as the words 'in Spirit' do not mean internal as contrasted with external observances, but spiritual, in-wrought by God's Spirit, as opposed to what man's natural power can effect, so the words 'in truth' do not mean hearty, sincere, upright. In all the worship of the Old Testament saints, they knew that God sought truth in the inward parts; they sought Him with their whole hearts, and most uprightly—and yet they obtained not to that worship in spirit and truth, which Jesus brought us when He rent the veil of the flesh. Truth here means the substance, the reality, the actual possession of all that the worship of God implies, both in what it demands and what it promises." [8]

Jesus does not outline a true form of worship, or a true doctrine of worship, but rather says the Father is seeking "true worshipers" (verse 23). These are people who are led by the Spirit and do not worship according to the dictates of sinful human nature. These are people who daily are seeking the power of the Holy Spirit in their lives and are seeing victories plus the fruit and gifts of the Spirit in their Christian experience. As you give the Holy Spirit a chance to fill your life you will be a true worshiper who will be found by God.

Listen to this from *The Desire of Ages*: "Religion is not to be confined to external forms and ceremonies. The religion that comes from God is the only religion that will lead to God. In order to serve Him aright, we must be born of the divine Spirit. This will purify the heart and renew the mind, giving us a new capacity for knowing and loving God. It will give us a willing obedience to all His requirements. This is true worship. It is the fruit of the working of the Holy Spirit. By the Spirit every sincere prayer is indited, and such prayer is acceptable to God. Wherever a soul reaches out after God, there the Spirit's working is manifest, and God will reveal Himself to that soul. For such worshipers He is seeking. He waits to receive them, and to make them His sons and daughters." [9] Worship in truth is Paul's emphasis in Romans 12:1: "Therefore, I urge you, brothers, in view of God's mercy, to offer your bodies as living sacrifices, holy and pleasing to God—this is your spiritual act of worship" (NIV).

While the New Testament does not seem to outline any order of service for public worship in large groups, the early Christian church, known as the Way, obviously followed some basic format. Perhaps Paul was alluding to this when he says, "But this I confess to you, that according to the Way which they call a sect, so I worship the God of my fathers, believing all things which are written in the Law and in the Prophets" (Acts 24:14).

The New Testament gives a number of hints as to what the Holy Spirit may have included in this public worship of "the Way." There would have been music and prayer (1 Corinthians 14:15); testimonies (1 Corinthians 14:26); the Lord's Supper (1 Corinthians 11:20-34); offerings (1 Corinthians 9:13, 14); the teaching or preaching of the Bible (2 Timothy 4:2). You will observe even from these few verses that I have quoted that it is very difficult to give many firm details of New Testament public worship. You may find some better examples than I have, showing the ingredients that were considered important.

Any worship that does not include a key segment for the exposition of the Scriptures will lack both Spirit and truth. When church members and the pastor are praying in the Word and allowing God to speak privately and in small groups, there will be a delight in hearing the Scripture in any congregational gathering. As a Spirit-filled, praying preacher proclaims the Word to people who have also been open to the Spirit there will be co-incidence between the Word proclaimed and the preparation for the Word in the hearts of the worshipers. Dennis Kinslaw, president of Asbury United Methodist College, calls this the law of the second witness. "A source of great comfort to a preacher of God's Word is what I call the 'law of the second witness.' It is an unfailing principle at work whenever the gospel is proclaimed: The preacher is never God's first witness in the hearer's life; God Himself is already there before the preacher. The Holy Spirit has been at work in every person's life in numerous ways long before a preacher speaks the Word of truth to him. So the preacher never approaches someone 'cold'; he can be sure that the Spirit of God is already at work in his hearer's life before the first word of his testimony is uttered or before the first point of his sermon is expounded." [10]

The Spirit-filled preacher will also always leave room, even during the delivery of the Bible message, for the Holy Spirit to direct his or her mind, to allow Scripture to meet the needs of those who listen. Those who hear the Word should be able to respond spontaneously to God and the congregation in worship, repentance, and praise.

Unfortunately, 1700 years of the dominance of the Roman emperor Constantine's model for public worship has clouded the ability of many modern Christians to see the New Testament's simplicity and beauty of Spirit-filled worship. In the time of Constantine the church became a building, rather than a group of Spirit-filled Christians. One or two star performers replaced the spontaneity that involves the participants in small group worship. Constantine's domination of Christianity has gone on long enough. It can and will be broken by the power of the Holy Spirit as people learn to worship in spirit and in truth.[11]

Let's go back to the spring morning tour with which we began this chapter. Actually it is a tour I made a number of times years ago searching for a place to worship God. Over the years I have periodically surveyed the public options that are available. Some denominations have divided on the basis of worship format. New church organizations have formed on the foundation of worship and ministry methodologies rather than theology.

Understanding and experiencing the filling of the Holy Spirit in my life in the past few years has given me a new perspective. While there will always be some personality, cultural, and ethnic differences in worship styles, the basic principles will apply. "It is we, not they, who have received the true circumcision, for we worship God by means of his Spirit and rejoice in our life in union with Christ Jesus. We do not put any trust in external ceremonies" (Philippians 3:3, TEV). "Jesus answered, 'Most assuredly, I say to you, unless one is born of water and the Spirit, he cannot enter the kingdom of God. That which is born of the flesh is flesh, and that which is born of the Spirit is spirit. Do not marvel that I said to you, "You must be born again" ' " (John 3:5-7). "And as Moses lifted up the serpent in the wilderness, even so must the Son of Man be lifted up" (verse 14). "But the hour is coming, and now is, when the true worshipers will worship the Father in spirit and truth; for the Father is seeking such to worship Him. God is Spirit, and those who worship Him must worship in spirit and truth" (John 4:23, 24).

One spring morning I walked into a building where 300 or 400 people were worshiping God. I didn't come to criticize, judge, or even observe, but to worship "Abba, Father." I was greeted warmly by friendly people and was able to pray quietly for a few moments before the service began. There were no star performers; we sang together songs old and new as a music leader asked the congregation for songs of experience that had been meaningful for them during the week. Then came a time of prayer, when the people circled into small groups of six or seven and ministered in prayer to each other's needs. They praised and blessed God together. When these small groups concluded, every worshiper sang reverently the Lord's Prayer in unison. Now it was time for three or four people to tell the whole congregation of ways the Lord had ministered to them or through them during the past week. Some were able to give words of exhortation, edification, and comfort the Holy Spirit had impressed them to share from His Word. It seemed in this congregation all members were considered to be ministers. The ministry focus of this church seemed to be on small group fellowships, in which all members could meet needs with spiritual gifts. Prayer targets locally and around the world were pinpointed. The pastor excitedly shared stories from his ministry with the small group leaders and led in a short, in-depth study of a portion of Scripture. Many of the small groups would be praying through that same Scripture portion during the next week. Almost before I realized what had happened, it was 12:30 p.m., the service was over, and as I walked out of the sanctuary I had the opportunity to deposit the tithes and offerings I had put aside during the week. People seemed to enjoy each other so much that it was after 1:00 p.m. when I left the building. There was no doubt where I would be worshiping next week.

Give the Holy Spirit a chance, and He will make worship more meaningful for you than ever before. As far as I know, the church I have just mentioned does not exist. It is my ideal, and I recognize there will most likely be some things you will want to change. I know, however, that now is the time to begin to worship in spirit and in truth, and God is still seeking worshipers like this.

SMALL GROUP STUDY
Chapter Eleven

Cohesive Contrasts

Is your small group getting together apart from your regular meeting time? Some very successful groups appoint a social leader who will organize outings, picnics, potlucks, family gatherings, events for Mother's Day, etc. If you haven't already, why not plan a social time together for your group. This will be a wonderful opportunity to deepen friendships and to minister to one another.

Here is a sharing question to begin: What has been the most beautiful worship experience that you have ever enjoyed? What made it special?

Concentrating on the Word
Study Text: John 4:10-24

In John 4:10-24 how many indications does Jesus give of the ministry of the Holy Spirit? List these in their order of importance.

Why do you think that Jesus would use water as a symbol of the Holy Spirit?

Describe how worship changed for you following your conversion or Spirit baptism.

Can you give some reasons Jesus would have been so definite about the three "musts" in John 3 and 4?

What good things have you seen become bad or dangerous when people have made them objects of worship?

In what ways could an "order of service" in public worship be good or bad?

Why is looking up in worship, above buildings, people, organizations, or rituals, most important?

When you discovered that Jesus is actually "seeking" for true worshipers, how did you feel?

What do you think is the difference between true worshipers and true worship? Which is more important?

Conversation With the Lord

Begin this time of prayer by looking up to God in praise—worshiping Him as a group together, praying and singing as the Holy Spirit leads. Pray also for needs in the group and intercede for other situations of special need outside the group. Continue to pray for the "empty chair," and conclude by holding hands around the circle as you share the Lord's Prayer together.

Committing the Word to Memory

This week, write out a verse from John 4:10-24 and share it with someone as soon as possible.

Chapter Twelve

Give the Holy Spirit a Chance
To Give You Visions and Dreams

Did a red flag go up when you read the title of this chapter? The idea of dreams and visions coming from God today makes many good Christians nervous and skeptical. If you don't believe that, just announce at a Christian gathering that you have received a vision, or say, "I would like to tell you about a dream God gave me last night." The reaction may make you wonder how God can possibly fulfill this promise of the Holy Spirit: "And it shall come to pass in the last days, says God, that I will pour out of My Spirit on all flesh; your sons and your daughters shall prophesy, your young men shall see visions, your old men shall dream dreams. And on My menservants and on My maidservants I will pour My Spirit in those days; and they shall prophesy" (Acts 2:17, 18). The context of this prophecy from Joel makes it very clear that now is the time for this special ministry of visions and dreams as the Holy Spirit is poured out in latter rain power.

In a Sydney suburb I was speaking to a large crowd on biblical archaeology when a women stood up and shouted in a foreign accent, "Why is the Bible so much against 'vimin'?" I tried to give a brief answer regarding the role of women in Scripture, but it was obviously unsatisfactory. Paula, as I later found her name to be, interrupted every meeting for a number of weeks with the same question, so that eventually I almost felt negative to "vimin" myself. One day Paula called my home and said that she wanted to tell me about a special dream she had received. I don't often enjoy listening to people's dreams, so it was with reluctance that I visited with her. She told me of a specific scene she had dreamed of, with details of hills and valleys and homes. In this vivid dream she noticed that there was a bright light shining on one special building. Paula was a well-educated woman who wrote regularly for the *Australian Catholic Weekly*. Her husband was a retired general who served as an official in the Yugoslavian Embassy. One day Paula called and informed me that she would be away for a few weeks in Los Angeles. I almost jumped for joy that I would have no more meeting interruptions. About a month later Paula called again and said with great excitement, "I am home again, and I have an amazing story to tell you." Her story was so amazing that I have never forgotten it.

In Los Angeles Paula had inquired about a TV personality whom she knew quite well and discovered that he was very sick in a Glendale hospital. As soon as she visited the hospital location, her forgotten dream came to mind, because she recognized that she was in the very place with the hills and valleys she had seen as she had slept a few months before. *Where is the building with the light on it?* she thought. Sure enough, the building was there exactly as she had seen it in her dream. On the front of the building were three words: "Voice of Prophecy." Paula entered the building and met the famous radio speaker H.M.S. Richards, whom the Holy Spirit used to study the Bible with her and lead her to accept Jesus as her Saviour and Lord. When I met Paula back in Sydney, she was a changed person; in fact, I had the opportunity soon after to baptize Paula in the name of the Father, Son, and Holy Spirit (Matthew 28:19, 20). On top of this, the church eventually elected her leader of "vimin's" ministries. Did God give Paula her dream? One thing we can be sure of—it certainly wasn't Satan. He would not have wanted Paula converted and baptized.

Sometimes the Bible uses dreams, visions, and prophecy interchangeably (e.g., Numbers 12:6) to describe a specific ministry of the Holy Spirit. The Holy Spirit enables people to see things that are normally out of the range of human vision. Ezekiel said, "The Spirit lifted me up between earth and heaven, and brought me in visions of God to Jerusalem" (Ezekiel 8:3). John described the source of his visions as being "in the Spirit" (Revelation 1:10; 4:2; 17:3). When Stephen was full of the Holy Spirit, he saw the glory of Jesus in heaven (Acts 7:55). Sometimes the Holy Spirit uses angels as the agents of God in visions and dreams. "Then he said to me, 'These words are faithful and true.' And the Lord God of the holy prophets sent His angel to show His servants the things which must shortly take place" (Revelation 22:6). This reminds me of an experience recorded by some Adventist pioneers. "We held a meeting in an upper room of a house in Oakland, while prayer was wont to be made. We knelt down to pray, and while we were praying, the Spirit of God like a tidal wave filled the room, and it seemed that an angel was pointing across the Rocky Mountains to churches in this [the eastern] part of America. Brother [John I.] Tay, who is now sleeping in Jesus, rose from his knees, his face as white as death, and said, 'I saw an angel pointing across the Rocky Mountains.' " [1]

Dreams were very directly used by God at the beginning of Jesus' ministry. The Wise Men were told in a dream not to return to Herod (Matthew 2:12). Joseph was told in a dream when to go to Egypt and when to return (verses 13, 19, 22). At the end of Jesus' ministry, Pilate's wife received a warning for her husband in a dream (Matthew 27:19). In view of this understanding that New Testament Christians had concerning the Holy Spirit's communication to human minds, they would not have considered Joel's words unusual at all. "And it shall come to pass afterward that I will pour out My Spirit on all flesh; your sons and your daughters shall prophesy, your old men shall dream dreams, your young men shall see visions; and also on My menservants and on My maidservants I will pour out My Spirit in those days" (Joel 2:28, 29).

Testing! Testing!

Because visions and dreams can be easily counterfeited and cannot be objectively studied like a loaf of bread or a bunch of wildflowers, it is necessary to test all claims to visions and dreams by the Word of God. "Do not restrain the Holy Spirit; do not despise inspired messages. Put all things to the test: keep what is good and avoid every kind of evil" (1 Thessalonians 5:19-21, TEV). The spiritual gift of discernment will also be valuable as the Holy Spirit uses people in the body of the household of faith to discern the source of a vision or dream. Was the dream or vision caused by drugs, indigestion, vivid imagination, or satanic forces, or was it the hand of God clearing the curtain of human limitation and enabling a man or woman, a child or youth, to see what only the Holy Spirit can reveal? It is important not to make important decisions on the basis of a dream or vision from one's own mind or from one other source, but remember this Bible principle, "This will be the third time I am coming to you. 'By the mouth of two or three witnesses every word shall be established' " (2 Corinthians 13:1).

Satanic forces always have and always will work with intense activity to counterfeit the prophecy of visions and dreams in Joel 2:28, 29. As time draws near for the second coming of Jesus, this counterfeit activity will greatly increase. "For false christs and false prophets will arise and show great signs and wonders, so as to deceive, if possible, even the elect" (Matthew 24:24). These false prophets will give convincing stories of visions they have received. "And the Lord said to me, 'The prophets prophesy lies in My name. I have not sent them, commanded them, nor spoken to them; they prophesy to you a false vision, divination, a worthless thing, and the deceit of their heart' " (Jeremiah 14:14).

The safeguard provided by the Holy Spirit's ministry in a small group is clearly seen as Paul speaks of the testimony of prophets in the church. "Two or three prophets should speak, and the others should weigh carefully what is said. And if a revelation comes to someone who is sitting down, the first speaker should stop. For you can all prophesy in turn so that everyone may be instructed and encouraged. The spirits of prophets are subject to the control of prophets. For God is not a God of disorder but of peace" (1 Corinthians 14:29-33, NIV). The Holy Spirit inspired the Scriptures, and it is through those Scriptures that He enables men and women to judge the claims of modern prophets and visionaries. "All Scripture is given by inspiration of God, and is profitable for doctrine, for reproof, for correction, for instruction in righteousness, that the man of God may be complete, thoroughly equipped for every good work" (2 Timothy 3:16, 17).

In the early history of the American colonies Jonathan Edwards was a dynamic revival preacher who later became the president of the college that is now Princeton University. Surrounding Edwards' preaching were many visions and Spirit manifestations, and these according to Edwards were to be judged by both the orchard and the fruit. "According to Edwards, neither a negative nor a positive judgement should be based on the manifestation alone, 'because the Scripture nowhere gives us any such rule.' How then is a manifestation to be judged? Partly by the orchard—the setting the manifestation occurs in, the kind of preaching the subject has listened to. And partly by the fruit—effects on the life, the on going testimony and subsequent character of the person in whom the manifestation is observed." [2] I am really impressed with Edwards' five tests of visions, dreams, and prophetic utterances. "Jonathan Edwards gave five signs that determine whether a work is or is not the work of the Holy Spirit. They form part of an exposition of 1 John 4, which according to Edwards must deal both with rules and fact—rules from the passage he was expounding, and facts from the careful observation of manifestations or the examination of reliable reports. All the rules (which are summarized as follows) have to do with the eventual effects of the work in the person's life, which should be—

"1. Giving more honor to the historic Jesus, the Son of God and the Saviour of the world;

"2. Opposing Satan's kingdom by discouraging sin, lust, and the world (the lust of the flesh, of the eyes, plus the pride of life);

"3. Holding Scripture in high esteem;

"4. Increasingly realizing that life is short, that there is another world, that they . . . must give an account of themselves to God, that they are sinful by nature and practice, and that they are helpless to overcome this without Christ; and

"5. Expressing love of Christ and for others, especially toward fellow Christians which should not be characterized by hostility.

"Edwards points out that you can be more certain that the work is not some sort of delusion when it is observed in many people, of many different types, in various places, than when it is only seen in a few places among a few people who know each other well. His point is not that the size of a movement matters. Instead, if the outbreaks occur in widely scattered areas, the chances of a sort of infection are minimized. He agrees that ideological fashions could account for beliefs, but the more widespread and varied it is, the more seriously it must be taken." [3]

Seeing as God Sees

There is an even more significant meaning of visions and dreams that I believe the Holy Spirit wants us to understand today. It is the ability to visualize the incredible potential of what God can do in lives, communities, societies, and countries through the outpouring of the Holy Spirit. When the 3,000 were converted on the day of Pentecost, Peter explained that this was a fulfillment of Joel's prophesy of dreams and visions. Christianity was not to remain a tiny sect of battered believers. It was to explode into a mighty movement that would sweep across the world, conquering in the name of Jesus. Now, in this understanding of visions and dreams I want to ask you, "Do you have a dream, a vision, of what the Holy Spirit can do in these end time days of earth's history?" Have you prayed until the Holy Spirit has been able to show you that His plans for mighty final movements of the everlasting gospel are far greater than you ever imagined?

"I feel good about the success of our church in this city," a man told me as I visited his church building.

"Why is that?" I asked.

"Just look at this," he replied with a tone of pride in his voice. "Our church building is full."

"Praise God," I said. "But how many people does your church hold?"

"About 150."

"What is the population of this city?"

"About 57,000."

"Brother," I concluded in surprise, "God may have enough people in this town to fill 100 of these churches; it may be possible to open 1,000 households of faith." He looked at me in amazement and shook his head as if he had met a wild-eyed fanatic.

A church of almost 1,000 members in an Oregon city of 17,000 was looking forward to a new pastor, who would replace the one who had recently moved away. A church member called me and requested a pastor who was dedicated to leading the church family in soul winning, and helping new members grow strongly in the church body. I said, "Brother, one person in 17 in your city is now a member of your church."

His reply was "What about the other 16?"

That is the vision that God will use in the finishing of His work.

Special faith is a gift of the Holy Spirit (1 Corinthians 12:9). The Bible definition of faith describes the type of vision that the Holy Spirit gives so that people can see beyond the present circumstances to the reality of all that is possible in life and geographical areas as the Holy Spirit is poured out. "Now faith is the assurance of things hoped for, the conviction of things not seen" (Hebrews 11:1, RSV).

Why is there so little vision today? Vision clinics offering eyeglasses and contact lenses are a common sight in most cities, but they cannot cure spiritual blindness. Spiritual vision is dependent on spiritual life and light. Spiritual darkness has its source in the "rulers of the darkness of this age" (Ephesians 6:12). Notice what they do. "But even if our gospel is veiled, it is veiled to those who are perishing, whose minds the god of this age has blinded, who do not believe, lest the light of the gospel of the glory of Christ, who is the image of God, should shine on them" (2 Corinthians 4:3, 4).

For these blinded minds to be opened, three things must happen. First, the life of Jesus must be revealed in our mortal body (verse 11). This resurrection life, which creates living eyes, is the work of the Holy Spirit. "But if the Spirit of Him who raised Jesus from the dead dwells in you, He who raised Christ from the dead will also give life to your mortal bodies through His Spirit who dwells in you" (Romans 8:11). Second, the eyes must be anointed with the eyesalve of the Holy Spirit (Revelation 3:18). Third, there must be light in which the eyes can see (2 Corinthians 4:6).

When Daniel was filled with the Spirit he had light, understanding, and wisdom (Daniel 5:11, 14). With life, open eyes, and light, born-again, Spirit-filled Christians, transformed by the Holy Spirit into the image of Jesus (1 Corinthians 3:18), can have visions and dreams of the mighty final work of the gospel reaching every part of the world in fulfillment of the prophecy of Revelation 14:6-12.

John Dawson, director of Youth With a Mission, has a vision that is vital in today's world. "Over one half of the world's population lives in urban centers. In developed nations like the United States, the percentage of urban dwellers is much higher. In California, for example, 90 percent of the population lives in cities.... By the year 2010, three out of every four people on earth will live in cities, which means cities must become the prime target of the missionary....

"A century ago London was the world's only super-city, but now 42 cities of the world have a population surpassing 4 million. Most of these cities are either Asian or Islamic. When we add those that are Marxist, we get some idea of the challenge Christians face in world evangelization. . . . We must have a new vision of Christian service; missions has always had a romance in it, with visions of primitive tribes and palm trees in the setting sun. We need to plant another dream in the hearts of our young pioneers. We must fill their minds with a more realistic and compelling picture. Our new vision of Christian missions must focus on cities. If we want to bring nations to Christ, we must win their cities." [4]

Life, open eyes, and light will mean that God's people will be able to see and hear all the communication of the Holy Spirit that will be profitable for the Gospel to light the earth with God's glory. Paul and his missionary team were very much aware of the leading of the Holy Spirit both verbally and visually. "Now when they had gone through Phrygia and the region of Galatia, they were forbidden by the Holy Spirit to preach the word in Asia. After they had come to Mysia, they tried to go into Bithynia, but the Spirit did not permit them. So passing by Mysia, they came down to Troas. And a vision appeared to Paul in the night. A man of Macedonia stood and pleaded with him, saying, 'Come over to Macedonia and help us.' Now after he had seen the vision, immediately we sought to go to Macedonia, concluding that the Lord had called us to preach the gospel to them" (Acts 16:6-10). Do you have a vision today for your neighborhood, community, state, or country? Pray about it. Ask God to help you see the potential as He sees it. As with Paul, perhaps the Holy Spirit will say no about some areas of service you have been planning, while opening up others of vastly greater potential.

A number of years ago I journeyed around the world visiting many countries, meeting church leaders and speaking to congregations and small groups of Christians. I had flown into Tehran and planned to fly on to Iraq in just a few days. At the airport in Iran I discovered to my shock that I did not have a visa to visit Iraq. The officials informed me that I could not leave Iran without that visa and that it might take many weeks to obtain. I prayed earnestly, asking the Lord whether this was the Holy Spirit telling me not to go to Iraq at that time. Was He closing the door to that country, as He did to Asia and Bithynia in the time of Paul? I prayed for a vision, understanding, and wisdom. "Lord, if only I could hear Your voice or see a person calling me as Paul did, what a help it would be." You have probably had moments when you have felt that way also. Iranian church leaders told me that it would be very difficult to get the visa. They had friends who had waited six months. We prayed about it, and as I spoke to a large congregation I asked if they would pray about it also. The next morning I arrived at the Iraqi Embassy only to find a line almost a block long waiting for visa information. After standing in line for about two hours, I entered the visa office and began to speak to the official behind the desk. His only English vocabulary seemed to be limited to "Get out and don't come back." I suspected that he had thought I was an American, so I joined the line again, this time hoping to tell him I had a New Zealand passport. After another two hours I reached the visa office, only to be forcibly removed by armed soldiers. I joined the line for the third time, praying now more earnestly than ever before to hear the direction of the Holy Spirit. After another two hours I was within 10 feet of the door of the visa office when I heard the Holy Spirit say "Five-Day Plan." Just three words. The Holy Spirit instructed me to speak these three words as I entered the visa office. "Five-Day Plan." I was puzzled; what did this have to do with my situation? As soon as I walked through the door I obediently yelled out, "Five-Day Plan."

The official looked at me in a moment of stunned silence. Then he said, "Five-Day Plan to Stop Smoking?"

I replied quickly, "In Australia I teach the Five-Day Plan to help people to stop smoking."

I could not believe what I heard in reply. "The Five-Day Plan is very good; it has helped many of my people in Iraq. Your church is the only one that helps our people. Please come with me into the back office." We walked back as he talked to me about health in his country. Then he asked me for my passport and stamped it with the visa. Praise God!

When I arrived back at the church headquarters, the excitement was great. "This is a miracle; we have never seen anything like this," a pastor exclaimed as he praised God.

Seeing in the Night

God's Holy Spirit vision enables Christians to see even in the darkness of difficult circumstances. Paul understood nocturnal vision. Like the New Zealand kiwi, Paul could see when there was almost no light. "We are hard pressed on every side, yet not crushed; we are perplexed, but not in despair; persecuted, but not forsaken; struck down, but not destroyed" (2 Corinthians 4:8, 9). This type of sight is the work of the Holy Spirit, who gives Christians miraculous night vision glasses. "And you became followers of us and of the Lord, having received the word in much affliction, with joy of the Holy Spirit" (1 Thessalonians 1:6).

In the darkness of racial discrimination Dr. Martin Luther King, Jr., had this type of nocturnal vision. In Washington, D.C., he moved the crowds with his August 28, 1963, "I Have a Dream" speech. In 1964 he was awarded the Nobel Peace Prize. His dream made a difference for millions of people.

To Give You Visions and Dreams

God gave Peter a vision that broke down the barriers between Jews and Gentiles in the early Christian church. Peter had seen an upside-down parachute containing wild beasts and strange birds raised and lowered three times. "While Peter thought about the vision the Spirit said to him, 'Behold, three men are seeking you. Arise therefore, go down and go with them, doubting nothing; for I have sent them' " (Acts 10:19, 20). The darkness of racial and religious prejudice was broken by the power of the Holy Spirit.

A few months ago I was preaching in a beautiful church in the London suburb of Brixton. Barbara and I had received a warm welcome from these enthusiastic Christians, and I had announced that student missionary Lonna Chase would sing at the close of my sermon. Lonna had spent about nine months in Brixton teaching more than 40 energetic West Indian children in a classroom beside the sanctuary. It was not an easy assignment, but Lonna had learned from her mother how to pray and have a personal relationship with God. The people in that Brixton church loved Lonna. She had taught their children many wonderful songs, but today she would sing for them a song that for me has become a favorite. "After the song," I informed the people, "please come forward if you hear God's Spirit speaking to you and leading you to make a new surrender to Jesus, to be used by Him to share His love in the darkness of this world." Listen to the words that Lonna sang at the conclusion of my sermon in Brixton.

>Lily of the Valley, let Your sweet aroma fill my life.
>Rose of Sharon, show me
>How to grow in beauty in God's sight.
>Fairest of ten thousand,
>Make me a reflection of Your light.
>Daystar, shine down on me.
>Let Your love shine through me in the night.
>
>Chorus:
>Lead me, Lord, I'll follow,
>Anywhere You open up the door.
>Let me know Your wisdom.
>Show me things I've never seen before.
>Lord, I want to be a witness.
>You can take what's wrong and make it right.
>Daystar, shine down on me.
>Let Your love shine through me in the night.

> Lord, I see a world that's dying,
> Wounded by the master of deceit,
> Groping in the darkness,
> Haunted by the years of past defeat.
> Then I see You standing near me,
> Shining with compassion in Your eyes.
> Daystar, shine down on me.
> Let Your love shine through me in the night.[5]

Even before the song was completed, people began to walk to the front of the sanctuary. The Holy Spirit moved so powerfully that many cried and praised God. There were great victories that day as the Holy Spirit gave the nocturnal vision that enabled people to see God's love shining in the night.

Give the Holy Spirit a chance to give you nocturnal vision now—vision that will enable you to see the great realities beyond trouble, tragedy, and the trauma of this age. Nocturnal vision will help you see the final rapid movements of the gospel as it is empowered by the Holy Spirit right in the community where you live. Don't be satisfied with mediocrity. Allow God to use you to do something miraculous for His kingdom.

Seeing the Unseen

"For our light affliction, which is but for a moment, is working for us a far more exceeding and eternal weight of glory, while we do not look at the things which are seen, but at the things which are not seen. For the things which are seen are temporary, but the things which are not seen are eternal" (2 Corinthians 4:17, 18). People of visions and dreams see what is humanly unseen. You could call this notional vision. It is beyond the visible; it exists in the mind; it is, as Paul says, seeing the unseen. Notional vision sees the Bible not as a volume of paper and ink, but as the power Word the Holy Spirit uses to change lives. Notional vision sees people not as worthless masses but as individuals who can be saved eternally as the Holy Spirit leads them to the cross of Jesus. Notional vision sees closed nations open to the gospel and filled with the Holy Spirit.

During the time of the Soviet Union I visited Russia and had the opportunity to meet openly and secretly with church leaders. On the day before I was to leave the Soviet Union, one leader gave me a small piece of paper on which was his name, address, and other important information that he said must not fall into the hands of the KGB. I was carrying a small zippered Bible with me, so I carefully placed the paper in the Bible, thinking that it would be safe.

The next day when I boarded the train for Finland I was surprised to find myself placed, in an otherwise empty railroad car, in a small sleeping compartment with three women. After a lot of protest the guard finally moved me to another compartment, where I was joined by a young man who was a university student. About 11:00 p.m. we reached the Finnish border, and I discovered to my amazement that some KGB officers had boarded the train and wanted to arrest me. I refused to be arrested, so some armed guards who were brought on tried to push me off the train. Once again I clung to the bunk in my compartment and still refused to leave. Now the search began; they threw everything out of my suitcase, undressed me, and checked all my clothes and possessions. Finally they came to the Bible. I watched and prayed as they opened the zipper and shook apart each page many times over. Finding nothing, the KGB reluctantly let me go and allowed the train to move on. It was now 1:00 a.m. and broad daylight in the Land of the Midnight Sun. Soon we were in the freedom of Finland.

A few hours later, after recovering from my two-hour ordeal, I remembered the piece of paper that had strangely disappeared from my Bible. Where was it? What had happened to it? If it had been found, the Christian leader would have been sent to a prison camp. Reverently I opened the Bible, and there was the piece of paper sitting loosely, just as I had placed it between the first two pages. I praised God for this incredible miracle, but at the same time wondered about the Soviet Union. Would it ever be open to the gospel?

In Finland, as I spoke at a beautiful youth camp, we prayed for Russia. "Lord, give us faith to believe that one day the iron curtain will be opened to the gospel." We saw the possibility of thousands converted and baptized in a day in this great country. It was a vision that seemed impossible. It was notional vision, seeing the unseen.

With the collapse of Communism and the Soviet Union at the beginning of the last decade of the twentieth century, the vision for Russia became a reality. Huge evangelistic series across the country have brought the knowledge of Jesus to millions of spiritually hungry souls. This year Australian evangelist John Carter held the largest baptism the country had ever seen for more than 1,000 years. "We've often looked forward to the latter rain of the Holy Spirit," Carter said in a recent interview. "I believe it is happening in Russia."

For 42 nights the Palace of Sport in Gorki (Nizhni Novgorod) was filled to capacity. So many people came out for the opening weekend meetings that five sessions were held, each filling completely the auditorium with more than 6,500 people. One 70-year-old man found an open window and started crawling in when police stopped him and told him to wait for a later session. "I've been waiting 70 years to hear about Jesus," he replied. "Don't make me wait any longer."

In total, almost 6,000 people accepted Jesus and signed a covenant to be baptized in that one series of meetings in this formerly closed city. Another evangelist, Mark Finley, had the opportunity to preach for 10 nights to crowds of more than 12,000 people in two sessions right in the Kremlin Hall of Congress.

Give the Holy Spirit a chance to fulfill Joel's prophecy where you live today. "And it shall come to pass afterward that I will pour out My Spirit on all flesh; Your sons and your daughters shall prophesy, your old men shall dream dreams, your young men shall see visions; and also on My menservants and on My maidservants I will pour out My Spirit in those days. And I will show wonders in the heavens and in the earth: blood and fire and pillars of smoke. The sun shall be turned into darkness, and the moon into blood, before the coming of the great and terrible day of the Lord. And it shall come to pass that whoever calls on the name of the Lord shall be saved. For in Mount Zion and in Jerusalem there shall be deliverance, as the Lord has said, among the remnant whom the Lord calls" (Joel 2:28-32). God has a vision and a dream for you. He wants you to see the world as He sees it, and when you do, you will be amazed at the Holy Spirit's plans for the final work of the everlasting gospel.

SMALL GROUP STUDY
Chapter Twelve

Cohesive Contrasts

We have discussed three of the four stages of small group development, namely, honeymoon, disillusionment, and synthesis. Now, as we near the end of this series of study guides, we need to talk about the fourth stage, which is often called culmination. Will the group break up at the end of this series, or will it move on to another study course and recovenant to stay together for another extended period of time? Pray about this. Discuss various possibilities. Perhaps there are other study guides that can be used or the group may decide to pray together through a book of the Bible, discussing the light that the Holy Spirit brings from each verse.

Here is a sharing question to begin your group today. When you were attending school, what did you visualize as your future destiny as far as occupation, family, and travel were concerned? How has it worked out?

Concentrating on the Word
Study Text: Acts 2:14-21

How many evidences do you find in Acts 2:14-21 that this prophecy of the Holy Spirit will be fulfilled again before the return of Jesus?

_____
_____

If a friend rushed into your small group and said, "I have had a vision from God," how would you react?

I don't believe it _____ Let me listen to this _____
Does God have a message for me? _____
I'd better leave now _____
Who said this is from God? _____ Other _____

What are some of the ways a Spirit-filled small group can be a safeguard against counterfeit dreams and visions?

_____
_____

How would you apply the two or three witnesses principle (2 Corinthians 13:1) to understanding God's will in a certain situation in relationship to visions and dreams?

Why do you think God would increase the frequency of dreams, visions, and prophecy just before Jesus' second coming?

List some ways the Bible, rather than dreams, should always be the final authority for truth—for example, about the return of Jesus.

What are some of the visions and dreams you have for God's work in your community and nation?

Are you willing to have the Holy Spirit poured out on you now, even if it means a special ministry for you?

Conversation With the Lord

Praise the Lord for the promises of His Spirit and evidence you see of this in your life and group. Pray for true spiritual vision and intercede for any situations of spiritual darkness the Lord brings to your attention. Pray about the transition into a new group after next week's meeting and close as usual with the Lord's Prayer.

Committing the Word to Memory

This week, write out a verse from Acts 2:14-21 and share it with someone as soon as possible.

Chapter Thirteen
▼

Give the Holy Spirit a Chance
To Bring the Great Revival

For some Christians "revival" is an exciting word. "We are planning revival meetings for our church," a pastor informed me enthusiastically. "We will be singing, praying, and preaching, and we are going to see the Holy Spirit work in a mighty way. There will be a lot of conversions as sinners come to Jesus. Our church members can't wait for this to happen."

Other Christians are nervous about revival. They are comfortable with powerful movements of the Holy Spirit in the past or in distant lands, but when it comes close to home, revival seems as dangerous as a box of matches beside an open can of gasoline. They fear that revival will bring out strong emotions and divide congregations. Revival brings radical opposition to sin in society, churches, and lives, and usually this is not popular.

Psychiatrist John White, having surveyed some of the positive and negative factors in revivals since the time of the Reformation, says, "What we have called revival during the last 300 years represents an unusual work of the Holy Spirit with the following characteristics.

"1. Converted and unconverted men, women, and children, stunned by a vision both of God's holiness and His mercy, are awakened in large numbers of repentance, faith, and worship.

"2. God's power is manifest in human lives in ways no psychological or sociological laws can explain adequately.

"3. The community as a whole becomes aware of what is happening, many perceiving the movement as a threat to existing institutions.

"4. Some men and women exhibit unusual physical and emotional behaviors. These create controversy. They can be an offense to opponents of the revival and a snare to its supporters.

"5. Some revived Christians behave in an immature and impulsive way, while others fall into sin. In this way the revival appears to be a strange blend of godly and ungodly influences, of displays of divine power and of human weakness.

"Wherever the revival is extensive enough to have national impact, sociopolitical reform follows over the succeeding century. In this way Christ's kingdom begins to be exercised over the evils of oppression and injustice."[1] After reading White's summary, are you still interested in praying for a revival? If you give the Holy Spirit a chance He will shatter some of the myths about revival and help you to be part of the great movement that will precede the second coming of Jesus.

The Spirit of Revival

Like a number of other common Christian words, "revival" is not found in the Bible, although "revive" or "revived" appear two times in the New Testament and 12 times in the Old. These words mean to live again; to restore to life; to be whole. As we have studied a number of times, this resurrection life comes only through the power of the Holy Spirit as He applies to each born-again Christian the benefits of the cross. "I will put My Spirit in you, and you shall live" (Ezekiel 37:14). "But if the Spirit of Him who raised Jesus from the dead dwells in you, He who raised Christ from the dead will also give life to your mortal bodies through His Spirit who dwells in you" (Romans 8:11). "And you He made alive, who were dead in trespasses and sins. . . . But God, . . . even when we were dead in trespasses, made us alive together with Christ (by grace you have been saved)" (Ephesians 2:1-5). "For Christ also suffered once for sins, the just for the unjust, that He might bring us to God, being put to death in the flesh but made alive by the Spirit" (1 Peter 3:18).

It is impossible to have the Spirit and not have life. The Holy Spirit doesn't bring revival; He is revival. He is the Spirit of life in Jesus Christ (Romans 8:2).

"Pastor, I think the Holy Spirit is dormant in our congregation," a young man informed me at a Holy Spirit seminar in the United Kingdom.

It was an overcast, showery day, so I asked him, "Is the sun dormant?"

"No," he replied, "that is impossible. The sun is always shining, but may not always be seen because of clouds or an object that causes shade or darkness."

"Neither is the Holy Spirit ever dormant," I explained. "He is life. He is always alive."

As Christians we may allow some cherished sin or material god to shade us from the Spirit. We may even be spiritually asleep. This is why it is often necessary to become involved in a time of special spiritual emphasis that can allow the Spirit to be revealed again in all His power, exalting the glory of Jesus.

"Therefore He says: 'Awake, you who sleep, arise from the dead, and

Christ will give you light' " (Ephesians 5:14). On the basis of Ephesians 5:14 and other similar verses, revivals have sometimes been called "awakenings," especially in the dynamic history of Christianity in the United States of America.

One spring we planted some tomatoes alongside our house, making sure the soil was good and they were well watered. In the past we'd planted tomatoes in other locations and enjoyed large crops, but this year there was very little fruit. "The problem is not enough sun," an expert told us. There was a lot of light, but the plants spent most of the day in the shade.

A revival takes place when we allow the Holy Spirit to move Christians out of the shade and into the full sunshine of Jesus' love. Then there is an awakening of each life by the full power of God so that there follows rapid growth and abundant fruit and gifts of the Spirit. The result of this revival will always be powerful evangelistic outreach with the everlasting gospel of Jesus.

Revival in Action

We could discuss many theories of revival, but I want to let the Holy Spirit show you one in action. From this example you will see that we have laid the foundation for revival in the earlier chapters of this book, building also on *How to Be Filled With the Holy Spirit and Know It*. As we look at this example of revival and discover the seven revival principles, pray that you may experience personal revival and also be an agent for revival in your church and community.

The book of Nehemiah was written about events that happened to the Jewish people who returned to their land after 70 years of exile in Babylon. In the midst of a great work of rebuilding their city the Holy Spirit led the people into a spiritual revival. Now, this event, which happened more than 400 years before the time of Jesus, may seem very distant today, but you will find here in this story basic principles of revival that apply right now.

"Now all the people gathered together as one man in the open square that was in front of the Water Gate; and they told Ezra the scribe to bring the Book of the Law of Moses, which the Lord had commanded Israel" (Nehemiah 8:1). This was the time for the Feast of Trumpets, and it seems that it was the Holy Spirit who drew the people together from all of the cities of Israel early in the morning, as there is no historical record of any gathering call. This was the civil new year's day, and not only did the men assemble, but the women and young people were present (verse 3). Even children and youth were affected by this revival (Nehemiah 10:28). In fact, as Peter said at Pentecost, the gift of the Holy Spirit is available to people of all ages (Act 2:17, 18, 39).

The crowd assembled in front of the Water Gate, and it is significant that Jesus, more than 400 years later, in the same city would use water as a symbol of the Holy Spirit. "He who believes in Me, as the Scripture has said, out of his heart will flow rivers of living water. But this He spoke concerning the Spirit, whom those believing in Him would receive; for the Holy Spirit was not yet given, because Jesus was not yet glorified" (John 7:38, 39).

The people who gathered in Nehemiah 8 came with the urgent request to hear the Word of God. The book of the Law of Moses (the first five books of the Bible) not only contained the Ten Commandments, which defines sin, but also many vivid details of the sanctuary and its services, which pointed forward to Jesus and His sacrifice for the sins of the world.

Here is **revival principle 1: As you have personal fellowship with the Holy Spirit, pray that He will lead you to a gathering where there is an anointing of the Spirit on the Word of God.** As we noticed in chapter four of this book there is a very intimate connection between the Spirit and the Word. In all true revivals the Holy Spirit exalts the Word. "And my speech and my preaching were not with persuasive words of human wisdom, but in demonstration of the Spirit and of power. . . . These things we also speak, not in words which man's wisdom teaches but which the Holy Spirit teaches, comparing spiritual things with spiritual" (1 Corinthians 2:4-13).

Philipp Spener was a German pastor who lived about 100 years after the time of the European Reformation. God used him in a mighty way to bring revival in the reformed churches that had moved from the bright sunlight of Jesus' love and truth into the shade of lifeless traditionalism. He led congregations into small groups for pastoral care with special emphasis on Bible study fellowship. As these groups prayed in the Word they asked: 1. What does it teach? 2. What does it command? 3. What promise or hope is given?[2] It was this emphasis on the Spirit and the Word that led to the great Moravian revival under the leadership of Count Zinzendorf. This revival and the 100-year prayer meeting that followed laid the foundation for the mighty Wesleyan revival, the beginning of extensive missionary activities, and the great awakenings across North America. Here is the basis for revival today. "In Spener's view, the best hope for renewal of the church was the recovery of the Word of God in the context of a gathered expression of the spiritual priesthood. Not only preaching but also 'reading, meditating, and discussion' (see Psalm 1:2) of the Word 'must be the chief means for reforming something. . . . The Word of God remains the seed from which all that is good in us must grow.' Through eager and diligent searching of the Scriptures together, believers 'will become altogether different people.' "[3]

People often say to me, "We are waiting for revival; we wish it would happen now. When will the latter rain of the Holy Spirit take place?" My answer is that revival is happening now in many parts of the planet as the Bible is proclaimed in the power of the Holy Spirit. Thousands are being converted, lives of Christians are being transformed, there are great victories for God. That is revival. What more can we want, except to see it happening where we live as the revival principles are applied?

The Roseville, California, Adventist Church is an exciting example of Holy Spirit revival today. "Powerful good news" was the theme of their fourth 40-hour revival weekend of prayer and fasting. Pastor Ron Clouzet reports that more than 800 people from a number of denominations participated in the revival meetings, which included intercessory prayer, Bible study, and fasting, as well as congregational singing and praise. Ten days prior to the weekend 25 people came together from 6:00 to 8:00 a.m. to pray especially for the weekend of prayer and fasting.

"What has been the result of these Spirit-filled revival weekends?" I asked Ron a few days ago as he spoke to me on the phone.

"Not only has our church attendance risen from 100 to an average of 550 in three years, but the Word of God has had a life-transforming effect on many people as great victories have taken place" was Ron's enthusiastic reply. Many of the members of the Roseville congregation are involved in small group ministries, and the evangelistic emphasis of this church exalting Jesus gives evidence that this is a genuine Holy Spirit revival.

In Nehemiah 8 the Holy Spirit brings us to the next step in revival. "And Ezra opened the book in the sight of all the people, for he was standing above all the people; and when he opened it, all the people stood up. And Ezra blessed the Lord, the great God. Then all the people answered, 'Amen, Amen!' while lifting up their hands. And they bowed their heads and worshiped the Lord with their faces to the ground" (verses 5, 6). What a remarkable picture this is of worship and praise in the Holy Spirit.

The psalmist says, "I will bless the Lord at all times; His praise shall continually be in my mouth" (Psalm 34:1). Baptist preacher Charles Spurgeon said in London, "When we bless God for mercies, we prolong them. When we bless Him for miseries, we usually end them."

"Bless the Lord, O my soul; and all that is within me, bless His holy name!" (Psalm 103:1). Often this blessing of God involves singing songs of praise. "Sing to the Lord, bless His name; proclaim the good news of His salvation from day to day" (Psalm 96:2). The responses of the people indicated their involvement in this worship. "Blessed be the Lord God of Israel from everlasting to everlasting! And let all the people say, 'Amen!' Praise the Lord!" (Psalm 106:48). The repetition of "Amen" in Nehemiah 8:6 indicates intensity, earnestness, and the fact that this was just not a brief moment of prayer but occupied a significant portion of the six-hour revival meeting.

It is the anointing of the Holy Spirit that replaces the spirit of heaviness with the garment of praise (Isaiah 61:3). When Jesus was rejoicing in the Spirit, He praised the Father (Luke 10:21). As the church in Antioch ministered to the Lord, they were able to discern the communication of the Holy Spirit (Acts 13:2). So it was in the time of Nehemiah. Praise, worship, and ministering to God prepared the way for the Holy Spirit to speak through the Word.

Revival principle 2: Earnest personal and public prayer and worship always accompany revival. The Welsh revival at the beginning of the twentieth century is often referred to as a power-packed example of the great work of the Holy Spirit. God used a young man, Evan Roberts, as His instrument to clear away the shade of external lifeless religion and allow the sun to shine into the lives of hundreds of thousands of people. Dr. Oswald J. Smith in his book *The Revival We Need* quotes from Evan Roberts as he shares his prayer experience. " 'I said to myself: "I will have the Spirit" and through every kind of weather and in spite of all difficulties, I went to the meetings. Many times, on seeing other boys with the boats on the tide, I was tempted to turn back and join them. But no. I said to myself: "Remember your resolve," and on I went. I went faithfully to the meetings for prayer throughout the 10 or 11 years I prayed for a revival. It was the Spirit who moved me thus to think.' " [4]

Dr. John White tells what happened to Roberts. "In 1904 he underwent a profound anointing of the Holy Spirit in Blaenannerch. He went back to his home in Loughor and began to hold prayer meetings which in a matter of days drew larger and larger crowds as revival swept the whole region. After one such meeting, Roberts wrote, 'After many had prayed, I felt some living energy or force entering my bosom, restraining my breath, my legs trembling terribly: this living energy increased and increased as one after another prayed. Feeling strongly and deeply warmed, I burst forth in prayer.' " [5]

The result of this last great revival in Britain was amazing. "The revival was to have a global embrace. In some strange providence of God the little land of Wales was chosen as a place to play a vital role in the world-revival of Pentecost already touching 40 times more people than the entire Welsh population."⁶

There can be no doubt that revival can be expected only in answer to prayer. The experiences of the disciples before the great revivals in Acts 2 and 4 show the Holy Spirit leading His people into prayer and then filling them for a mighty evangelistic thrust as the Word of God is proclaimed and Jesus is exalted.

A group of pastors and their spouses met to study the Word and pray for a few days. As the Holy Spirit fellowship began, there were beautiful songs of worship intermingled with many heartfelt prayers and tears of repentance. For a while we wrestled with mental images of the hectic world we had temporarily left behind. But as the Holy Spirit penetrated the darkness, Jesus' love began to shine, and we were able to bless God and worship Him in Spirit and truth. Revival came, and we were awakened and renewed. Two years later I met some of the pastors who were present at that little chapel. "We want to praise God for the way the Holy Spirit has led in our ministry since that time" was their unanimous testimony. Revival had brought new life to ministries in a remarkable way.

In Nehemiah 8, prayer and praise were followed by the study of the Word. "So they read distinctly from the book, in the Law of God; and they gave the sense, and helped them to understand the reading" (verse 8). Not only was the Word of God read, but it was explained; its meaning was exposed; the listeners understood how to apply it to their own lives and situations. The books of Moses were a thousand years old, but they were very relevant to the crowd near the Water Gate that day in old Jerusalem. It is through the Word of God that the Holy Spirit leads us into all truth, and it is through the Word of truth that the Holy Spirit exalts Jesus (John 16:13, 14). Revival preaching and teaching allows the Holy Spirit to magnify the cross of Jesus, showing the gospel in all its beauty and power. "This is He who came by water and blood—Jesus Christ; not only by water, but by water and blood. And it is the Spirit who bears witness, because the Spirit is truth. . . . And this is the testimony: that God has given us eternal life, and this life is in His Son. He who has the Son has life; he who does not have the Son of God does not have life" (1 John 5:6-12). As Ezra and his helpers read from the books of Moses, the listeners learned of the significance of the sacrificial lambs. When Jesus came to be baptized more than 400 years later, John could say, "Behold! The Lamb of God who takes away the sin of the world!" (John 1:29).

Revival principle 3: From the Bible the meaning of the cross and full significance of the gospel is proclaimed and explained. As Paul says: "For I am not ashamed of the gospel of Christ, for it is the power of God to salvation for everyone who believes, for the Jew first and also for the Greek" (Romans 1:16). "For our gospel did not come to you in word only, but also in power, and in the Holy Spirit and in much assurance, as you know what kind of men we were among you for your sake" (1 Thessalonians 1:5).

Grant came to our revival series expecting either a lot of emotionalism or hellfire preaching. During the meetings Kathy sang a number of beautiful songs about the cross, including "Via Dolarosa," which traces the terrible path of suffering that took Jesus to Calvary. My revival sermons exalted Jesus and told how He had taken the cross, a symbol of horror and tragedy, and changed it into a sign of triumph, so that we can say with Paul, "But God forbid that I should glory except in the cross of our Lord Jesus Christ" (Galatians 6:14). Grant saw the meaning of the cross as he had never seen it before, and as the call was made to surrender fully to Jesus, he came forward with a number of others to make a new commitment to God. There was rejoicing that day in Grant's family, and great happiness as he was later baptized. Once again the gospel had been preached by the Holy Spirit (1 Peter 1:12), and the fruit of the Spirit was revealed in "all goodness, righteousness, and truth" (Ephesians 5:9).

The teaching and preaching of the Word in Nehemiah 8 brought a deep conviction of sin. "And Nehemiah, who was the governor, Ezra the priest and scribe, and the Levities who taught the people said to all the people, 'This day is holy to the Lord your God; do not mourn nor weep.' For all the people wept, when they heard the words of the Law" (verse 9). The Holy Spirit always convicts of sin, righteousness, and judgment (John 16:8). By the law comes the knowledge of sin (Romans 3:20), and the law is our tutor that leads us to Jesus (Galatians 3:24). Godly sorrow for sin leads to repentance and is always important for salvation (2 Corinthians 7:10).

Revival principle 4: In the Spirit-filled atmosphere of a revival meeting the sunlight of Jesus' love will show sin as hateful and evil. Participants will experience a deep desire to confess to God and turn away from all that is unlike Jesus. On the day of Pentecost the people who heard Peter's Spirit-empowered sermon were deeply moved. "Now when they heard this, they were cut to the heart, and said to Peter and the rest of the apostles, 'Men and brethren, what shall we do?'" (Acts 2:37). Jonathan Edwards said, "The characteristic of revival is that a profound consciousness of sin is produced in many persons at the same time by the awareness of God." [7]

At the conclusion of a camp meeting sermon I was led by the Holy Spirit to ask if the conviction of sin and the need for repentance were stirring in the hearts of any of the audience. I gave the invitation first for pastors to come forward if they recognized their need of deep repentance. Twenty or 30 came forward, and their prayers were earnest and sincere. Soon they were joined by hundreds of other people and there was much evidence of genuine revival. Later a young man came to me and spoke in amazement. "I can't believe that you gave that invitation to pastors. I was sure that none of them would admit a need of repentance. When they came forward, it had a profound effect on me, and I knew that God wanted me to surrender also. I came forward and found myself standing beside a pastor I had treated in a very negative way. When I asked him to forgive me, we hugged each other and cried. Praise God."

Even as the speaker I needed to come to God in true repentance that night. And I recognize repentance deepening in my life as the Holy Spirit continues to show me what I am really like in contrast to Jesus.

It is the conviction of sin that leads people to reformation and changed lives, but only revival can make reformation more than empty resolutions or vain hopes. This definition of terms helped clarify this for me: "A revival and a reformation must take place, under the ministration of the Holy Spirit. Revival and reformation are two different things. Revival signifies a renewal of spiritual life, a quickening of the powers of mind and heart, a resurrection from spiritual death. Reformation signifies a reorganization, a change in ideas and theories, habits and practices. Reformation will not bring forth the good fruit of righteousness unless it is connected with the revival of the Spirit. Revival and reformation are to do their appointed work, and in doing this work they must blend." [8]

Remaining in sorrow after accepting the forgiveness and love of Jesus denies God's great grace and does not represent God's plan for those who have been revived by the power of the Holy Spirit. "Then he said to them, 'Go your way, eat the fat, drink the sweet, and send portions to those for whom nothing is prepared; for this day is holy to our Lord. Do not sorrow, for the joy of the Lord is your strength.' So the Levites quieted all the people, saying, 'Be still, for the day is holy; do not be grieved.' And all the people went their way to eat and drink, to send portions and rejoice greatly, because they understood the words that were declared to them" (Nehemiah 8:10-12). Unless a revival ends in joy and praise, it will not be strong, "for the joy of the Lord is your strength." In his interesting book *Laughter, Joy, and Healing* Dr. Donald Demaray says, "But what about joy? For the Christian the presence of Christ, which is joy, brings stability through the experiences of life. It is rather like a wheel: the rim goes over the bumpy turf of life's disappointments, but the hub of joy remains firm and steadies the ride. The crunch comes if we allow the hurts of life to inject their poison against the very joy God gives in His Son, Jesus Christ." [9]

Joy is a beautiful fruit of the Holy Spirit (Galatians 5:22), and is a foundation of the kingdom of God as the Holy Spirit dwells in the hearts of born-again Christians (Romans 14:17). But in what way is the joy of the Lord a strength? There is no strength in misery or discouragement. Nor is there any strength in unhappiness. The joy of the Lord is strength. Joy in prosperity, people, possessions, power, position, prestige, popularity, or personality can disappoint in the end. In contrast, Jesus promises joy that is full and complete (John 16:24). Revival focuses each life on God, and because He becomes the joy of life, rather than anything of the world that Satan can manipulate, there is strength that is supernatural. "That He would grant you, according to the riches of His glory, to be strengthened with might through His Spirit in the inner man" (Ephesians 3:16).

Revival principle 5: Let the Lord become the focus of true joy. This joy may not initially be a feeling of exuberance, but will, through faith, become the outward expression of the indwelling presence of the Holy Spirit. The joy of true revival has its source in God. "Also that day they offered great sacrifices, and rejoiced, for God had made them rejoice with great joy; the women and the children also rejoiced, so that the joy of Jerusalem was heard afar off" (Nehemiah 12:43). This joy can find its expression in music with instruments, congregational singing, and choirs (verses 27-43). When this type of revival begins to move in churches, its effect will be dramatic in the community and society. People will know that something is happening. Lives will be changed, and joy will radiate. It will be noticed "afar off."

If this sounds to you like a lot of festivity and happiness you are right, but there is need for a caution flag, because many lives have gone off the track and smashed into the wall right here. Joy, excitement, and festivity are not the revival in themselves; they are the fruit of the revival. Satan can easily counterfeit a revival, basing it on emotion and not on the Word of God and sincere repentance. Notice this warning regarding camp meeting revivals that was given at the beginning of this century: "The Holy Spirit never reveals itself in such methods, in such a bedlam of noise. This is an invention of Satan to cover up his ingenious methods for making of none effect the pure, sincere, elevating, ennobling, sanctifying truth for this time. . . . A bedlam of noise shocks the senses and perverts that which if conducted aright might be a blessing. The powers of satanic agencies blend with the din and noise, to have a carnival, and this is termed the Holy Spirit's working.

"When the camp meeting is ended, the good which ought to have been done and which might have been done by the presentation of sacred truth is not accomplished. Those participating in the supposed revival receive impressions which lead them adrift. They cannot tell what they formerly knew regarding Bible principles."[10]

Following the great revival in Nehemiah 8, the people made booths, and the influence of the Word of God as it had been read and explained during the revival meetings was continued in small group meetings (Nehemiah 8:13-18).

Revival principle 6: Integrate all the revival participants into small group fellowships for continued nurture, Bible study, prayer, worship, and the safeguarding of the new revival experience. Dr. Howard Snyder, professor of church renewal at United Theological Seminary, concludes his study of the great movements of renewal and revival in church history by stating that lay leadership and small cell groups were an important factor in each of the great revivals.[11] Snyder lists some of the reasons for the importance of lay-led small group fellowships in revival history. We can summarize what he says in this way.

1. These small group structures provided an immediately available social context for stabilizing new converts and for leading to conversion those who had been "awakened" through other means.

2. Relatedly, the small groups and similar structures conserved evangelistic fruit by stabilizing new converts or adherents who otherwise would likely have become discouraged or disaffected and fallen away.

3. The vital, disciplined small group structures tended to keep the revival movement dynamic and its identity and mission clear. They provided continuity while acting as a check against institutionalism and legalism.

4. These small group structures provided the context for experiencing the fellowship of the Holy Spirit and the convicting, correcting, discerning, and encouraging word of the Spirit and the Word.[12]

Longtime evangelist Arnold Scherencel says that he has seen the fruitage of revival meetings almost double as he has integrated them with small group ministries. Over many years the Holy Spirit has used Arnold and his wife, Margaret, in a mighty way. "Small groups are the only ministry strong enough to establish new Christians and church members," Arnold testifies. "I have seen good results where there are small groups already functioning in a church. If there are no groups, I make sure some are established by the conclusion of my evangelistic meetings."

The great revival in the time of Nehemiah did not leave the people on a high that lasted throughout their lives. Nor did it push them away from God so that the pendulum swung into apostasy and rejection of God's Word. The continued emphasis on the reading of Scriptures enabled the Holy Spirit to lead the people into growing spiritual cycles of repentance and praise. Twenty-four days after the revival began, the people were assembled again and once more came into confession and repentance as the Law was read. They opened their hearts in surrender and worship, and once again the people were led into praise and blessing of God (Nehemiah 9:1-5).

Revival principle 7: Give your friend the Holy Spirit a chance to deepen your relationship with the Lord through daily emphasis on the Word of God and prayer. The great Welsh revival was closely connected to small groups and cottage meetings. My wife and I recently had the opportunity to trace some of our Welsh ancestry, and so we journeyed to a few of the sites of the great Welsh revival. Along the way we asked the pastor-scholar Brian Phillips, who accompanied us, why this great revival had died out so quickly. His answer confirmed the importance of revival principle 7 and is underscored by George Canty: "A strong criticism of the Welsh revival was its lack of the Word of God, making the latter part of it more a revival of Welshness and emotion, and its fires burned down too quickly." [13]

It is the Word of God that lasts. It is through the Word of truth that the Holy Spirit can continue to work with fire burning in individual lives and churches. This is why I want to encourage you to continue to pray in the Word, as we studied in chapter four. Allow the Holy Spirit to speak to you through the Scriptures every day. Give the Holy Spirit a chance to bring you back again and again to revival principle 1 and on through all the principles of true revival.

One evening, as we discussed the topic of revival in our small group, Sonna shared an experience that happened during her freshman year in a North Dakota academy. During a special Week of Prayer a great revival took place that students still remember more than 15 years later. There was much evidence of the Holy Spirit on the campus. Groups of students prayed together, others would join in singing Scripture songs. "Everyone seemed to care for everyone else," Sonna said. "Students came very close to each other, and many were baptized. The last quarter was the best I had ever known at school."

But older Christians in the community warned, "Revival doesn't last; it just fades away." Rather than this observation being a negative, it should be recognized that the joyous high of revival does level out and that the Christian is always brought to the place of repentance once more as he or she sees new and deeper revelations of Jesus in the Scriptures. The cycle of revival happens again and again, as we noticed in Nehemiah, and each time the Word of God strengthens its hold on the hearts and minds of those who continue to pray and grow in their devotional experience. In this way the results of true revival are stabilized and conserved and the Holy Spirit is able to lead those who are open to the love of God back to corporate joy, worship, and evangelism again.

Now could be the time for the last great revival. Give the Holy Spirit a chance to lead you into revival right now in the community where you live. Pray about it today. Open God's Word and begin to pray for the outpouring of the Holy Spirit. The revival can begin with you and me and spread to thousands as we share the Word of God. Revival is evangelism, and evangelism is revival. This is the fulfilling of the great prophecy of the three angels in Revelation 14:6-12. The people who are able in the power of the Holy Spirit to be part of the true latter rain revival and God's final message of truth for this world will be involved in a combination of Spirit and truth that will shatter the grip of evil forces on millions of lives and will rejoice in seeing the second coming of Jesus.

"And this gospel of the kingdom will be preached in all the world as a witness to all the nations, and then the end will come" (Matthew 24:14). If you give the Holy Spirit a chance personally and publicly, you will have a part in the last great revival.

Father, in the name of Jesus we thank You for the Holy Spirit, who is leading us into the great final work of the gospel. Holy Spirit, I open my life today to give You the chance to fill me again with God's love and Your mighty power so that Jesus can be glorified as never before. Show me needs that will enable me to manifest Your spiritual gifts so that there can be healing and resurrection life. Keep me close to Your Word, Father, so that all that I do and say will be directed by Your truth. Thank You for the cross of Jesus. I come in repentance and rejoice today in Jesus' forgiveness and victory. I praise You now and bless and glorify Your holy name as You put a new song in my heart. Amen.

SMALL GROUP STUDY
Chapter Thirteen

Cohesive Contrasts

Since this is the last study guide in this series, it may be helpful if the group spends a few moments in evaluation. Questions can be asked, such as: Was this series of studies helpful? What did I learn? Did I grow closer to the people in the group? Did we achieve our goals for this study? What would I do differently if I were to do this study again?

The group by now have most likely discussed plans for new studies or disbanding. Because of the bonding that has taken place, many of the group members will most likely want to stay together; or perhaps this may be a good time to divide and start a number of new groups with alternative locations and times.

Here is a sharing question to begin. As this series of studies concludes, what is the most valuable "gift" each person in the group has given you?

Concentrating on the Word
Study Text: Nehemiah 8:1-9:5

Although the Holy Spirit is not mentioned in Nehemiah 8:1-9:5, what evidences or symbols of the Holy Spirit can you find in these verses?

_____

_____

What do you think Christians can learn today from the praise and worship at the beginning of the revival in Nehemiah 8:6?

_____

_____

What reasons would you give to explain why the leaders of the revival requested the people to turn from sorrow to rejoicing (Nehemiah 8:9)?

_____

_____

Has joy in the Lord ever been a strength to you? What happened? How did it contrast to other joy you have experienced?

Some people after the "high" of a revival become discouraged and even fall into temptation. How can small groups be a safeguard against this?

How would you feel if someone informed you that he or she was enjoying an exciting revival, but was not interested in studying or praying in the Scriptures and obeying its teachings in the power of the Holy Spirit?

Glad the person is liberated _____
Eager to join the individual _____
Fearful that the person will be deceived _____
Suspicious of the person's sincerity _____
Doubtful that the revival is genuine _____
Happy for the individual _____

How has the Bible helped you in your experience with the Lord? Has it been a stabilizing influence, or a troubling one?

Conversation With the Lord

Begin by ministering to God, praising and blessing His Holy name. Now pray especially for revival, remembering that this prayer may lead you and group members into deep repentance. Pray for special needs inside and outside the group and conclude by holding hands in a circle as you pray the Lord's Prayer together.

Committing the Word to Memory

This week, write out a verse from Nehemiah 8:1-9:5 and share it with someone as soon as possible.

References

Chapter One

[1] John Rea, *The Holy Spirit in the Bible* (Altamonte Springs, Fla.: Creation House, 1990), pp. 20, 21.
[2] Garrie F. Williams, *How to Be Filled With the Holy Spirit and Know It* (Hagerstown, Md.: Review and Herald Pub. Assn., 1991), pp. 42, 43.
[3] C. Peter Wagner, *The Third Wave of the Holy Spirit* (Ann Arbor, Mich.: Vine Books, 1988).
[4] Kevin and Dorothy Ranaghan, *Catholic Pentecostals* (New York: Paulist Press, 1969), pp. 11-22.
[5] Peter E. Gillquist, *Let's Quit Fighting About the Holy Spirit* (Grand Rapids: Zondervan Pub. House, 1974), p. 13.
[6] G. B. Thompson, *The Ministry of the Spirit* (Washington, D.C.: Review and Herald Pub. Assn., 1914), p. 152.
[7] Jack Hayford, *Spirit-filled* (Wheaton, Ill.: Tyndale House, 1988), p. 66.
[8] James White, in *Spiritual Gifts* (Battle Creek, Mich.: Seventh-day Adventist Pub. Assn., 1864), vol. 3, pp. 29, 30.

Chapter Two

[1] London: Faber and Faber, 1976.
[2] For a basic study on the Holy Spirit in relationship to a converted or unconverted person, see *How to Be Filled With the Holy Spirit and Know It*, chap. 3.
[3] Ellen G. White, *The Desire of Ages* (Mountain View, Calif.: Pacific Press Pub. Assn., 1940), p. 172.

Chapter Three

[1] E. G. White, *The Desire of Ages*, p. 671.
[2] ———, *Christian Service* (Washington, D.C.: Review and Herald Pub. Assn.), p. 254.
[3] New York: Harper and Row, 1965, p. 161.
[4] Roy W. Fairchild, *Finding Hope Again* (San Francisco: Harper and Row, 1980), pp. 49, 50.
[5] *The Works of John Wesley* (Grand Rapids: Zondervan), vol. 1, p. 222.

Chapter Four

[1] John Williams, *The Holy Spirit* (Neptune, N.J.: Loizeaux Brothers, 1980), p. 69.
[2] *The Works of John Wesley*, vol. 5, p. 3.
[3] E. G. White, *The Desire of Ages*, p. 390.
[4] H. Lincoln Wayland, ed., *Autobiography of George Müller* (Grand Rapids: Baker Book House, 1981), p. 207.
[5] Questions based on Paul E. Little, *How to Give Away Your Faith* (London: Intervarsity Press, 1966), pp. 136-138.
[6] *The Works of John Wesley*, vol. 8, p. 483.
[7] Billy Graham, *The Holy Spirit* (Waco, Tex.: Word Books, 1978), p. 48.
[8] "A Mighty Fortress," *The Seventh-day Adventist Hymnal* (Hagerstown, Md.: Review and Herald Pub. Assn., 1985), No. 506.

Chapter Five

[1] "Come, Holy Spirit." Words by William J. and Gloria Gaither. Music by William J. Gaither. Copyright © 1964 by William J. Gaither. All rights reserved. Used by permission.
[2] Ellen G. White, *Testimonies for the Church* (Mountain View, Calif.: Pacific Press Pub. Assn., 1948), vol. 6, p. 175.
[3] ———, *Christ's Object Lessons* (Washington, D.C.: Review and Herald Pub. Assn., 1900), pp. 118-121.
[4] E. M. Bounds, *The Complete Works of E. M. Bounds* (Grand Rapids: Baker Book House, 1990), pp. 283, 284.
[5] *Ibid.*, p. 281.
[6] A. W. Pink, *The Holy Spirit* (Grand Rapids: Baker Book House, 1970), p. 145.
[7] Bounds, p. 287.
[8] *Ibid.*, p. 289.
[9] Becky Tirabassi, *Releasing God's Power* (Nashville: Oliver Nelson Pub., 1990), pp. 9, 10.
[10] Ellen G. White, in *Review and Herald*, Jan. 3, 1907.
[11] *Ibid.*, May 28, 1895.
[12] *Ibid.*, May 21, 1901.

Chapter Six

[1] Bill Hybels, *Too Busy Not to Pray* (Downers Grove, Ill.: Intervarsity Press, 1988), p. 51.
[2] E. G. White, *The Desire of Ages*, p. 131.

REFERENCES

Chapter Seven

[1] *People*, Feb. 10, 1986. (Italics supplied.)
[2] Andrew Murray, *The Believer's Full Blessing of Pentecost* (Minneapolis: Bethany House, 1984), p. 105.
[3] R. A. Torrey, *The Person and Work of the Holy Spirit* (Grand Rapids: Academie Books, 1974), p. 100.
[4] *Ibid.*, p. 101.
[5] *Review and Herald*, Sept. 10, 1904.
[6] Ron Lee Davis, *Gold in the Making* (Nashville: Thomas Nelson Pub., 1983), p. 69.

Chapter Eight

[1] Ellen G. White, *Temperance* (Mountain View, Calif.: Pacific Press Pub. Assn., 1949), p. 113.
[2] ———, *Selected Messages* (Washington, D.C.: Review and Herald Pub. Assn., 1958), book 2, p. 129.
[3] ———, *Testimonies to Ministers* (Mountain View, Calif.: Pacific Press Pub. Assn., 1962), p. 79.
[4] ———, *The Desire of Ages*, p. 173.
[5] William A. Miller, *When Going to Pieces Holds You Together* (Minneapolis: Augsburg Pub. House, 1976), p. 24.
[6] White, *The Acts of the Apostles* (Mountain View, Calif.: Pacific Press Pub. Assn., 1911), p. 49.

Chapter Nine

[1] Ralph W. Neighbour, Jr., *Where Do We Go From Here?* (Houston: Torch Pub., 1990), p. 114.
[2] *Ibid.*, p. 121.
[3] Beth Lester, 1992.
[4] Carl George, *Prepare Your Church for the Future* (New York: Fleming H. Revell Co., 1991), p. 131.
[5] Neal F. McBride, *How to Lead Small Groups* (Colorado Springs: NavPress, 1990), pp. 22, 23.
[6] Howard Snyder, *Signs of the Spirit* (Grand Rapids: Academie Books, 1989), pp. 290, 291.
[7] *Ibid.*, p. 305.
[8] *Ibid.*, p. 133.
[9] *Christian History*, vol. 1, No. 1, p. 32.
[10] Richard B. Wilke, *And Are We Yet Alive?* (Nashville: Abingdon Press, 1986), pp. 80, 81.
[11] *Ibid.*, pp. 82, 83.

Chapter Ten

[1] Neighbour, *Where Do We Go From Here?* pp. 151, 152.
[2] *The Works of John Wesley*, vol. 1, p. 141.
[3] Davis, *Gold in the Making*, p. 79.
[4] *Ibid.*, pp. 44, 45.
[5] Neighbour, pp. 160, 161.
[6] Gillquist, *Let's Quit Fighting About the Holy Spirit*, p. 90.
[7] William McRae, *The Dynamics of Spiritual Gifts* (Grand Rapids: Zondervan, 1976), pp. 128, 129.
[8] Snyder, *Signs of the Spirit*, p. 162.
[9] August G. Spangenberg, *The Life of Nicholas Lewis, Count Zinzendorf* (London: Holdsworth, 1838), p. 138.
[10] Neighbour, p. 153.
[11] E. G. White, *The Desire of Ages*, p. 823.
[12] *The Works of John Wesley*, vol. 5, p. 141.

Chapter Eleven

[1] Andrew Murray, *The Spirit of Christ* (Fort Washington, Pa.: Christian Literature Crusade, 1985), p. 29.
[2] Raymond E. Brown, trans., *The Gospel According to John* (*Anchor Bible*) (Garden City, N.Y.: Doubleday & Co., Inc., 1966), p. 172.
[3] M. Bickerstaff, *There Was a Man Sent*, p. 9.
[4] Ellen G. White, in *General Conference Bulletin*, Mar. 30, 1903.
[5] ———, *Steps to Christ*, (Mountain View, Calif.: Pacific Press Pub. Assn., 1956), p. 104.
[6] ———, *Selected Messages* (1980), book 3, p. 332.
[7] ———, *In Heavenly Places* (Washington, D.C.: Review and Herald Pub. Assn., 1967), p. 288.
[8] Murray, p. 27.
[9] White, *The Desire of Ages*, p. 189.
[10] Dennis F. Kinlaw, *Preaching in the Spirit* (Grand Rapids: Francis Asbury Press, 1985), p. 81.
[11] See James H. Rutz, *1700 Years Is Long Enough* (Colorado Springs: Open Church Ministries).

Chapter Twelve

[1] Ellen G. White, in A. L. White, *Ellen G. White: The Progressive Years* (Hagerstown, Md.: Review and Herald Pub. Assn., 1986), p. 419.

[2] John White, *When the Spirit Comes With Power* (Downers Grove, Ill.: Intervarsity Press, 1988), p. 82.

[3] *Ibid.*, pp. 149, 150.

[4] John Dawson, *Taking Our Cities for God* (Altamonte Springs, Fla.: Creation House, 1989), pp. 34, 35.

[5] "Daystar (Shine Down on Me)." Words and music by Steve Richardson. Copyright © 1988 by Ariose Music. All rights reserved. Used by permission.

Chapter Thirteen

[1] John White, *When the Spirit Comes With Power*, pp. 32, 33.

[2] *Christian History*, vol. 5, No. 2, p. 18.

[3] Snyder, *Signs of the Spirit*, p. 99.

[4] In *Herald of His Coming*, June 1990, p. 7.

[5] John White, *When the Spirit Comes With Power*, p. 29.

[6] George Canty, *The Hallmarks of Pentecost* (London: Marshall Pickering, 1989), p. 86.

[7] *Ibid.*, p. 57.

[8] E. G. White, *Christian Service*, p. 42.

[9] Donald E. Demaray, *Laughter, Joy, and Healing* (Grand Rapids: Baker Book House, 1986), p. 117.

[10] E. G. White, *Selected Messages*, book 2, pp. 36, 37.

[11] Snyder, p. 252.

[12] *Ibid.*, pp. 259-261.

[13] Canty, p. 95.